About the editors

Felicity Thomas is a lecturer at the University of Exeter and a research associate at the University of Sussex. She has worked, published and taught in the areas of migrant health and wellbeing, HIV/AIDS and international development, and been involved in a number of NGO projects with refugees and asylum seekers in sub-Saharan Africa and the UK. She has authored a number of journal publications on migration and health, and recently edited *Mobility, Sexuality and AIDS* (2010).

Jasmine Gideon is a lecturer in development studies at Birkbeck College, University of London. She has worked and published on issues relating to gender and health policy in Latin America, economic and social rights and access to health care services, and is currently writing *Gender, Globalisation and Health: The Latin American Context*. She is currently working with Latin American migrants in the UK, exploring their health seeking behaviour.

Migration, health and inequality

EDITED BY FELICITY THOMAS
AND JASMINE GIDEON

Zed Books
LONDON | NEW YORK

Migration, health and inequality was first published in 2013 by
Zed Books Ltd, 7 Cynthia Street, London N1 9JF, UK and Room 400,
175 Fifth Avenue, New York, NY 10010, USA

www.zedbooks.co.uk

Set in OurType Arnhem and Monotype Futura by
Ewan Smith, London
Index: ed.emery@thefreeuniversity.net
Cover design: www.reactor15.com
Printed and bound by CPI Group (UK) Ltd, Croydon,
CRO 4YY

Distributed in the USA exclusively by Palgrave Macmillan, a division of
St Martin's Press, LLC, 175 Fifth Avenue, New York, NY 10010, USA

A catalogue record for this book is available from the British Library
Library of Congress Cataloging in Publication Data available

ISBN 978 1 78032 125 7 hb
ISBN 978 1 78032 124 0 pb

Contents

Tables and figures

Tables

Figures

control or contain various migrant populations (Coker, 2003). Such attitudes have undoubtedly played a key role in the establishment of protectionist approaches and policies that restrict and monitor the behaviour, rights and entitlements of particular migrant groups.

Alongside such protectionist approaches however, most governments have also signed up to a range of human rights conventions and, in some cases, have portability arrangements around social security entitlements that help to ensure that certain migrants have comparable rights to citizens. Yet despite such seemingly positive developments, the global policy arena on migrant health remains largely uncoordinated and often vague, with inconsistencies and contradictions existing across and within policies and their implementation. Partly in response to this situation, a considerable literature has now emerged across a range of academic disciplines, including development studies, geography, anthropology, law and public health, which stresses the importance of understanding migration, health and equality from a rights-based perspective.

Such approaches have stressed the importance of considering the unique health-related vulnerabilities that individual migrants may face at various stages during the often complex process of migration. A key finding here has been that many migrant groups consistently report low levels of health and wellbeing relative to the host population (McDonald and Kennedy, 2004). Even where portability arrangements do exist, these are often limited to high income professionals and are predominantly North–North migrants. At present only 23 per cent of migrants worldwide are able to enjoy access to and portability of social rights (Avato et al., 2010: 456). A major challenge regarding migrants' rights and entitlements to healthcare concerns those who are unable to work or who work in the 'informal' economy, where such rights are particularly difficult to monitor and to enforce (Kofman, 2007). However, even migrants who do, in theory, have rights and entitlements can face a range of practical barriers that limit their access to, and use of, healthcare services in host countries. The living and working conditions experienced by many such migrants can also negatively impact on their health, with research from a wide range of countries frequently reporting that a disproportionate number of migrants are more likely to be located in low paid, low status jobs relative to the host population (Benach et al., 2011; Kosny et al., 2011). At the same time, migrants often live in relatively poor-quality housing and do not have access to a healthy diet and lifestyle; all of this can contribute to their worsening health situation (Sabates-Wheeler, 2009). These

Introduction

FELICITY THOMAS AND
JASMINE GIDEON

In recent decades, processes of globalisation have fundamentally transformed the intensity, scale and diversity of global connections. In turn, improved communications and transportation have led to an intensification of population movement as people are more easily able to migrate to seek to better their lives in other countries, regions or localities. Reflecting such changes, migration is, for many people, increasingly seen as a complex, often multi-staged process rather than a singular transition from one place to another. Population migration is thus undoubtedly a key global policy issue at the start of the twenty-first century. Nevertheless, there has been a noticeable absence in the discussion of the so-called 'migration-development-social policy' nexus (Hujo and Piper, 2010; Piper, 2009). As such, important questions are now being raised regarding the rights, entitlements and equalities available to migrant populations seeking to access key welfare services in host countries and communities, and regarding the impact of migration on the welfare of populations in the home communities from which migrants have come.

While most governments recognise health as an essential human right, significant debates remain – and have indeed been amplified in the current global recession – over the extent to which non-citizens share the same rights and entitlements as citizens in relation to accessing healthcare services. At an international level, policy-making on migration has tended to be undertaken from what have been widely described as policy sector 'silos' (Zimmerman et al., 2011), with different, and often competing goals, and little specific focus on issues of health. At the same time, concerns have long been voiced regarding the possible links between migration, health and the wellbeing of host communities, with migrant populations commonly being seen in the public psyche as a health threat. Perhaps nowhere has this been more apparent in recent times than with widespread public fear concerning the migration of people from the Global South to the Global North, leading to a popularly perceived need to in some way

ILO	International Labour Organization
ILR	indefinite leave to remain
IOM	International Organization for Migration
ISAPRE	institución de salud previsional (health insurance institution) (Chile)
IVF	in vitro fertilisation
LAWRS	Latin American Women's Rights Service
NGO	non-governmental organisation
NHS	National Health Service (UK)
NRI	non-resident Indian
NRM	National Referral Mechanism (UK)
OAS	Organization of American States
OECD	Organisation for Economic Co-operation and Development
OFW	overseas Filipino workers
PCT	primary care trust (UK)
PIO	people of Indian origin
PTSD	post-traumatic stress disorder
SEF	statement of evidence form
TB	tuberculosis
UDHR	Universal Declaration of Human Rights
UKBA	United Kingdom Border Authority
UKHTC	United Kingdom Human Trafficking Centre
UNAIDS	Joint United Nations Programme on HIV/AIDS
UNCRC	United Nations Convention on the Rights of the Child
UNHCR	United Nations High Commissioner for Refugees
UNICEF	United Nations Children's Fund
WHA	World Health Assembly
WHO	World Health Organization

Abbreviations

A&E	accident and emergency
ACHR	American Convention on Human Rights
AIDS	acquired immune deficiency syndrome
ART	anti-retroviral therapy
BMA	British Medical Association
BME	black and minority ethnic
CASEN	Caracterización Socio-Económica Nacional (National Socioeconomic Characterization survey) (Chile)
CAT	Convention Against Torture
CEDAW	Convention on the Elimination of All Forms of Discrimination Against Women
CERD	Committee on the Elimination of Racial Discrimination
CESCR	Committee on Economic, Social and Cultural Rights
CRPD	Convention on the Rights of Persons with Disabilities
DH	Department of Health (UK)
ECAT	European Convention on Action Against Trafficking in Human Beings
ECHR	European Convention on Human Rights
ECtHR	European Court of Human Rights
ESC	European Social Charter
EU	European Union
FGM	female genital mutilation
FONASA	Fondo Nacional de Salud (National Health Fund) (Chile)
GATS	General Agreement on Trade in Services
GP	general practitioner
HIV	human immunodeficiency virus
HRC	Human Rights Committee
ICCPR	International Covenant on Civil and Political Rights
ICERD	International Convention on the Elimination of All Forms of Racial Discrimination
ICESCR	International Covenant on Economic, Social and Cultural Rights
ICJ	International Court of Justice
ICPRMW	International Convention on the Protection of the Rights of All Migrant Workers and Members of their families

Acknowledgements

A number of the chapters in this book stem from the conference 'Migration and the Right to Health', which was held in London in May 2010. Special thanks are due to the London International Development Centre and the School of Advanced Study, University of London, who generously funded and hosted this event. Thanks are also due to the Leverhulme Trust, whose support for one of the editors via a research fellowship helped enable this book to get underway.

We are also grateful to the authors and publishers who gave permission to reprint various excerpts for some of the chapters collected here:

- Palgrave Macmillan, for permission to reprint excerpts from Shah, R. S. (2010) 'The right to health, state responsibility and global justice', in R. S. Shah (ed.) *The International Migration of Health Workers*, Chapter 5.
- Elsevier Limited, for permission to reprint excerpts from Thomas, F. (2010) 'Transnational health and treatment networks: Meaning, value and place in health seeking amongst southern African migrants in London', *Health and Place*, 16(3) and Thomas, F., P. Aggleton and J. Anderson (2010) '"Experts", "partners" and "fools": Exploring agency in HIV treatment seeking among African migrants in London', *Social Science and Medicine*, 70(5).
- Emerald Group Publishing, for permission to reprint excerpts from Gideon, J. (forthcoming) 'Exploring migrants' health seeking strategies: The case of Latin American migrants in London', *International Journal of Migration, Health and Social Care*, 7(4), www.pierprofessional.com/ijmhscflyer/.

processes can be exacerbated by a wide range of other factors that can make certain migrant groups especially vulnerable to poor health, and particularly prone to marginalisation from healthcare services and support. Such factors include temporal issues that relate to different vulnerabilities associated with various points in the migration process, the blame and stigma associated with infectious diseases such as HIV (human immunodeficiency virus), and socio-cultural factors such as local 'constructions' of migrants and the ways in which these may be cross-cut by gender, age, race or legal status (Spitzer, 2011; Sundquist, 1995).

Importantly, migration not only impacts on those who move, but can also impact upon the health and rights of communities that are left behind. This is particularly stark when those migrating are themselves trained health workers, who seek to better their lives by leaving already under-resourced health sectors in the Global South to enter the health services of foreign, usually economically wealthier and better resourced nations (Mackintosh et al., 2006). At the same time, however, it is important to recognise that migration flows are not always unidirectional and do not always involve movement from the Global South to the Global North. Recent years have witnessed a rise in South–South movement, as well as an increase in more flexible and temporary forms of migration, and as such, attention must be given to the range of transnational and diasporic networks and links upon which migrant and home-based populations can call.

In relation to this, academic analysis is beginning to recognise the need to examine the ways in which individuals exert agency and adapt their lifestyles to the circumstances in which they find themselves (Dyck and Dossa, 2007). In particular, issues of access are framed within a discussion of 'the problem of the management of cultural difference' (Dyck, 2006: 2). Within the migration field more broadly many scholars have rejected the notion of assimilation that, as Dyck argues, in essence underpins the medicalised approach to health and migration. Of central importance here is the need to look beyond host country responses and 'biomedical' frameworks of understanding to also examine the role of transnational and diasporic health networks and to explore indigenous, popular or lay ideas about health and wellbeing as they relate to different constructions of illness aetiology and treatment seeking. At the same time it is important to recognise that while on the one hand networks can provide valuable support to migrant groups, on the other hand they can also be a source of stress as people may seek to conceal information about poor health from those 'back home' (Escandell and Tapias, 2010) or reinforce gendered roles around informal healthcare provision (Menjívar, 2002). Such analysis in turn raises important and challenging questions regarding the health-related rights and equalities that people are, or should be, entitled to, particularly when their understandings and perceived requirements fall beyond, or even contradict, normative biomedical frameworks of health and wellbeing.

Migration, health and inequality attempts to consolidate some of the key developments that have emerged across the social sciences and public health literature by bringing together this array of issues in an examination of the interface between migration, health and various forms of inequalities. The volume emerged from the editors' sense of the potential importance of such insights for those working at the intersections of migration and health, either as practitioners or as academics, and from the extremely insightful papers that were presented at two conferences held in 2010 with which the editors were involved. We felt that this new book could help increase understanding of the complex inter-linkages between these new insights, and deepen knowledge of the wide range of priorities, needs and experiences of migrant populations and of the home and host communities with whom they liaise.

We have tried to organise the book in a way that will provide insight as to how migration, health and inequality intersect within the wider social, political, economic and cultural structures and processes that take place at different scales: from the macro level of health and migration-related policy-making to the micro level of individual and household experience. In so doing, we have organised the book around four overarching themes: current migration patterns and processes; migration and the right to health in the context of global policy-making and implementation; migration, health and rights among particularly vulnerable populations; and migration, health and rights as they relate to transnational and diasporic networks and links. Particular issues – such as global power relations and geopolitics, the interconnections between structure and agency, the potential role of local, host and home-based communities, and the gendered nature of health experiences – appear in a number of the chapters. At the same time, certain geographical areas where research on migration and health has been particularly strong, such as in parts of Europe, and among migrant workers moving between parts of sub-Saharan Africa, Latin America, southern Asia and the Global North are discussed in several chapters. A number of these chapters are, in turn, framed within the specific context of the UK's National Health Service (NHS).

4

Current migration patterns and processes

Chapter 1 sets the context of the book by providing an important overview of current issues affecting migration and health. In this chapter, Mary Haour-Knipe provides a clear account of current global migration patterns, focusing on the ways in which globalisation processes have unsettled traditional linear migration patterns and resulted in a much more diverse range of migration trajectories and experiences. Attention is given to the potential impacts on health that may be experienced by different migrants at different stages of the migration process, and the global level policy and legal frameworks that may affect this. The author calls for more rigorous data collection on which to base important policy formulation, and stresses the need to create linkages and build a more coordinated response to migration and health between countries and sectors.

In Chapter 2, Sally Hargreaves and Jon Friedland build upon many of these themes via analysis of the health experiences of 'new migrants' who have arrived in Europe in the past decade. In this chapter they highlight the variety of approaches taken by host governments in Europe, and the resulting inconsistencies in health-related entitlements that are available to migrants. Particular focus is placed on the stark inequalities that migrants may face as they seek to access public healthcare services and the ethical dilemmas that healthcare professionals face as a result of this.

Global policy-making and implementation

The section on global policy-making and implementation brings together three chapters that examine some of the crucial issues that governments face as they seek to respond to health provision needs at a range of levels. Key here is the way that governments seek to provide for and protect the health of their own citizens, while simultaneously negotiating the entitlements and rights of various migrant groups. These issues are examined in depth by Sue Willman (Chapter 3), who focuses on the effectiveness of international laws and policies pertaining to migrant health. Providing a detailed examination of current international human rights law, Willman argues that major discrepancies exist between such policy and its implementation. A key factor here, she argues, is that while international treaties are binding between states, they are rarely enforceable at an individual level, and when they are they tend to be impeded by a lack of power and resources. Drawing upon evidence from a range of well-known and test cases in international legal practice, Willman usefully highlights both the opportunities and obstacles that migrants may face in seeking to use various human rights laws to access health services.

In Chapter 4, Rebecca Shah examines the impact of international health worker migration, focusing specifically on healthcare workers who migrate from developing countries to work in the healthcare sectors of economically wealthier and better resourced nations. While it has frequently been stated that such migration has a damaging 'brain-drain' impact on home countries, with severe repercussions for healthcare provision, Shah argues that a more nuanced approach that considers the wide range of moral and ethical issues at play is necessary to more fully understand the actual and potential harms associated with health worker migration. Inherent within this is the need to consider the coexistence of often competing healthcare rights and entitlements among the populations of both home and host countries, and the rights of migrant workers wishing to seek greater opportunities for themselves and their families by relocating overseas. Considering the ways in which human rights frameworks and concepts of international responsibility pose both opportunities for and limitations on healthcare, Shah argues that we need to recognise and address the broader global and geopolitical inequalities under which current migration takes place at the expense of poorer nations.

Providing a more focused regional example of health inequalities facing particular groups of migrants, Báltica Cabieses and Helena Tunstall (Chapter 5) examine how different migrant groups from across Latin America can experience very different levels of access to healthcare provision in Chile. As such, the authors call for researchers and policy-makers to recognise the heterogeneity of migrant experience. At the same time however, they highlight the need to recognise and understand the ways in which healthcare inequalities not only face migrant populations, but also citizens of host countries.

Health, migration and vulnerable groups

While many migrants have been found to face difficulties accessing healthcare services in host countries, attention should also be given to the more specific inequalities and vulnerabilities that can be faced by certain migrant groups. The three chapters in this section focus on particular groups of migrants who have been found to be especially vulnerable in terms of accessing adequate and appropriate healthcare services in host countries.

In Chapter 6, Elaine Chase examines the diverse and often harrowing experiences of unaccompanied young people seeking asylum in the UK.

While previous research has focused on the mental health of young asylum seekers and refugees, and the need to mitigate past trauma through clinical and therapeutic interventions, Chase takes this argument further, putting forward a convincing case for the recognition of ontological security as a key factor influencing health status. Seeking this kind of security and belonging, she argues, is often at odds with invasive UK immigration processes, leaving young people with a sense of uncertainty, anxiety and frustration that adversely impacts on their health and wellbeing.

The provision of healthcare entitlements to people who have experienced forms of human trafficking is another key issue faced by policy-makers. In Chapter 7, Siân Oram examines the health-related entitlements of women trafficked to the UK since the ratification of the Council of Europe Convention on Action against Trafficking in Human Beings (ECAT) policy in 2008, and the related introduction of the National Referral Mechanism that now governs healthcare and support for trafficked persons. Oram argues that despite such measures being enforced in order to facilitate healthcare access, trafficked women continue to have to rely upon NGOs and other support services to get these entitlements, and indeed, that in some cases, such mechanisms have inadvertently made the process more difficult.

Drawing upon her experiences as Director of Maternity Action, Rosalind Bragg (Chapter 8) examines the impacts of NHS healthcare charging upon migrant women seeking ante- and post-natal healthcare in the UK. In so doing, she explores how concerns over health tourism have adversely affected migrant access to maternity-related healthcare, and in some cases, led to harmful outcomes for both mother and child. Bragg highlights the need for greater research and knowledge generation regarding the maternal health issues facing migrants and calls for urgent action to be taken to get midwives and other health professionals to engage much more directly with such potentially vulnerable migrant groups.

Transnationalism, diaspora and health

The chapters in the final section of this book recognise the need to look beyond host country responses to also examine the ways that transnational and diasporic networks and links can impact upon migrant health. While the structural barriers to healthcare identified in the earlier chapters of this book must not be underestimated, Felicity Thomas (Chapter 9) argues that it is important to also recognise the diversity of ways in which migrants understand health and wellbeing, and to recognise that such understandings may differ considerably from conventionally accepted biomedical frameworks of illness aetiology and treatment. Using data gathered from southern African migrants in the UK, Thomas explores the moral, ethical and individual and public health dilemmas that can result when the hegemony of biomedicine pushes 'alternative' understandings and treatments underground.

In Chapter 10, Meghann Ormond explores what has become a fast growing phenomenon in certain areas of the Global South – medical tourism. Challenging previous literature that sees such opportunities as exploitative and restricted to people from wealthier countries, Ormond's chapter demonstrates how, in an ever-globalising world, countries such as India and the Philippines are increasingly able to obtain benefit from the wealth, success and prestige of their own migrant diasporas as they contribute to their homeland as both health-care consumers and providers.

In Chapter 11, Jasmine Gideon considers the health seeking strategies of Latin American migrants in the UK. Even where migrants have legal entitlements to use healthcare services, a number of informal barriers may constrain their access and they remain marginalised from formal services. The chapter highlights how some Latin American migrants draw on social networks to identify alternative means of securing healthcare but that often the solutions may push people towards informal providers and further exacerbate health inequalities.

In the final chapter (Chapter 12) Eleni Hatzidimitriadou and Gülfem Çakır examine the role of community self-help groups and community activism as mechanisms of empowerment for migrants' claims to welfare and health rights. Focusing upon the role of Turkish women's groups, they argue that community organisations in the diaspora have the potential to mediate and act as a bridge in identifying and addressing the health needs of ethnic minority and migrant groups and in so doing, empower community members to more effectively voice their healthcare needs.

References

Avato, J., J. Koettel and R. Sabates-Wheeler (2010) 'Social security regimes, global estimates, and good practices: The status of social protection for international migrants', *World Development*, 38(4): 455–66.

Benach, J., C. Muntaner, C. Delclos, M. Menéndez and C. Ronquillo (2011) 'Migration and "low-skilled" workers in destination countries', *PLoS Med* 8(6): e1001043.

Coker, R. (2003) 'Migration, public health and compulsory screening for TB and HIV', *Asylum and*

Migra-tion Working Paper 1, IPPR, London.

Dyck, I. (2006) 'Travelling tales and migratory meanings: South Asian migrant women talk of place, health and healing', *Social and Cultural Geography*, 7(1): 1–18.

Dyck, I. and P. Dossa (2007) 'Place, health and home: Gender and migration in the constitution of healthy space', *Health and Place*, 13: 691–701.

Escandell, X. and M. Tapias (2010) 'Transnational lives, travelling emotions and idioms of distress among Bolivian migrants in Spain', *Journal of Ethnic and Migration Studies*, 36(3): 407–23.

Hujo, K. and N. Piper (2010) 'Linking migration, social development and policy in the south – an introduction', in K. Hujo and N. Piper (eds) *South–South Migration: Implications for Social Policy and Development*, Palgrave Macmillan, Basingstoke and New York: 1–45.

Kofman, E. (2007) 'Gendered migrations, livelihoods and entitlements in European welfare regimes', in N. Piper (ed.) *New Perspectives on Gender and Migration: Livelihoods, Rights and Entitlements*, Routledge/UNRISD, New York: 59–101.

Kosny, A., E. MacEachen, M. Lifshen, P. Smith, G. Joya Jafri, C. Neilson, D. Pugliese and J. Shields (2011) 'Delicate dances: Immigrant workers' experiences of in-jury reporting and claim filing', *Ethnicity & Health*, DOI:10.1080/13 557858.2011.614327.

McDonald, J. and S. Kennedy (2004) 'Insights into the "health immigrant effect": Health status and health service use of immigrants to Canada', *Social Science and Medicine*, 59(8): 1613–27.

Mackintosh, M., K. Mensah, L. Henry and M. Rowson (2006) 'Aid, restitution and international fiscal redistribution in health care: Implications of health professionals' migration', *Journal of International Development*, 18(6): 757–70.

Menjívar, C. (2002) 'The ties that heal: Guatemalan immigrant women's networks and medical treatment', *International Migration Review*, 36(2): 437–66.

Piper, N. (2009) 'The complex interactions of the migration-development nexus: A social perspective', *Population, Space and Place*, 15(2): 93–101.

Sabates-Wheeler, R. (2009) 'The impact of irregular status on human development outcomes for migrants', *United Nations Development Programme Human Development Reports Research Paper*, July, No. 26, UNDP, New York.

Spitzer, D. (2011) *Engendering Migrant Health: Canadian Perspectives*, University of Toronto Press, Toronto.

Sundquist, J. (1995) 'Ethnicity, social class and health. A population-based study on the influence of social factors on self-reported illness in 223 Latin American refugees, 333 Finnish and 126 South European labour migrants and 841 Swedish controls', *Social Science and Medicine*, 40(6): 777–87.

Zimmerman, C., L. Kiss and M. Hossain (2011) 'Migration and health: A framework for 21st century policy-making', *PLoS Med* 8(5): e1001034.

1 | Context and perspectives: who migrates and what are the risks?

MARY HAOUR-KNIPE

Introduction

Since the 2010 conferences in London and Washington DC on which the chapters for this book are based, migration has become a major issue in Europe. As important political shifts occur on Africa's northern coast, and against a background of economic crisis, the possibility that massive numbers of people fleeing conflict and instability will cross the Mediterranean to Europe's southern coast has been liberally evoked in the press. Political parties in a number of countries have used the fears and stereotypes that migration evokes to appeal to voters – sometimes in blatant disregard of facts. At the same time, and perhaps in reaction, calls have been made to discuss migration policies in a more dispassionate way, for individual countries and for Europe as a whole. This is thus a good time to evoke migration's often neglected health aspects, and especially to discuss these in the contexts of equality and of human rights.

This chapter attempts to put the subject of migration, health and inequality into perspective, geographically by sketching current world migration patterns, time-wise by discussing potential health effects related to the successive phases of the migration process, and normatively by evoking the policy and legal frameworks that affect migrant health.

The larger context: international migration today

As any visit to an airport, train station or major highway will amply demonstrate, population movement has become a taken-for-granted fact of life at the beginning of the twenty-first century. Countless millions of people cross international borders every year for tourism, to visit family and friends, to do business or to seek employment or asylum. Approximately 3 per cent of the world's population has crossed international borders in a longer-term way, to live in a country other than that in which they were born. Most international migration world-wide takes place within regions, in other words from one developing country to another, or from one developed country to another; only about 37 per cent of all international migration takes place from a developing to a developed country (UNDP, 2009).

Migration patterns have changed in several very significant ways over the past 10 to 20 years. First of all, the numbers of international migrants have increased, going from about 150 million in 2000 to 214 million today, and predicted to reach 405 million by 2050 (IOM, 2010). A major underlying reason is the substantial – and increasing – differences in income trends that encourage people to seek better lives in other countries. The social and economic benefits of migration can be significant in fact: people from low human development index countries earn 15 times as much subsequent to migrating, are able to enrol twice as many of their children in schools, and experience 16 times less child mortality (UNDP, 2009). Other reasons underlying increases in migration include growing demographic disparities (by about 2025 new entrants to the labour force in developing countries will exceed the total number of working age people currently living in developed countries, for example) (ibid.) and possibly environmental factors, as climate change increases environmental stress in lands that are already marginal.

An additional factor is quite simply that the journeys involved are easier than in previous generations: better transport networks and significant decreases in air fares mean that more people can travel, both within and between countries. At the same time, the rapid expansion of the use of mobile telephones and of internet communication means that it is simple and inexpensive to keep in contact with family and friends while one is away. Together, these changes mean that migrating to another country is less daunting than it undoubtedly once was. Short-term and circular migration have increased as people can relatively easily go abroad for a few months or years, keep in contact while they are away, return home for visits, or move on to other countries. A corollary of such population movement is that it is not uncommon for migrants to hold more than one nationality.

Migration specialists used to talk about 'push' and 'pull' factors to differentiate between voluntary and forced migration, but have now tended to back away from such distinctions, noting that any particular individual is very often both pushed and pulled in a decision to migrate. One may be pushed by conflict and/or by the fact that there are few opportunities for decent employment at home, for example, and also pulled by curiosity, or by the stories of family and friends who have migrated. Along similar lines, official migration categories in destination countries can be somewhat fluid: migration status may well change, for example when a visa expires and a tourist becomes an irregular migrant, when an asylum seeker is granted refugee status, or when a spouse admitted under family reunification takes up employment.

A factor that may be underestimated in individualistic societies is that migration is very often not an individual matter but a family affair. Families may select certain of their members to work abroad, in hopes of bettering the situation of the entire group, directly through the financial remittances sent back, and also indirectly, for example by making it possible for the next generation to attend better schools. In some societies, in addition, migration is a normal and expected part of growing up, or an important part of the heritage of families or of entire communities (c.f. Anarfi et al., 2005 for parts of West Africa; and Thomas-Hope, 1999 for the Caribbean).

The demographics of migration have also shifted. A greater proportion of international migrants are skilled labourers, such as information technology specialists or healthcare workers. And half of the world's labour migrants are now women, who go abroad as primary migrants rather than migrating to join family members as they did a generation ago. Female migrants work in all sectors of the economy and at all levels, although they tend to be concentrated in occupations associated with traditional gender roles such as education, social work and health, particularly nursing (Jolly and Reeves, 2005). They also work in factories, as domestics, and – as women throughout the world increasingly work outside their homes – to care for children and the elderly (Carling, 2005; Orozco, 2009).

From the point of view of destination countries, massive, active and official recruitment of labour migrants ceased quite some time ago, although there is still a market for undocumented migrant workers to carry out unskilled and poorly paid jobs, in restaurants, agriculture and construction for example. Most countries that receive migrants have recently seen increased calls for control of in-migration, however, and especially for repressive measures to attempt to limit irregular migration. Economic crisis and uncertainty have undoubtedly heightened such calls. Reception in destination countries is no longer necessarily welcoming, and may be hostile as anxiety feeds xenophobia (IOM, 2010).

In sum, former migration patterns still exist – young men still set out alone to take up jobs abroad, then establish their families in the new country and settle permanently. But this traditional linear

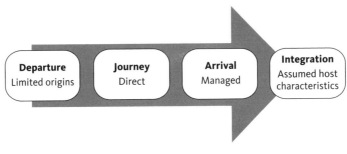

TRADITIONAL MIGRATION PATTERN

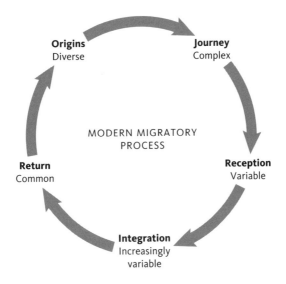

1.1 Traditional and modern migration paradigms (*source*: Gushulak, 2010)

pattern has become more of a circle, and also more complex, with people leaving from, transiting, going to a wider range of countries then going back again. Figure 1.1 sketches the traditional migration paradigm and today's migration patterns.

Phases of the migration process and health effects

In a phenomenon sometimes referred to as the 'healthy migrant effect', it has been noted that those who migrate may well be in better health than those who do not. People who deliberately set out to find work or to join family members are, after all, those with energy and social capital sufficient to engage in the risks of leaving their communities, to seek new experiences in hopes of creating better conditions for themselves and their families. This section discusses the possible health effects of migration, following the migratory process just sketched.

During transit Travel between countries of origin and of destination is uneventful for most migrants, but may be dangerous or have health consequences for a minority. Those attempting to cross borders clandestinely, for example, may hide during the voyage, cramped into freight containers or trucks, under trains or in boats that are entirely unsuited to carrying large numbers of people. The press regularly reports dramatic deaths of tens or even of thousands of men, women and children in the course of such unsafe journeys, as for example when a boat carrying some 300 Eritrean and Somali refugees from Libya capsized off the Italian coast in April 2011, leaving some 250 people unaccounted for (Associated Press, 2011). Other migrants or would-be migrants experience harassment and/or health-damaging exploitation during their journeys. Examples include forced sex experienced by women – and also men – as they flee conflict or live in refugee situations (c.f. Rowley et al., 2008), or as they seek to cross borders in search of employment (c.f. Bronfman et al., 2002).

For other migrants the transit phase of the migration process may last for long periods of time, for example as they move from one country to another in search of stable employment. Access to routine healthcare is often inadequate during such periods of extended transit, and prevention measures such as periodic health examinations, dental care and vaccinations may be totally lacking (Gushulak and MacPherson, 2004), potentially leading to long-term damage to health.

At destination Studies of immigrants in Canada and the United States (McDonald and Kennedy, 2004; Singh and Siahpush, 2001), Nicaraguan migrants in Costa Rica (Herring et al., 2008) and Turkish living in Germany (Razum et al., 1998), among others, have documented the good level of health of recent immigrants. Migrants' initial health advantage tends to dissipate over time, however, as documented in detailed studies in a number of Organisation for Economic Co-operation and Development (OECD) countries (UNDP, 2009). For example a major review of the health and wellbeing of children in immigrant families in the US showed good health for first generation immigrant children, but that their advantages faded: immigrant young people living in the US for longer periods tended to be less healthy and to report more risk behaviours, with rates of most behaviours approaching or exceeding

those of US born majority adolescents by the third and later generations (Hernandez et al., 1998). These findings are similar to those of
other studies that report the disappearance of health advantages for
immigrant young people with time in the destination country, in the
US and also internationally (c.f. Brindis et al., 1995; Gfroerer and Tan,
2003; McKay et al., 2003).

Several factors may account for such declines, including changes
in health behaviours, limitations in access to health services, and
especially working, housing and other social conditions. Immigrants
may adopt poorer health behaviours and lifestyles in the destination
country, such as the risk behaviours just referred to, or diet changes
that lead to increases in obesity for example (Antecol and Bedard,
2005). More importantly for this book, and as elaborated by Scheppers
et al. (2006), migrants often face barriers to health services, at the level
of the patients, of providers, or of health and social systems. At the
level of the patient, one's own health may simply not be a priority
when one feels responsible for sending funds home to pay for basic
essentials, or for a child's education. In such cases the possibility
of illness may simply be ignored for as long as possible. Cultural
differences in health beliefs and attitudes, in perceived illness, in
health practices and in assumptions about models of medical care
also create potential barriers to migrants' use of health services. For
example people from communities in which medical care is paid for
on a fee-for-service basis may be unaware of, or unfamiliar with, the
provision of nationally insured services that should be available to
them (see also Hargreaves and Friedland, this volume). At the level of
the provider, potential barriers include services that are inappropriate
or ill-adapted: opening hours may not be convenient, distance or cost
may be prohibitive, language or cultural misunderstandings may create
barriers, or migrants may not trust health services in the destination community. Other barriers occur at the level of health and social
systems, where in fact access to services may be limited for migrants.
Legal status – or having one's immigration status in order – is often
a determining factor for such access (Scheppers et al., 2006).

Of all the factors that may account for declines in migrants' health
after their arrival in destination countries, however, it is perhaps the
structural factors that are most important. The literature contains
numerous descriptions of the housing problems of migrant workers,
for example. Such workers often find themselves living in poor quality
lodging and paying exploitative rents. Men and women who migrate
without their partners often attempt to keep expenses down by

crowding in with other migrants when they first move to a new place (Parrado et al., 2010). In places that range from migrant labour hostels of South Africa (Ramphele, 1993), tea plantations in Kenya (Ondimu, 2010) and palm oil plantations in Papua New Guinea (Wardlow, 2010), studies have described situations in which entire families crowd into spaces that were originally built for single male workers. The communities that arise are overcrowded, noisy and insecure, and not likely to be good for the physical or the mental health of the families that live in them.

Another important set of structural factors, those related to employment, were explored by a specific network of the World Health Organization (WHO) Commission on Social Determinants of Health; the Employment Conditions Knowledge Network pointed out that although many of today's migrants are professionals and skilled workers, migrant workers also tend to be concentrated at the opposite end of the employment spectrum, in dangerous industries and in hazardous jobs, occupations and tasks. In most countries, migrant workers are concentrated in agricultural, food processing, construction, semi-skilled or unskilled manufacturing jobs and in low wage service jobs that natives of the host country prefer to avoid if they can. Their jobs are often precarious, with wages that cannot support their families. The Commission further pointed out that migrant day labourers are often exposed to a variety of work-related hazards such as chemicals, pesticides, dust and other toxic substances. They may not receive proper protective equipment, safety and other on-the-job training, insurance, healthcare or compensation in case of injury, and may fear reprisals if they demand better working conditions. Irregular migrant workers are especially vulnerable to coercion, abuse and exploitation at the workplace – since they fear job loss, incarceration and deportation, they can be hired at extremely low wages and are often underpaid or not paid at all (Benach et al., 2011, 2010). The effects of job insecurity on psychological distress and overall health constitute yet another burden for migrant workers and their families. Working below one's level of qualification is a source of stress for others, for example when migrants trained as teachers work as nannies, or doctors work as aides.

Women may be particularly vulnerable. Unskilled female migrant labourers work as domestics, hotel cleaners, waitresses and in hospitality and entertainment industries (Ehrenreich and Hochschild, 2003), while others are active in retail sales, in labour intensive factory work and in the informal sectors. Such women often face low remuneration, heavy workloads, long working hours and poor career development.

Their jobs are often not covered by labour legislation or other social security or welfare provisions, or are only covered inadequately (ILO, 2004). This is especially the case for domestic work, where protection is often flimsy and medical care inadequate, and where psychological, physical and sexual abuse has frequently been noted (CARAM Asia, 2004; Engle, 2004).

It is through the potential health consequences for young people and children that the structural conditions of the migration process are perhaps most pertinent, however. Children and young people are affected by migration in a number of ways: when they move with their families, when their parents migrate and leave them in the home country, or when they migrate alone (see Chase, this volume). As with other groups, the health consequences for physical and mental health depend to a large degree on the conditions and circumstances under which the migration takes place, and can range from significant benefits and increased resilience for those whose move is voluntary, planned and perceived as a family step forward (Haour-Knipe, 2001; Scalabrini Migration Center, 2003), to ill-health and damaging exclusion from educational and health systems among those who move to live clandestinely with parents who are irregular migrant workers (Bryant, 2005). Unaccompanied minors, especially, are at risk of violence, child trafficking, exploitation, discrimination, sexual and other abuses, and of being coerced into begging, drug dealing or prostitution (Commission on Human Rights, 2004) – or they may tell of feeling intense pride at having helped support their families in difficulty by proactively seeking a better life abroad (Anarfi et al., 2005).

One of the most eloquent – and also most alarming – studies to examine such factors is the 'Children of Immigrants Longitudinal Study' in the United States, which has been following a large sample of second generation youths in a major migration destination country. The authors had previously noted that children of immigrants encounter social contexts in schools and neighbourhoods that may lead to 'downward assimilation', such as dropping out of school, joining youth gangs, and using and selling drugs (Portes and Zhou, 1993 cited in Portes et al., 2005). By early adulthood the majority of second generation youth in the longitudinal study were moving ahead educationally and occupationally, but a significant minority was being left behind. Those slipping behind were children of immigrants with lower levels of education and income. Their families were less likely to be intact, to be closely integrated into ethnic networks or to have dense ties to their communities. For these young people, lack of skills, poverty and a hostile context of reception accumulate into difficulties that are frequently insurmountable. The authors observe that the results from their study are 'almost frightening' in revealing the power of structural factors such as family human capital, family composition and attachment to the community in shaping the lives of the young immigrants (Portes et al., 2005). Quite similarly, but in a more general remark, the UNDP Human Development Report devoted to population mobility notes that countries' concerns about migration, security and crime may reinforce each other, in what becomes a vicious circle:

> Migrants who are marginalized – due, for example, to temporary or irregular status or high levels of unemployment – may resort to anti-social or criminal behaviour, confirming the security fears of locals. If this leads to further discrimination in the labour market and in policy formation, such migrants may turn away from the new society back to the old, possibly forming gangs or other anti-social organizations that threaten local populations. (UNDP, 2009: 91)

In sum, where labour market disadvantage leads to social exclusion, repercussions for social cohesion can quickly follow: the health consequences affect not only migrants themselves, but entire societies.

Returning to communities of origin

The potential health effects of migration in communities of origin and in those of return are mirror images of each other. Returning, or visiting, migrants may be responsible for introducing new pathogens or increasing the prevalence of infections among the local population when they return, as has been shown for HIV in South Africa, for example (Lurie et al., 2003), or – in both directions – across the border between India and Nepal (Nepal, 2007).

As has already been mentioned, migration is often a family affair: the remittances sent home can increase the economic situations of households, and also bring social remittances, the increased social capital and new ideas, practices and identities that increase the family's wellbeing. Such economic and social remittances can help a family afford a healthier lifestyle and better healthcare for the returning migrant, the members of his or her family, or even for entire communities, as, for example, when returnees or migrants in diaspora set up hospitals or other health facilities in their communities of origin (Ganguly, 2003).

On the negative side, reintegration may be more difficult than expected for the returning migrant (Long and Oxfeld, 2004). An excellent study of return migration to Barbados, for example, describes how many returnees found that conditions in the community had changed, and that they themselves had changed in ways they had not realised. The welcome was different when the return home was permanent than it had been when it had been for a visit; expectations turned out to have been unrealistic; not all friendships had weathered the separations; and jealousies were frequent (Gmelch, 2004). In addition, returnees may encounter family difficulties, such as returning back to dependency, or not having fulfilled all that had been (sometimes unrealistically) expected of them (King, 2000; Tiemoko, 2003).

The return of former migrant workers home to their families for care when they are seriously ill or at the end of their lives gives rise to particularly difficult and tragic situations (Haour-Knipe, 2009). Individuals returning to low resource settings with life-threatening, disabling or chronic health concerns that require ongoing or high-tech treatment, such as cancer, diabetes or HIV, may have difficulty identifying or paying for adequate care when they return (Zimmerman et al., 2011). Occupational illnesses that appear long after the employee has left a particular job (such as those related to asbestos) pose particular challenges to responsibility: defining responsibilities between employers and former employers, or policy implications between source and host nations, have been defined as some of the unmet challenges concerning migrant health (IOM, 2005; Shah, this volume).

Policy frameworks affecting migrant health, and the role of international organisations

The lopsided demographic patterns, economic imbalances and conflicts that push and pull people to migrate show every sign of persisting. And – more positively – simple curiosity and adventurousness will also incite people to leave home, to live in other communities to see what life is like elsewhere. Yet entry policies prevailing in destination countries have generally been marked by denial and delay, by increasing legal and administrative barriers to migration, and by heightened border controls that mainly simply encourage illegal stays. When policy on migration *is* formulated, the discussions have been nicely described as being conducted from policy sector 'silos'. The policy areas of international aid, security, immigration enforcement or trade or labour, for example, have different or even incompatible goals, and in addition they rarely include health (Pace and Gushulak, 2010; Zimmerman et al., 2011).

For many years, policy-making in the area of migrant health was dominated by notions of disease control and containment. Migration was viewed in terms of its 'threats' or the historical fear that entering migrants would bring diseases with them. The approach emphasises public health security and control of communicable disease, relying heavily on monitoring and screening for such conditions as tuberculosis (TB) and HIV. More recently, fears of healthcare costs potentially incurred by entering migrants have been added to these concerns. In recent years the health of migrants has increasingly been set in terms of human rights discourse, however, or the idea that some rights are universal, whatever one's migration status. Several legally binding international human rights treaties have been signed, assuring equality and non-discrimination. Examples are the International Convention on the Elimination of All Forms of Racial Discrimination (ICERD), the Convention on the Rights of the Child and the Convention on the Elimination of All Forms of Discrimination against Women. A more specific example is the International Convention on the Protection of the Rights of All Migrant Workers and Members of their Families (ICPRMW). These instruments – and their limitations – are discussed in detail in other chapters of this book (see in particular, Willman). Such agreements help focus on the most vulnerable and marginalised, thus recognising the special vulnerabilities of migrants that have been discussed in this chapter. The approach thus moves migration health discourse towards social equity discourse.

Migrant health has been the specific object of several resolutions, agreements or promises signed over the past few years. A WHO World Health Assembly (WHA) resolution on the health of migrants, endorsed in May 2008, for example, promotes migrant-sensitive health policies. In 2001 the United Nations General Assembly Special Session on HIV/AIDS called for developing national, regional and international strategies that facilitate access to HIV/AIDS prevention programmes for migrants and mobile workers, including the provision of information on health and social services. The call was reinforced in 2009 when the UNAIDS Programme Coordination Board requested that mobile populations, including migrants and forcibly displaced persons, be incorporated into strategies to achieve universal access to HIV prevention, treatment, care and support (NGO representatives, 2009). Several European projects are currently being carried out on migrant health (see http://migheath.net/eu/index.php/Main_Page for regularly updated information on these), and a number of countries are providing access to healthcare for migrants, including for those whose status is irregular.

International organisations have a significant role in such efforts. WHO and UNAIDS have already been mentioned, as has the commission on social determinants of health. Each of these has specifically evoked the importance of assuring migrant health. Other critical actors include such specialised agencies as the International Organization for Migration (IOM), which deals with migration in general, and the United Nations High Commissioner for Refugees (UNHCR), which concentrates on forced migration. These, and other inter-governmental and non-governmental organisations, are able to cover populations that otherwise tend to fall between the cracks of equity efforts carried out by governments, taking leadership in issues outside the realm of national interests and relating to people who do not necessarily 'belong' in the country in which they are residing. They, along with NGOs, may be able to develop and carry out specific projects related to migrant health that would be impossible for an official government agency to carry out, for example because 'the government' is not trusted by the target population, or simply because the target population does not officially exist (migrants living in irregular situations in a given country are an excellent example of the latter).

Such agencies can build bridges between countries of origin, transit and destination, creating opportunities and spaces for discussions that would not otherwise happen, such as the International Dialogues on Migration organised by the IOM. Several such consultative processes have been held over the years, for example to discuss asylum, refugee and migration policies throughout Europe; overseas employment and contractual labour in Asia; irregular migration and trafficking of persons in East and Southeast Asia; or migration and transit in the Caribbean, in the Mediterranean, in southern Africa or in West Africa. Contrasting perspectives and needs can be aired during such exchanges, information can be shared, confidence can be built, and collaborative approaches can be explored. Such agencies can also play an important role carrying out research and documenting needs regarding neglected issues with regard to migrant health, such as the UNHCR has done concerning refugees' coverage in national AIDS plans and in Global Fund grants for HIV and malaria (Spiegel et al., 2010).

Such documentation, along with information campaigns, advocacy, workshops and capacity building training, helps raise appropriate awareness to issues that would otherwise have been left behind. They can define – and begin to address – complex policy issues, such as who should be responsible for healthcare and support when a former migrant worker returns home too ill to work, or when a migrant's elderly parent or child living in a different country needs help. In the best of cases the combined efforts of such international organisations and NGOs can lead to policy advances in relation to migrant health. One good example is a convention produced by the Governing Body of the International Labour Organization (ILO) in June 2011 to protect the rights of migrant domestic workers, including that to a safe and healthy working environment (ILO, 2011). Another took place subsequent to intensive efforts of an International Task Team on HIV-related Travel Restrictions, which urged states to replace any existing HIV-specific restrictions on entry, stay and residence with access to prevention, treatment, care and support for citizens and non-citizens alike (UNAIDS, 2008), and after which several countries lifted bans on travel and immigration by people living with HIV (www.hivtravel.org).

Needs and challenges

Needs in the field of migrant health start with the generation of better data, on migration in general, on the health of migrants, and on such issues as migrants' access to health services. Until authors begin to clearly spell out the definitions they are using when they discuss migrants and migration, and until information about such denominators as the numbers of migrants present in a given community is readily available, it will be difficult to document and advocate for needs in the field of migrant health, and/or to carry out evaluations of programmes and propose lessons for good practice.

Another need is to create linkages, or to build bridges between countries and regions, and between sectors on a broad spectrum of health issues. The linking with the wider focus on social equity just mentioned is a good step in this direction. Until countries of origin, transit, destination and return sit down to discuss policy issues together – along with representatives of migrant groups – and until such discussions range beyond the healthcare sector, policy-making will continue to be carried out in silos doomed to remain largely ineffective. Related to this need is a significant challenge: that of working though differences between laws, policy and practice. Laws that are fundamentally equitable must be backed up by the official policies that regulate their application. However neither laws nor policies will be pertinent until the individual border officer, teacher or health worker is enabled and willing to apply them to the individual migrant standing in front of her in search of a decent job, a school or care for an illness.

As for other major challenges, the economic crisis swirling around the world as this chapter is being written is likely to have a heavy impact on migrant workers, due to the vulnerability factors described. Migrants, especially migrant women, are likely to be affected in several ways: through restrictions on new admissions of migrant workers and non-renewal of work permits; through job losses in sectors that employ migrant workers; through the availability of fewer working days, deterioration in working conditions and increased abuses that are more likely to affect workers with weaker bargaining power; through hardship upon loss of employment that is further complicated when precarious workers are not eligible for social benefits; through discrimination and xenophobia against workers mistakenly perceived to be 'stealing' local workers' jobs; and through return of unemployed migrants to communities of origin that are also facing high unemployment and poverty (IOM, 2009).

A fundamental challenge in the field of migrant health, perhaps *the* fundamental challenge, is that the presence of migrant workers and their families poses questions about 'us' and 'them'. The presence of migrants in a community raises tension about equity, about access for all, and about deciding how to distribute limited resources. This tension becomes worse during economic downturn, as the vulnerable move to protect themselves. Meeting this fundamental challenge will require creative thinking, for defining and advocating for models of what works. It will require leadership and advocacy in developing models of equality that reach beyond our own families and our own communities, to include new forms and models of sharing.

References

Anarfi, J., S. Gent, I. Hashim, V. Iversen, S. Khair, S. Kwankye, C. A. Tagoe, D. Thorsen and A. Whitehead (2005) *Voices of Child Migrants: A Better Understanding of How Life Is*, Sussex Centre for Migration Research, Sussex.

Antecol, H. and K. Bedard (2005) 'Unhealthy assimilation: Why do immigrants converge to American health status levels?', *IZA Discussion Paper No. 1654*, IZA, Bonn.

Associated Press (2011) 'Up to 250 missing after migrant boat sinks off Italy', AP, www.ap.org/.

Benach, J., C. Muntaner, H. Chung and F. G. Benavides (2010) 'Immigration, employment relations, and health: Developing a research agenda', *American Journal of Industrial Medicine*, 53(4): 338–43.

Benach, J., C. Muntaner, C. Delclos, M. Menendez and C. Ronquillo (2011) 'Migration and "low-skilled" workers in destination countries', *PLoS Med*, 8(6): e1001043.

Brindis, C., A. L. Wolfe, V. McCarter, S. Ball and S. Starbuck-Morales (1995) 'The associations between immigrant status and risk-behavior patterns in Latino adolescents', *Journal of Adolescent Health*, 17(2): 99–105.

Bronfman, M. N., R. Leyva, M. J. Negroni and C. M. Rueda (2002) 'Mobile populations and HIV/ AIDS in Central America and Mexico: Research for action', *AIDS*, 16(Suppl. 3): S42–9.

Bryant, J. (2005) *Children of International Migrants in Indonesia, Thailand, and the Philippines: A Review of Evidence and Policies*, UNICEF, Innocenti Research Centre, Florence.

CARAM (Coordination of Action Research on AIDS and Mobility) Asia (2004) *The Forgotten Spaces: Mobility and HIV Vulnerability in the Asia Pacific*, CARAM, Kuala Lumpur.

Carling, J. (2005) *Gender Dimensions of International Migration*, Global Commission on International Migration, Geneva.

Commission on Human Rights (2004) 'Specific Groups and Individuals: Migrant Workers, Report of the Special Rapporteur, Ms. Gabriela Rodríguez Pizarro. Addendum: Mission to the Philippines', United Nations Economic and Social Council, New York.

Ehrenreich, B. and A. R. Hochschild (2003) *Global Woman: Nannies, Maids, and Sex Workers in the New Economy*, Metropolitan Books, New York.

Engle, L. (2004) *The World in Motion; Short Essays on Migration and Gender*, IOM, Geneva.

Ganguly, D. (2003) *Return Migration and Diaspora Investments in the Indian Healthcare Industry*, Indian Institute of Management, Bangalore.

Gfroerer, J. C. and L. L. Tan (2003) 'Substance use among foreign-born youths in the United States: Does the length of residence matter?', *American Journal of Public Health*, 93(11): 1892–5.

Gmelch, G. (2004) 'West Indian migrants and their rediscovery of Barbados', in L. Long and E. Oxfeld (eds) *Coming Home? Refugees, Migrants, and Those Who Stayed Behind*, University of Pennsylvania Press, Philadelphia: 206–23.

Gushulak, B. (2010) *Monitoring Migrants' Health. Global Consultation on Migrant Health*, WHO, IOM, National School of Public Health, Geneva.

Gushulak, B. and D. W. MacPherson (2004) 'Population mobility and health: An overview of the relationships between movement and population health', *Journal of Travel Medicine*, 11(3): 171–4.

Haour-Knipe, M. (2001) *Moving Families: Expatriation, Stress and Coping*, Routledge, London.

— (2009) 'Families, children, migration and AIDS', *AIDS Care*, 21(S1): 43–8.

Hernandez, D. J., E. Charney, National Research Council and Committee on the Health and Adjustment of Immigrant Children and Families (1998) *From Generation to Generation: The Health and Well-being of Children in Immigrant Families*, National Academy Press, Washington DC.

Herring, A. A., R. E. Bonilla-Carrion, R. M. Borland and K. H. Hill (2008) 'Differential mortality patterns between Nicaraguan immigrants and native-born residents of Costa Rica', *Journal of Immigrant Minority Health*, 12: 33–42.

ILO (International Labour Organization) (2004) *Towards a Fair Deal for Migrant Workers in the Global Economy*, ILO, Geneva.

— (2011) 'Text of the Convention Concerning Decent Work for Domestic Workers', International Labour Conference, ILO, Geneva.

IOM (International Organization for Migration) (2005) *Health and Migration: Bridging the Gap*, IOM, Geneva.

— (2009) *The Impact of the Global Economic Crisis on Migrants and Migration*, IOM, Geneva.

— (2010) *World Migration Report 2010: The Future of Migration: Building Capacities for Change*, IOM, Geneva.

Jolly, S. and H. Reeves (2005) *Gender and Migration: Overview Report*, Institute of Development Studies, Brighton.

King, R. (2000) *Generalizations from the History of Return Migration. Return Migration: Journey of Hope or Despair?*, IOM, Geneva.

Long, L. and E. Oxfeld (2004) *Coming Home? Refugees, Migrants, and those who Stayed Behind*, University of Pennsylvania Press, Philadelphia.

Lurie, M. N., B. G. Williams, K. Zuma, D. Mkaya-Mwamburi, G. Garnett, A. W. Sturm, M. D. Sweat, J. Gittelsohn and S. S. Abdool Karim (2003) 'The impact of migration on HIV-1 transmission in South Africa: A study of migrant and nonmigrant men and their partners', *Sexually Transmitted Diseases*, 30(2): 149–56.

McDonald, J. T. and S. Kennedy (2004) 'Insights into the "healthy immigrant effect": Health status and health service use of immigrants to Canada', *Social Science and Medicine*, 59(8): 1613–27.

McKay, L., S. Macintyre and A. Ellaway (2003) *Migration and Health: A Review of the International Literature*, MRC, Medical Research Council's Medical Sociology Unit – Public Health Research Unit, University of Glasgow, Glasgow.

Nepal, B. (2007) 'Population mobility and spread of HIV across the Indo-Nepal border', *Journal of Health, Population and Nutrition*, 25(3): 267–77.

NGO representatives (2009) *Report by the NGO representative: 24th Meeting of the UNAIDS Programme Coordinating Board*, UNAIDS, Geneva.

Ondimu, K. (2010) 'Labour migration and risky sexual behavior: Tea plantation workers in Kericho District, Kenya', in F. Thomas, M. Haour-Knipe and P. Aggleton (eds) *Mobility, Sexuality and AIDS*, Routledge, London and New York: 154–67.

Orozco, A. (2009) *Global Care Chains*, United Nations International Research and Training, Institute for the Advancement of Women (INSTRAW), Santo Domingo, Dominican Republic.

Pace, P. and B. D. Gushulak (2010) *Policy and Legal Frameworks Affecting Migrants' Health. Global Consultation on Migrant Health*, WHO, IOM, National School of Public Health, Geneva.

Parrado, E., C. Flippen and L. Uribe (2010) 'Concentrated disadvantages: Neighbourhood context as a structural risk for Latino immigrants in the USA', in F. Thomas, M. Haour-Knipe and P. Aggleton (eds) *Mobility, Sexuality and AIDS*, Routledge, London and New York: 40–54.

Portes, A., P. Fernandez-Kelly and W. Haller (2005) 'Segmented assimilation on the ground: The new second generation in early adulthood', *Ethnic and Racial Studies*, 28(6): 1000–40.

Ramphele, M. (1993) *A Bed Called Home: Life in the Migrant Labour Hostels of Cape Town*, D. Philip, Cape Town.

Razum, O., H. Zeeb, H. S. Akgun and S. Yilmaz (1998) 'Low overall mortality of Turkish residents in Germany persists and extends into a second generation: Merely a healthy migrant effect?', *Tropical Medicine and International Health*, 3(4): 297–303.

Rowley, E. A., P. B. Spiegel, Z. Tunze, G. Mbaruku, M. Schilperoord and P. Njogu (2008) 'Differences in HIV-related behaviors at Lugufu refugee camp and surrounding host villages, Tanzania', *Conflict and Health*, 17 October: 2–13.

Scalabrini Migration Center (2003) *Hearts Apart: Migration in the Eyes of Filipino Children*, Scalabrini Migration Center, Manila.

Scheppers, E., E. van Dongen, J. Dekker, J. Geertzen and J. Dekker, J. (2006) 'Potential barriers to the use of health services among ethnic minorities: A review', *Family Practice*, 23(3): 325–48.

Singh, G. and M. Siahpush (2001) 'All-cause and cause-specific mortality of immigrants and native born in the United States', *American Journal of Public Health*, 91(3): 392–9.

Spiegel, P. B., H. Hering, E. Paik and M. Schilperoord (2010) 'Conflict-affected displaced persons need to benefit more from HIV and malaria national strategic plans and Global Fund grants', *Conflict and Health*, 4: 2–6.

Thomas-Hope, E. (1999) 'Return migration to Jamaica and its development potential', *International Migration*, 37(1): 183–207.

Tiemoko, R. (2003) *Migration, Return and Socio-Economic Change in West Africa: The Role of Family*, Sussex Centre for Migration Research, Sussex.

UNAIDS (Joint United Nations Programme on HIV/AIDS) (2008) *Report of the International Task Team on HIV-related Travel Restrictions: Findings and Recommendations*, UNAIDS, Geneva.

UNDP (United Nations Development Programme) (2009) *Overcoming Barriers: Human Mobility and Development*, UNDP, New York.

Wardlow, H. (2010) 'Labour migration and HIV risk in Papua New Guinea', in F. Thomas, M. Haour-Knipe and P. Aggleton (eds) *Mobility, Sexuality and AIDS*. Routledge, London and New York: 176–86.

Zimmerman, C., L. Kiss and M. Hossain (2011) 'Migration and health: A framework for 21st century policy-making', *PLoS Med*, 8(5): e1001034.

2 | Impact on and use of health services by new migrants in Europe

SALLY HARGREAVES AND JON S. FRIEDLAND

New migration to Europe

In recent years Europe has become a major destination for international migrants, increasing from 14.7 million in 1990 to 73 million in 2010 and now representing a third of the global total (IOM, 2010). Today, migrants have a considerable impact on the population demographics of most European Union (EU) countries, with the largest numbers of migrants residing in Russia, Germany, Spain, UK and France, and of whom up to half are now young women. One of the key aspects of this new migration is the range of countries from which migrants now come, and the plethora of reasons they have for migrating to European countries. In the UK, for example, commentators have referred to this phase as 'the new migration', noting that the diversity of new migrants is now exceeding anything previously experienced (Vertovec, 2006). For the purposes of this chapter, we adopt the term 'new migrant' to encompass migrants entering since the 1990s in this new wave of immigration, and to enable a distinction to be made between new migrants and more settled migrants.

Migrants come to Europe for many different reasons, with considerable numbers now entering on work or student visas. In 2009 261,000 applicants registered for asylum in the EU-27, from 151 different countries (Eurostat, 2010). Indeed, it was the dramatic rise in asylum seekers during the last two decades of the twentieth century, following the collapse of the Soviet Bloc and the conflict of Bosnia and Herzegovina, that forced EU governments to confront the issue of immigration to and within Europe. The Maastricht and Amsterdam Treaties, in 1992 and 1997 respectively, saw the development of common asylum and migration policies, with a focus on stemming the rising number of migrants seeking political asylum across Western Europe (Castles et al., 2003). The result has been a strengthening of EU borders and the implementation of measures to deter asylum seekers and other migrants from coming to the EU. This 'fortress Europe' approach is associated with an increase in the number of people dying as they attempt to enter European countries through illegal channels, for example smuggled across borders in the back of lorries or by boat, but will inevitably have more subtle though important affects on migrant health. More recently, policy change at the EU level has focused on tackling growing levels of irregular migration. Irregular migrants are also referred to as illegal, undocumented or unauthorised migrants and include individuals entering by avoiding immigration inspection, entering using false documents, overstaying visas or otherwise violating visa conditions, having a rejected asylum claim but remaining in the host country (a 'failed' asylum seeker), as well as those who have already applied for asylum in another country. Estimates of numbers are difficult to ascertain; most recent estimates of numbers within EU member states are between 1.9 and 3.8 million (Clandestino Research Project, 2009).

In the past decade irregular migrants, asylum seekers and refugees have increasingly been depicted as competitors for scarce resources, including healthcare, in particular by increasingly xenophobic sections of the European population. Current policy debate has focused on the curtailment or denial of social security rights and – of particular relevance to this chapter – their rights to access publicly funded healthcare (Norredam et al., 2006; Médecins du Monde, 2009; Torres-Cantero et al., 2007). There are concerns that this more restrictive approach is short sighted and a breach of international human rights law, with implications for all migrants in Europe, whether entitled to access services or not. Policies to restrict and control access to health services will undoubtedly compound existing barriers to healthcare that many migrant groups face on arrival to the host country, and may impact on how these new migrants ultimately access and utilise health services. Furthermore, more restrictive policies pose ethical dilemmas for healthcare professionals tasked with meeting the needs of migrant and ethnic communities who face inequities in health status and disease risk.

What are the implications for health services?

The numbers and diversity of new migrants undoubtedly present organisational challenges to health services in host countries. The implication of migration from resource poor countries on health systems of richer nations is an issue that is growing in importance in research terms. Migrants as a group will be particularly affected by worldwide differences in disease patterns and social inequalities. Although it is impossible to generalise, some new migrants face destitution, poor housing and low socioeconomic status on arrival, with implications for health status and their ability to access services (Arai and Harding, 2002).

In 2007 the Portuguese Presidency of the EU defined migrant health as a core focus of EU health policy, with migrant health now considered a key indicator of integration within host societies. At present, however, there are major shortfalls in the development and evaluation of migrant health policies in Europe, with an urgent need for countries to better document and share their experiences and improve the research base and data collection around provision of healthcare to migrants (Mladovsky, 2009).

Health status of new migrants The health status of new migrants will vary considerably and be dependent on a number of variables including pre-migration and host country experiences, immigration status, ability to work, age, sex and family status. What is becoming increasingly clear, however, is the importance that health has in the lives of Europe's migrants, and the extent to which the migration context impacts on their health and subsequent integration. Both migration status and low social position are considered to be independent risk factors associated with poor health across all migrant groups (McKay et al., 2003). Poverty and destitution are well documented in refugee, asylum seeker and irregular migrant populations across Europe, with implications for physical and mental health (Médecins du Monde, 2009; Médecins Sans Frontières, 2005). International studies support the idea that irregular migrants from resource poor countries may face considerably worse living and working conditions and social disadvantage in host countries, and build up to a comparably worse health status over time (Romero-Ortuno, 2004). Immigrant women are considered particularly vulnerable. One study exploring pregnancy outcomes across migrant women in European countries found that these women showed a clear health disadvantage with higher risk of low birth weight, perinatal mortality, congenital malformations and preterm delivery (Bollini et al., 2009; see also Bragg, this volume). Recent calls have also been made to better understand inequities in care for chronic diseases in Europe's migrant community (Bhopal, 2009).

Migration is becoming a central theme in discourse and policy-making on infectious disease management in Europe, particularly with respect to HIV/AIDS, other sexually transmitted infections and TB. This relates primarily to the rise in number of migrants moving from resource poor countries, with higher rates of infectious diseases and poorly developed healthcare systems, to more affluent areas of the world where prevalence rates are low, as well as the inequalities in access to services they may face on arrival. Irregular migrants in Europe are considered to have a higher prevalence of infectious diseases including TB (Romero-Ortuno, 2004; Wolff et al., 2010). Other infectious diseases, including sexually transmitted infections, hepatitis B, HIV, malaria and parasitic infection are considered to be more prevalent among refugees and asylum seekers, prevalence rates that are compounded perhaps by high levels of social and economic deprivation faced on arrival. Hepatitis B and C infections are an increasing concern among migrants (Hahne et al., 2009). One study of infectious diseases departments across Italy reported a broad range of diseases in migrants, diseases directly correlated with conditions of poverty (Scotto et al., 2005).

Some European countries are now witnessing increases in migrant associated TB and HIV. The factors underlying the observed increases remain unclear but increased socioeconomic deprivation and migration from high risk regions are known to play a part (Abgrall et al., 2010; Gilbert et al., 2009; Xiridou et al., 2011). Black Africans, many of whom are considered to be new migrants, comprise a rapidly increasing population in terms of HIV infection. Over 90 per cent of heterosexually acquired HIV infections diagnosed in the UK during 2004, for example, were probably acquired in high prevalence countries of origin, mainly sub-Saharan Africa (UKCG, 2005), a trend that is being mirrored across Europe (Hamers and Downs, 2004). Current approaches to tackling TB and multi-drug-resistant TB among migrants in Europe too need to be re-evaluated. In the UK, Norway and Sweden three-quarters of cases of TB (1996–2005) were foreign-born (Gilbert et al., 2009). Yet screening policies for new migrants are considered inadequate in many EU countries (Coker et al., 2006; Hargreaves et al., 2009). International studies have shown that TB may be a particular issue for irregular migrants, yet they are often unable to access free screening and treatment (Romero-Ortuno, 2004).

Impact on European health services New migrants pose dilemmas and challenges for service providers in terms of the extra administration, support and clinical and interpreting services required, and have financial and resource implications that are often not formally considered in service budgets. They may require new services, outside of the mainstream, when they are formally blocked from accessing public health services (Médecins Sans Frontières, 2005). New migrants may be a substantial and diverse group who present a considerable workload to hospital services in particular, for example emergency departments in high migrant areas (Clément et al., 2010; Cooke et al., 2007; Hargreaves et al., 2006). New migrants may use emergency department services for non-urgent problems because they are unable to access primary care services, with calls for efforts to be made to address barriers to primary care that will ultimately prove more cost-effective. Indeed some fusion of services and lowering of barriers between primary and secondary care may benefit migrants. However, impact on and use of services by new migrants is likely to be complex. A Europe-wide systematic review highlights variations in healthcare use between migrants and non-migrants, making it hard to generalise, and with current shortfalls in data collection by European health services, comparability of data remains difficult (Norredam et al., 2010).

In addition, clinicians have speculated that rates of admission of more vulnerable new migrants such as refugees and asylum seekers at mental health services may be higher than the general population, which is considered to have resource and management implications (Murphy et al., 2002). A study of new migrants from eight Central and Eastern European countries at two central London genitourinary medicine clinics reported a substantial impact, with these migrants thought to account for 10 per cent of new attendances if current immigration rates continue, requiring services to adapt quickly (Burns et al., 2009). Language barriers may well have the biggest impact on the cost of healthcare for this group, in light of the need to fund costly interpreters (Bischoff and Denhaerynck, 2010). In addition, the diversity of new migrants presents challenges to service providers when addressing the health and social needs of patients and the provision of culturally appropriate services (Priebe et al., 2011; Rajamanoharan et al., 2004).

Barriers to healthcare and their influence on service use

Improving access to health services is now a major consideration in the field of migrant health Europe-wide, with international human rights law recognising access to basic healthcare for all individuals as a basic human right. Article 12 of the 1966 International Covenant on Economic, Social and Cultural Rights (ICESCR) is of most relevance to migrants, and recognises 'the right of everyone to enjoy the highest attainable standard of physical and mental health'. The ICESCR states that everyone has rights with regard to health, without mention of citizenship or legal residency. In addition, the ICESCR places a specific

TABLE 2.1 Key barriers to healthcare for new migrants

System and provider level barriers

Entitlement to publicly funded healthcare

Discriminatory practices and negative attitudes of frontline staff

Quality of care

Patient level barriers

Knowledge of health services and how to use them

Adaptation to a new healthcare system

Language barriers

Asylum seeker status

---

obligation on governments to ensure equality of access to healthcare for all people in the event of sickness. To what extent all migrant groups realise these rights, however, is known to differ considerably between countries, and Europe-wide policies to improve access to healthcare are now considered essential to reduce inequalities (Nielsen and Krasnik, 2010; Norredam et al., 2006; Romero-Ortuno, 2004).

Existing literature supports the notion that migrants face certain barriers to accessing healthcare, and these barriers will influence service use and may explain patterns of ill-health (Aria and Harding, 2002; Scheppers et al., 2006). Barriers include several personal factors, including: age, sex, socioeconomic status, ethnicity, language ability, proximity to health services, social exclusion, health seeking behaviour and health beliefs. In addition, barriers at the service provider level may also influence use, including health policy and certain character-istics of the healthcare delivery system. Barriers may operate at two levels: entry into the healthcare system (initial access); and access to appropriate care to meet needs once inside the system (relevant access) (Adamson et al., 2003).

What is becoming increasingly clear, however, is that new migrants may face a range of specific access issues that may not be relevant to other migrant groups presenting to health services (Hargreaves, 2007; Priebe et al., 2011). These factors include a lack of entitlement to access free publicly funded healthcare (whether actual or perceived), but also specific issues associated with asylum status (traumatic experiences, social deprivation) as well as their ability to access an appropriate quality of healthcare to meet needs, and a lack of knowledge about accessing a new health system on arrival. Discrimination towards new migrants by frontline staff, particularly towards asylum seekers and refugees, may reflect hostile public attitudes in some groups towards new migrants or confusion around their entitlements to healthcare. These factors will influence how new migrants approach and use health services, and need to be better explored if we are to improve health outcomes for this patient group.

Table 2.1 provides a summary of key barriers that may be of particular importance when considering new migrants specifically. We have categorised barriers to care for new migrants into two categories: barriers at the patient level and barriers at the system and provider level.

System and provider level barriers

Lack of entitlement to free healthcare One of the unique barriers to care faced by new migrants is a lack of entitlement to publicly funded healthcare. This may be perceived or actual, but in both cases can impact on the migrant's ability to access healthcare. There are concerns that restricted access to preventative healthcare and screening is not considered a cost-effective approach to delivering healthcare to migrants (Hargreaves, 2007; Lu et al., 2000; Veldhuijzen et al., 2010). Many new migrants – particularly irregular migrants – will face the constant fear that they may be charged for services, facing bills that they are unable to pay.

The approaches taken by host governments across Europe vary considerably on this issue. In the UK, for example, policies towards groups such as irregular migrants and failed asylum seekers are becoming increasingly restrictive with respect to access to free healthcare; recent attempts have been made to restrict free access to both primary and secondary care for these migrants in light of dramatically rising rates of immigration (Hargreaves et al., 2008; Hargreaves and Burnett, 2008). Europe-wide generally, however, irregular migrants are mostly not entitled to receive publicly funded healthcare free of charge; exceptions to this rule are emergency medical care and in many countries services for children and pregnant women (Médecins du Monde, 2009; Romero-Ortuno, 2004). Infectious diseases may be treated as an emergency but contact tracing, a difficult area in its own right, is seldom adequately resourced despite likely benefits to migrant and ethnic communities as a whole. In 6 of 11 European countries (Belgium, France, Italy, the Netherlands, Portugal and Spain) the law provides for the system to cover all or part of the costs for irregular migrants (Médecins du Monde, 2009). In Germany, Greece, Sweden and Switzerland access to healthcare is largely restricted to emergency care. In Spain, legislative changes in 2002 made it possible for irregular migrants to receive medical cards and free medical care on the same level as legal migrants. For asylum seekers in particular, the situation across European countries in terms of entitlements and access to services varies greatly (Norredam et al., 2006). Whereas in Austria, Denmark, Estonia, Finland, Germany, Hungary, Luxembourg, Malta, Spain and Sweden there are legal restrictions in access to healthcare for one or more of the three groups of asylum seekers investigated (adults, children and pregnant women), with these groups only entitled to emergency care and treatment. Some free medical screening is provided to asylum seekers upon arrival in all EU countries except Greece.

Research has shown that even where there is an entitlement to access free healthcare, inadequate knowledge among medical practitioners regarding the entitlements of a diverse range of migrants presents a barrier to accessing care and treatment (Hargreaves et al., 2008; Norredam et al., 2006; Priebe et al., 2011). A critical question remains as to whether health professionals across Europe support such restrictive policies towards particular migrant groups. It is likely that views will vary in individuals and regionally, depending on levels of migration and/or perceived levels of health tourism. The British Medical Association (BMA) has called for 'humane flexibility' in the system to ensure that all migrants, despite entitlement, can access healthcare (Sheather and Health, 2004); the BMA says there are ethical, clinical and humanitarian grounds for not supporting the exclusion of failed asylum seekers from free health services. Other professional bodies have called for health workers to treat people on the basis of clinical need alone (Singer, 2004). Concerns have been raised about the ethical implications for healthcare professionals when they have to decide whether or not to treat a patient, not on medical grounds but on the grounds of whether the patient has the right papers and/or the right illness, and the subsequent conflicts doctors may face with their employers (Ashcroft, 2005; Pollard and Savulescu, 2004). There have been calls for HIV treatment to be provided free of charge on both ethical and public health grounds. Indeed it seems illogical for Western governments to support and fund, on the one hand, improved access to HIV care and treatment in resource poor countries, yet to deny access to free HIV treatment to these same individuals on their arrival in Europe.

Crucially, across Europe there is an absence of safety nets for non-eligible migrants to ensure that those without resources to pay for expensive private care can have access to basic healthcare (McColl et al., 2006). Safety nets do exist, for example, in the Netherlands –

in the form of a special fund that finances healthcare to irregular migrants – and Belgium, France and Spain have special state health insurance. The international NGOs Médecins du Monde and Médecins Sans Frontières run clinics and health access projects across Europe (Médecins du Monde, 2009; Médecins Sans Frontières, 2005). Indeed a plethora of NGOs and voluntary groups are involved in the provision of healthcare to asylum seekers and irregular migrants across Europe, yet it is now acknowledged that they cannot meet the considerable and rising demands placed on their limited services.

Discrimination, distrust, and barriers to appropriate care Negative attitudes of staff and actual or perceived discrimination, stereotyping and racism are considered to be a barrier to accessing appropriate healthcare (Priebe et al., 2011; Torres-Cantero et al., 2007). One qualitative study exploring access to maternity information among recently arrived Somali women in the UK found that women perceived that they were denied information specifically due to punitive attitudes and prejudiced views among health professionals and that was associated with reduced access to necessary services (Myfanwy and Davies, 2001). General practitioners (GPs) may be reluctant to register asylum seekers and refugees and other new migrants because they perceive them to be highly mobile and so cannot be followed up for routine screening and vaccination (Hargreaves et al., 2008). Opportunities to treat and prevent diseases are therefore missed. Simple and cost-effective measures, such as vaccination, are not undertaken sometimes in the mistaken belief that migrants will not be in the country long enough for this to matter.

A critical question is whether new migrants gain access to a good quality of care and appropriate levels of care to meet their needs. A right to access free healthcare is not sufficient to ensure healthcare utilisation, with researchers calling for healthcare professionals to take more proactive steps, including making health services culturally responsive (Aung et al., 2010; Bischoff et al., 2009). Initiatives such as the Amsterdam Declaration, promoting 'migrant friendly hospitals' across the EU, are a welcome step and call for healthcare services to become more responsive to the specific needs of migrants (Bischoff et al., 2009). Concerns have been raised around the availability in European countries of appropriate medical services for migrants. One German study exploring delays to diagnosis and treatment among new migrants at a tropical medicine institute found that 20 per cent had not received a medical examination six months post-arrival, and half needed treatment upon presentation – researchers linked this high proportion of delayed diagnosis and treatment directly to a lack of appropriate medical services for migrants (Lenz et al., 2006). With respect to asylum seekers and refugees, many professionals may not understand their problems, especially those related to experiences in their home countries or to cultural issues and behaviour during illness (Eshiett and Parry, 2003). Destitution and high mobility may impact on the ability of migrants to gain permanent registration at particular health services; one qualitative study of the post-migration geographical mobility of the Somali community in London found that it took more than five years after arrival before most Somalis found permanent accommodation in London, with frequent changing of residential places between various deprived areas considered to impact on their ability to maintain continuous and effective healthcare access (Warfa et al., 2006).

Patient level barriers Migrants may lack understanding of the health system on arrival to their new host country and this represents a major barrier to new migrants accessing appropriate services. For many, they cannot communicate in the host language nor read leaflets, if indeed there are any. There is often a lack of information in local community languages and migrants are often uninformed about their rights and entitlements to access services. There may be delays experienced in accessing necessary health services on arrival because of poor understanding of the primary care system in particular and the complicated multilayered organisational structure of established health systems (Myfanwy and Davies, 2001; Papadopoulos et al., 2004; Priebe et al., 2011).

Adaptation to a new healthcare system may prove difficult and present an obstacle to access. These migrants, who may have been working and able to pay in their home country, may now find themselves destitute, jobless or unable to work because of visa restrictions or the asylum/immigration system. They may be unable to pay for private healthcare and so left to navigate a publicly funded healthcare system that is not responsive to their specific needs. One South American new migrant frustrated about the poor quality of services received in the UK commented:

> people from South America we don't have free healthcare … we need
> to pay for everything in South America – for GPs, for treatment, for
> everything, but we have the chance for very high levels of services. In
> this country it is very, very different. (Hargreaves, 2007: 197)

A consistent finding is that language and communication issues are important barriers to care for new migrants, and influence many aspects of service use. Communication difficulties have strong negative implications for all aspects of care and represent a key factor in delayed diagnosis. One Polish new migrant described the issues well:

> Another thing is the language problem – it's huge because even though they speak everyday basic English, and basic conversational skills, when they go to a doctor it is not that simple anymore. And medical language and the system is completely different here than in Poland and they just don't understand where to go, how to deal with some cases and on top of that even the diagnosis for that they need more language help. (ibid.: 199)

In addition, she stressed that language was more than just communicating with the doctor about a health issue: 'if people have very poor English and they can only get by and say basic things, and can't write or read, are depressed, unsure of themselves, they don't have the force, enough self-esteem to ask, to push for things'. Indeed, use of professional interpreters is associated with better quality care and improved outcomes (Bischoff and Denhaerynck, 2010).

Asylum status itself has been shown to present a specific barrier to health services. Destitution, poor housing and low socioeconomic status are key concerns among this group in particular. This group may also have experienced traumatic events in the countries from which they have left, so may have unique and unmet health needs on arrival (BMA, 2003). They are likely to have a poor health status and multiple health needs, impacted on by the stress and uncertainty of their precarious immigration status. There may be fears that staff at health services would somehow inform the immigration authorities of their immigration status, and that their medical condition may jeopardise their claim for political asylum, with immigration officers having access to their medical records.

Influence on service use These barriers undoubtedly have implications for how these new migrants approach and use health services and there are some specific issues in terms of service use that are relevant, even unique, to new migrants. A number of studies have concluded that new migrants may delay seeking care or that they experience a delay to testing, diagnosis and treatment (Carnicer-Pont et al., 2009; Thomas et al., 2010). Numerous reasons have been reported for delays in presentation, including social circumstances, distrust of the medical profession, stigma and discrimination, fear of repercussions from immigration authorities and not knowing where to go. In one Swedish study, 82 per cent of respondents (mostly failed asylum seekers) felt that their illegal status and lack of identity card stopped them from approaching health services (Médecins Sans Frontières, 2005). Most reported being reluctant to take their children to health services, despite the child's entitlement to receive free healthcare, because they feared repercussions for the family from immigration authorities. The use of private practitioners or alternative/complementary sources of healthcare, and even travel abroad for those migrants who are able to move freely across borders, have been reported (Hargreaves, 2007), as well as self-medication (Aung et al., 2010), but the implications of these on both health systems and health status are, to date, poorly documented and little understood.

Lastly, what is becoming increasingly clear is that barriers to accessing primary medical services may result in migrants presenting directly to secondary services, such as free open access accident and emergency (A&E) departments (Clément et al., 2010; Hargreaves et al., 2006). This may be a particular issue for migrants who are not entitled to receive free healthcare or who fear registering with family doctors. Such services may not be well organised for offering care to this patient group and may not offer vaccination, screening and other preventative healthcare. Initiatives that specifically encourage new arrivals to register with and use informed primary care services may alleviate pressures on acute services and could ultimately be a more cost-effective approach to providing healthcare to new migrants.

Conclusions

Increasing immigration to Europe has implications for both the organisation and development of health services, as well as for the healthcare professionals tasked with meeting the needs of new migrant patients. Although it is difficult to generalise, certain new migrant groups may have worse health outcomes and a range of additional service requirements, including legal, administrative and communication needs. New migrants may be a substantial and diverse group who may present an additional workload at key health services, particularly acute health services, in light of the unique barriers to services they may experience. In particular, there are concerns around the increasingly restrictive approach to migrants' rights to access free publicly funded healthcare in host countries and the implications that this will have on the ability of vulnerable migrant groups to access an appropriate level of care to meet their needs. A more restrictive approach results in considerable inequities in access and is short sighted, not least in light of the increasing levels of migrant-associated infectious diseases such as TB and HIV being reported across Europe. This approach runs contrary to Western governments' human rights commitments to ensure access to a basic level of healthcare for all, posing ethical dilemmas for healthcare professionals tasked with meeting the needs of these patients.

Rather than exclusive policies around healthcare access, European policy-makers should now be moving towards more inclusive policies to encourage new migrants – whether legal or illegal – to access primary healthcare and screening on arrival and to provide targeted and publicly funded health services that reflect the requirements of migrant populations. This would be to the benefit of both new migrants themselves and to the whole health economy. There is an urgent need for improved data collection and robust research in the field of migrant health, the promotion of greater organisational flexibility, improved resources and staff training at health services, and for greater dialogue Europe-wide so that countries can learn from each other's experience and work together to improve health outcomes for new migrants.

References

Abgrall, S., P. Del Giudice, G. Melica and D. Costagliola (2010) 'HIV-associated tuberculosis and immigration in a high-income country: Incidence trends and risk factors in recent years', *AIDS*, 24(5): 763–71.

Adamson, J., Y. Ben-Shlomo, N. Chaturvedi and J. Donovan (2003) 'Ethnicity, socio-economic position and gender – do they affect reported health-care seeking behaviour?', *Social Science and Medicine*, 57(5): 895–904.

Arai, L. and S. Harding (2002) *Health and Social Care Services for Minority Ethnic Communities in the United Kingdom: A Review of the Literature on Access and Use*, MRC Social and Public Health Sciences Unit, University of Glasgow, Glasgow.

Ashcroft, E. (2005) 'Standing up for the medical rights of asylum seekers', *Journal of Medical Ethics*, 31: 125–6.

Aung, N. C., B. Rechel and P. Odermatt (2010) 'Access to and utilization of GP services among Burmese migrants in London: A cross-sectional descriptive study', *BMC Health Services Research*, 10: 285.

Bhopal, R. (2009) 'Chronic diseases in Europe's migrant and ethnic minorities: challenges, solutions and a vision', *European Journal of Public Health*, 19(2): 140–3.

Bischoff, A. and K. Denhaerynck (2010) 'What do language barriers cost? An exploratory study among asylum seekers in Switzerland', *BMC Health Services Research*, 10: 248.

Bischoff, A., A. Chiarenza and L. Loutan (2009) '"Migrant-friendly hospitals": A European initiative in an age of increasing mobility', *World Hospitals and Health Services*, 45: 7–9.

BMA (British Medical Association) (2003) *Asylum Seekers and their Health Needs*, British Medical Association, London.

Bollini, P., S. Pampallona, P. Warner and B. Kupelnick (2009) 'Pregnancy outcome of migrant women and integration policy: A systematic review of the international literature', *Social Science and Medicine*, 68(3): 452–61.

Burns, F. M., C. H. Mercer, A. R. Evans, C. J. Gerry, R. Mole and G. J. Hart (2009) 'Increased attendances of people of eastern European origin at sexual health services in London', *Sexually Transmitted Infections*, 85: 75–8.

Carnicer-Pont, D., P. G. de Olalla and J. A. Caylà (2009) 'HIV infection late detection in AIDS patients of a European city with increased immigration since mid-1990s', *Current HIV Research*, 7(2): 237–43.

Castles, S., H. Crawley and S. Loughna (2003) *States of Conflict: Causes and Patterns of Forced Migration to the EU and Policy Responses*, Institute for Public Policy Research, London.

Clandestino Research Project (2009) 'Size and development of irregular migration to the EU. Clandestino Research Project. Counting the uncountable: data and trends across Europe', Clandestino Research Project, Brussels. http://clandestino.eliamep.gr/wp-content/uploads/2009/12/clandestino_policy_brief_comparative_size-of-irregular-migration.pdf

Clément, N., A. Businger, L. Martinolli, H. Zimmermann and A. K. Exadaktylos (2010) 'Referral practice among Swiss and non-Swiss walk-in patients in an urban surgical emergency department: are there lessons to be learnt?', *Swiss Medical Weekly*, 140: w13089.

Coker, R., C. Bell, J.-P. Pitman, J. P. Zellweger, E. Heldal, A. Hayward, A. Skulberg, G. Bothamley, R. Whitfield, G. de Vries and J. M. Watson (2006) 'Tuberculosis screening in migrants in selected European countries shows wide disparities', *The European Respiratory Journal*, 27(4): 801–7.

Cooke, G., S. Hargreaves, J. Natkunarajah, G. Sandhu, D. Dhasmana, J. Eliahoo, A. Holmes and J. S. Friedland (2007) 'Impact on and use of an inner-city London Infectious Diseases Department by international migrants: A questionnaire survey', *BMC Health Services Research*, 7: 113.

Eshiett, M. U. and E. H. Parry (2003) 'Migrants and health: A cultural dilemma', *Clinical Medicine*, 3(3): 229–31.

Eurostat (2010) 'Asylum decisions in the EU 27', Eurostat, Geneva, http://epp.eurostat.ec.europa.eu/cache/ITY_PUBLIC/3-18062010-AP/EN/3-18062010-AP-EN.PDF (accessed 5 January 2012).

Gilbert, R. L., D. Antoine, C. E. French, I. Abubakar, J. M. Watson and J. A. Jones (2009) 'The impact of immigration on tuberculosis rates in the United Kingdom compared with other European countries', *The International Journal of Tuberculosis and Lung Disease*, 13(5): 645–51.

Hahne, S., T. Wormann and M. Kretzschmar (2009) 'Migrants and hepatitis B: New strategies for secondary prevention needed', *European Journal of Public Health*, 19: 439.

Hamers, F. and A. Downs (2004) 'The changing face of the HIV epidemic in Western Europe: What are the implications for public health priorities?', *Lancet*, 364: 83–94.

Hargreaves, S. (2007) 'The impact on and use of the UK's National Health Service by new migrants', unpublished PhD thesis, University of London, London.

Hargreaves, S. and A. Burnett (2008) 'UK court decision: Healthcare and immigration', *Lancet*, 371: 1823–4.

Hargreaves, S., J. S. Friedland, P. Gothard, S. Saxena, H. Millington, J. Eliahoo, P. Le Feuvre and A. Holmes (2006) 'Impact on and use of health services by international migrants: Questionnaire survey of inner city London A&E attenders', *BMC Health Services Research*, 6: 153–8, www.biomed central.com/1472-6963/6/153 (accessed 5 January 2012).

Hargreaves, S., A. H. Holmes, S. Saxena, P. Le Feuvre, W. Farah, G. Shafi, J. Chaudry, H. Khan and J. S. Friedland (2008) 'Charging systems for migrants in primary care: The experiences of family doctors in a high-migrant area of London', *Journal of Travel Medicine*, 15(1): 13–18.

Hargreaves S., M. Carballo and J. S. Friedland (2009) 'Screening migrants for tuberculosis: Where next?', *Lancet Infectious Diseases*, 3: 139–49.

IOM (International Organization for Migration) (2010) *World Migration 2010. The Future of Migration – Building capacities for change*, IOM, Geneva.

Lenz, K., K. Bauer-Dubau and T. Jelinek (2006) 'Delivery of medical care for migrants in Germany: Delay of diagnosis and treatment', *Journal of Travel Medicine*, 13: 133–7.

Lu, M. C., Y. G. Lin, N. M. Prietto and T. J. Garite (2000) 'Elimination of public funding of prenatal care for undocumented immigrants in California: A cost/benefit analysis', *American Journal of Obstetrics and Gynaecology*, 182(1 Pt 1): 233–9.

McColl, K., S. Pickworth and C. Raymond (2006) 'Project:London – supporting vulnerable populations', *BMJ*, 332: 115–17.

McKay, L., A. MacIntrye and S. Ellaway (2003) *Migration and Health: A Review of the International Literature*, MRC Social and Public Health Sciences Unit, Glasgow.

Médecins du Monde (European Observatory on Access to Healthcare) (2009) *Access to Healthcare for Undocumented Migrants in 11 European Countries: 2008 Survey Report*, Médecins du Monde, Paris.

Médecins Sans Frontières (2005) *Experiences of Gomda in Sweden: Exclusion from Healthcare for Immigrants Living without Legal Status. Results from a Survey by Médecins Sans Frontières*, MSF, Brussels.

Mladovsky, P. (2009) 'A framework for analysing migrant health policies in Europe', *Health Policy*, 93: 55–63.

Murphy, D., D. Ndegwa, A. Kanani, C. Rojas-Jaimes and A. Webster (2002) 'Mental health of refugees in inner-London', *Psychiatric Bulletin*, 26: 222–4.

Myfanwy, M. and M. Davies (2001) 'The maternity information

concerns of Somali women in the United Kingdom', *Journal of Advanced Nursing*, 36: 237–45.

Nielsen, S. S. and A. Krasnik (2010) 'Poorer self-perceived health among migrants and ethnic minorities versus the majority population in Europe: A systematic review', *International Journal of Public Health*, 55: 357–71.

Norredam, M., A. Mygind and A. Krasnik (2006) 'Access to health care for asylum seekers in the European Union – a comparative study of country policies', *European Journal of Public Health*, 16(3): 285–9.

Norredam, M., S. S. Nielsen and A. Krasnik (2010) 'Migrants' utilization of somatic healthcare services in Europe – a systematic review', *European Journal of Public Health*, 20(5): 555–63.

Papadopoulos, I., S. Lees, M. Lay and A. Gebrehiwot (2004) 'Ethiopian refugees in the UK: Migration, adaptation and settlement experiences and their relevance to health', *Ethnicity and Health*, 9: 55–73.

Pollard, A. J. and J. Savulescu (2004) 'Eligibility of overseas visitors and people of uncertain residential status for NHS treatment', *BMJ*, 329: 346–9.

Priebe S., S. Sandhu, S. Dias, A. Gaddini, T. Greacen, E. Ioannidis, U. Kluge, A. Krasnik, M. Lamkaddem, V. Lorant, R. P. Riera, A. Sarvary, J. Soares, M. Stankunas, C. Straßmayr, K. Wahlbeck, M. Welbel and M. Bogic (2011) 'Good practice in healthcare for migrants: Views and experiences of care professionals in 16 European countries', *BMC Public Health*, 11: 187.

Rajamanoharan, S., E. F. Monteiro, R. Maw, C. A. Carne and A. Robinson (2004) 'Genitourinary medicine/HIV services for persons with insecure immigration or seeking asylum in the United Kingdom: A British Co-operative Clinical Group survey', *International Journal of STD and AIDS*, 15(8): 509–14.

Romero-Ortuno, R. (2004) 'Access to healthcare for illegal immigrants in the EU: Should we be concerned?', *European Journal of Health Law*, 11: 245.

Scheppers, E., E. van Dongen, J. Dekker, J. Geertzen and J. Dekker (2006) 'Potential barriers to the use of health services among ethnic minorities: A review', *Family Practice*, 23(3): 325–48.

Scotto, G., A. Saracino, R. Pempinello, I. El Hamad, S. Geraci, M. Panunzio, E. Palumbo, D. C. Cibelli and G. Angarano (2005) 'Simit epidemiological multicentric study on hospitalized immigrants in Italy during 2002', *Journal of Immigrant Health*, 7(1): 55–60.

Sheather, J. and I. Health (2004) 'Policing access to primary care with identity cards', *BMJ*, 329: 303–4.

Singer, R. (2004) 'Asylum seekers: An ethical response to their plight', *Lancet*, 363: 1904.

Thomas, F., P. Aggleton and J. Anderson, J. (2010) '"If I cannot access services, then there is no reason for me to test": The impacts of health service charges on HIV testing and treatment amongst migrants in England', *AIDS Care*, 22: 526–31.

Torres-Cantero, A. M., A. G. Miguel, C. Gallardo and S. Ippolito (2007) 'Healthcare provision for illegal migrants: May health policy make a difference?', *European Journal of Public Health*, 17: 483–5.

UKCG (United Kingdom Collaborative Group) (2005) *Mapping the Issues. HIV and Other Sexually Transmitted Infections in the United Kingdom*, Health Protection Agency Centre for Infections/The UK Collaborative Group for HIV and STI Surveillance, London.

Veldhuijzen, I. K., M. Toy, S. J. Hahné, G. A. De Wit, S. W. Schalm, R. A. de Man and J. H. Richardus (2010) 'Screening and early treatment of migrants for chronic hepatitis B virus infection is cost-effective', *Gastroenterology*, 138(2): 522–30.

Vertovec, S. (2006) *The Emergence of Super-diversity in Britain*, Working Paper No. 25, Centre on Migration, Policy and Society, University of Oxford, Oxford.

Warfa, N., K. Bhui, T. Craig, S. Curtis, S. Mohamud, S. Stansfeld, P. McCrone and G. Thornicroft (2006) 'Post-migration geographical mobility, mental health, and health service utilization among Somali refugees in the UK: A qualitative study', *Health and Place*, 12(4): 503–15.

Wolff, H., J. P. Janssens, P. Bodenmann, A. Meynard, C. Delhumeau, T. Rochat, P. Sudre, M. C. Costanza, J. M. Gaspoz and A. Morabia (2010) 'Undocumented migrants in Switzerland: Geographical origin versus legal status as risk factor for tuberculosis', *Journal of Immigrant and Minority Health*, 12(1): 18–23.

Xiridou, M., M. Van Veen, M. Prins and R. Coutinho (2011) 'How patterns of migration can influence the heterosexual transmission of HIV in The Netherlands', *Sexually Transmitted Infections*, March 25, Epub ahead of print, http://sti.bmj.com/content/early/2011/03/24/sti.2010.048512.abstract.

3 | Do migrants have an enforceable right to healthcare in international human rights law?

SUE WILLMAN

Introduction

Surprisingly, there is no single, comprehensive international legal provision covering either the right to health or the rights of migrants. This is the first obstacle in finding a 'migrant right to health'. In broad terms, international human rights law recognises the enjoyment of the highest attainable standard of health as a fundamental human right of every individual, regardless of race, religion, political belief, economic or social condition and immigration status. The right to health is recognised in numerous legal provisions and branches of international law, such as refugee law, international human rights law, ILO instruments, as well as in domestic law through constitutions and statutes.[1] But there is a wide gap between these provisions on paper and their implementation on the ground. While lawyers may refer to an international provision as 'legally binding', this generally means binding between states, rather than enforceable by the migrant patient, however desperate their need for treatment.

This uncertainty about the right to health in general is compounded by the growing trend for the states that host migrants to introduce laws and policies aimed at restricting migrants' access to healthcare, a situation exacerbated by the current global economic crisis (UN Human Rights Council, 2010: paras 9 and 14). The trend is particularly prevalent in wealthier states with developed healthcare systems, as in the EU. Governments use immigration control arguments to justify the discriminatory measures, and suggest healthcare restrictions will discourage so-called 'health tourism'. Governments also argue that resources must be protected for the benefit of those perceived to have the strongest claim on the state, such as citizens, or those with some form of lawful residence. These approaches and attitudes have increasingly become the norm, as the Special Rapporteur testified in UN Human Rights Council (ibid.) report: 'Most countries ... link access to non emergency healthcare to migrants' immigration status' (para. 27). This chapter considers whether such discriminatory rules can survive in courts and international tribunals. By investigating the differing legal foundations for a right to healthcare, from non-discrimination to 'special protection' rules, it aims to identify a binding right to healthcare for non-citizen migrants.

Is there a right to health?

The multitude of international treaties addressing the right to health gives the impression that anyone in need of healthcare, migrant or not, should be able to access it. Almost every country in the world has signed up to the (WHO) Constitution that begins 'Governments have a responsibility for the health of their peoples which can be fulfilled only by the provision of adequate health and social measures' (Preamble to the Constitution of the World Health Organization, 1948). Each of the UN's 192 state parties has ratified the Universal Declaration of Human Rights (UDHR): 'Everyone has the right to a standard of living adequate to the health and well-being of himself and his family including ... medical care' (article 25(1)). The Declaration also provides that all are equal before the law. The Preamble applies its standards to every individual and organ of society (which must include health professionals and authorities). Over time, all or parts of the UDHR have come to be accepted as 'customary international law', which means it is binding on states and must be taken into account by domestic courts even without domestic laws implementing it (Buergenthal, 1995: 29–38).

The UDHR was introduced as an interim measure in the aftermath of the Second World War, partly because states could not agree on the balance to be struck between civil and political rights and socio-economic rights such as healthcare. It was eventually followed by the International Covenant on Civil and Political Rights (ICCPR) and the ICESCR, which were intended as more concrete provisions. Regrettably, unlike the UDHR, the ICESCR does not expressly provide for medical treatment; instead state parties 'recognize the right of everyone to the highest attainable standard of physical and mental health' (article 12(1)). The steps to be taken to implement this include 'the creation of conditions which would assure to all medical service and medical attention in the event of sickness'. This vague wording reflects resistance to the development of socioeconomic rights in international law by states such as the US, which is not one of the 160 states that have ratified the ICESCR.

Against this backdrop, it must be acknowledged that many commentators have questioned the very existence of a general right to health, even before turning to the position of migrants. The most active proponents of the right recognise the difficulties of enforcing it (Chapman, 1997–8). The US State Department has forcefully denied that any right to health can be enforced, asserting that ICESCR article 12 is non-binding and dismissing UDHR article 25 as 'an aspiration' (US Department of State, 2008).

Does human rights protection extend to migrants?

The extent to which a human rights treaty covers migrants depends on the wording of the agreement, but there is ample authority to show that both international and regional human rights protection extend to migrants. The ICCPR applies to 'all individuals within the territory and subject to its jurisdiction' (article 2(1)). The Human Rights Committee (HRC) has interpreted this as meaning that 'in general, the rights set forth in the Covenant apply to everyone ... irrespective of his or her nationality or statelessness' (HRC General Comment No. 15, 1986, para. 1). Later the Committee extended this, stating:

> the enjoyment of Covenant rights is not limited to citizens of States parties but must also be available to all individuals, regardless of nationality or statelessness, such as asylum seekers, refugees, migrant workers and other persons, who may find themselves in the territory or subject to the jurisdiction of the State party. (HRC General Comment No. 31, 2004, para. 10)

The ICESCR has different wording, allowing governments to achieve its rights gradually according to their economic circumstances ('progressive realization'). However, the International Court of Justice (ICJ) has pointed out that it 'contains no provision on its scope of application' (*Advisory Opinion on the Legal Consequences of the Construction of a Wall in the Occupied Palestinian Territory*, para. 112). There are more examples of a universal approach to human rights protection in the regional human rights schemes that do not exclude migrants from access to rights. The American Convention on Human Rights (ACHR), for example, protects the rights and freedoms of all persons, emphatically stating that '"person" means every human being' (article 1(2)).

Equality arguments as a basis for migrants' entitlement to healthcare

Equality protection seems an obvious source for a migrant entitlement to healthcare. However, there is no consensus that anti-discrimination rules encompass migrants, in particular undocumented migrants. This is effectively because states can argue that such discrimination can be justified by the need for immigration control. Yet, at the post-war birth of human rights, the UDHR made it very clear that its rights and freedoms were to be applied without discrimination of any kind, including that based on national origin (article 2). The only specific reference to migrants is in UDHR article 14, which provides for a right to seek asylum from persecution, subject to limitations. This can be interpreted as permitting immigration control, but not permitting differential access to its fundamental rights. Unfortunately, although influential, as we have seen, the UDHR itself is limited when it comes to enforceable rights.

Ironically, the main treaty outlawing race discrimination, the ICERD, specifically excludes protection from discrimination as between citizens and non-citizens (article 1(2)). Its supervisory body, the Committee on the Elimination of Racial Discrimination (CERD) has attempted to offset this. It has recommended that state parties adopt measures to ensure that they 'respect the right of non-citizens to an adequate standard of physical and mental health, by, inter alia, refraining from denying or limiting their access to preventive, curative or palliative health services' (CERD General Recommendation XXX, para. 36).

Although there is no human rights instrument expressly outlawing discrimination against migrants, it is arguable that the principle of non-discrimination is now a principle of customary international law, taking into account its consistent inclusion in human rights instruments (e.g. ICESCR, article 2; ICCPR articles 2 and 26; ICPRMW, articles 1 and 7; European Convention on Human Rights (ECHR), article 14). According to the Committee on Economic, Social and Cultural Rights (CESCR), the principle of non-discrimination proscribes:

> any discrimination in access to health care ... on the grounds of race, colour, sex, language, religion, political or other opinion, national or social origin, property, birth, physical or mental disability, health status, sexual orientation and civil, political, social or other status. (CESCR General Comment No. 14, para. 18)

A migrant might be protected by either the 'nationality/national origin' or the 'other status' headings. Where a migrant worker was refused unemployment insurance, the approach of the European Court of Human Rights (ECtHR) was to decide this was discrimination based on nationality (*Gaygusz v Austria*, para. 42). The Human Rights Council has also interpreted non-discrimination provisions as protecting migrants by treating nationality as 'other status', which is protected from discrimination by the ICCPR (*Gueye et al. v France*, para. 189).

It is significant that the duty not to discriminate was the starting point when the CESCR (the supervisory body responsible for the ICESCR) issued detailed guidance on the ICESCR article 12 right to health (CESCR General Comment No. 14, para. 1, note 1, and para. 30). The Committee went on to say, 'States are under an obligation to respect the right to health by refraining from denying or limiting equal access for all persons, including ... asylum-seekers and illegal immigrants, to preventive, curative and palliative health services' (ibid., para. 34). When the Special Rapporteur on the right of everyone to the enjoyment of the highest attainable standard of physical and mental health investigated Sweden's healthcare system, he relied on this approach (UN Human Rights Council, 2007). While observing that 'the standard of living, health status and quality of health care in Sweden are among the best in the world', he found that asylum seeking adults did not have access to the same healthcare as other adults domiciled in Sweden 'which amounted to discrimination under international human rights law' (ibid., para. 69). In particular he highlighted the situation of undocumented migrants who could receive immediate healthcare but would be charged for it (ibid., paras 36–7). The Special Rapporteur concluded his report by recommending that the Swedish government reconsider its position with a view to offering all asylum seekers and undocumented persons the same healthcare, on the same basis, as Swedish residents, 'to bring itself into conformity with its international human rights obligations' (ibid., para. 75).

The 'justification' defence to discrimination against migrants

It is not enough to prove that a migrant has been discriminated against when a state denies them healthcare because there may be a defence of 'justification', for example based on the need for immigration control. The HRC has stressed that the enjoyment of equal rights does not necessarily require identical treatment, at least in the context of the ICCPR's non-discrimination provisions (HRC, 1989, General Comment 18, para. 7). It points out that human rights law allows extra protection for particular classes of individuals, such as pregnant women, and certain political rights may be linked to citizenship (ibid., para. 8). The Committee's approach is that different treatment will not necessarily amount to discrimination, 'if the criteria for such differentiation are reasonable and objective and if the aim is to achieve a purpose which is legitimate under the Covenant' (ibid., para. 12).

This idea that discrimination may be lawful if it is 'justified' and 'proportionate' has been developed in the regional courts. The ECtHR, in particular, has interpreted discrimination as meaning different treatment on prohibited grounds, for example race, nationality, other status, between people in analogous situations. Differences in treatment can be justified by a state if they pursue a legitimate aim, according to the principles that normally prevail in democratic society, and if there is a reasonable relationship of proportionality between the method used and the aim (which in the case of migrants is likely to be immigration control). The Court will also allow states wriggle room, known as a 'margin of appreciation', where allocation of scarce resources is concerned. So in *Sentges v Netherlands* the Court rejected a severely disabled person's complaint that his ECHR article 8 right to family life was violated by the refusal to provide an expensive robotic arm. The Inter-American Court has followed the ECtHR approach, finding 'a distinction is only discriminatory when it lacks an objective and reasonable justification' (*Proposed Amendments to the Naturalization Provisions of the Constitution of Costa Rica*, Advisory Opinion para. 56). The Court found it was not discriminatory to have preferential naturalisation rules for those of Central American descent. It observed that not all different treatment is discriminatory in itself and that in fact, it may sometimes be necessary in order to achieve justice.

Although states that refuse migrants access to healthcare and other resources may rely on justification as a defence to discrimination claims, they will not necessarily succeed. The ECtHR has upheld complaints of discrimination by non-EU migrants who were refused child benefit because they did not have a residence permit, rejecting the justification defence (*Niedzwiecki v Germany* and *Okpisz v Germany*). The Court found there was a breach of the right to respect for family life (ECHR article 8), which was discrimination on the basis of nationality (ECHR article 14). The Court has also found no objective and reasonable justification for aliens to be discriminated against because they did not have a residence permit (*Niedzwiecki v Germany* para. 32 and *Okpisz v Germany* para. 33).

Protection for special groups as a basis for migrants' entitlement to healthcare

To what extent can provisions designed to protect particular groups, such as women, children, disabled people or torture survivors fill the gap in migrant healthcare entitlement? The Convention on the Elimination of All Forms of Discrimination Against Women (CEDAW) clearly requires states to provide women with care during pregnancy, confinement and the post-natal period, 'granting free services where necessary'

(CEDAW article 12(2)). Few major governments (apart from the US) can argue that they are not bound by it since it is a widely ratified treaty, with 187 parties. Similarly, states that have ratified the United Nations Convention on the Rights of the Child (UNCRC) have agreed to take 'appropriate measures' to 'ensure the provision of necessary medical assistance and health care to all children' (article 24(2)(b)). Only the US and Somalia have failed to ratify the UNCRC. The newest relevant treaty, the Convention on the Rights of Persons with Disabilities (CRPD) requires states to 'provide those health services needed by persons with disabilities specifically because of their disabilities, including ... services designed to minimize and prevent further disabilities' (article 25 (b)). Again this has been widely ratified, including by the EU. Migrant torture survivors might rely on the Convention Against Torture (CAT), which requires state parties to provide for redress, 'including the means for as full rehabilitation as possible' (article 14). CAT has 149 parties, including the US.

Each of the treaties referred to above has a committee of independent experts to monitor implementation, which requires states to make periodical reports; each allows for individual complaints with the exception of the UNCRC. So for example, a disabled migrant could benefit from the CRPD Optional Protocol that has been ratified by a number of member states[2] and gives a disabled individual or groups of individuals the right to complain to the Committee on the Rights of Persons with Disabilities.

A migrant who is in an EU state and is the victim of a human trafficking offence may be entitled to assistance and support, including medical treatment[3] (Directive 2011/36/EU on preventing and combating trafficking in human beings, article 11). If member states decide to opt in to the Directive (as the UK has), they must introduce implementing legislation by 6 April 2013.

Ironically, migrants' legal rights to healthcare have perhaps been best protected in the prison or detention setting. The Standard Minimum Rules for the Treatment of Prisoners, which were first adopted by the UN in 1955, provide for medical services in prison and detention centres, including 'at every institution there shall be available the services of at least one qualified medical officer who should have some knowledge of psychiatry' (Standard Minimum Rules for the Treatment of Prisoners, 233). The rules have been taken into account in ECtHR decisions and can be considered to have reached the status of customary international law, which means they should be taken into account by domestic courts.

Regional human rights protection as a basis for migrants' entitlement

As explained above, the regional human rights treaties generally apply to migrants, just as they apply to citizens who are present in the state. But as yet there is no regional court decision that directly considers migrants' entitlement to healthcare. Part of the reason for this is the difficulty in identifying a concrete entitlement to healthcare, or even a right to health, which could then be applied to migrants. The only regional human rights treaty that specifically includes a right to health is the African Charter on Human and Peoples' Rights (article 16(1)). The African Commission, which considers individual complaints of violations of the Charter, has found violations of this right in a number of cases (see for example *World Organization Against Torture, Lawyers' Committee for Human Rights, Jehovah Witnesses, Inter-African Union for Human Rights v Zaire* and *D. R. Congo v Burundi, Rwanda and Uganda*). But even in the African regional system, with its explicit right to health, it is more difficult to demonstrate a state responsibility to provide healthcare outside the detention context; in the '*Saro-Wiwa*' case, the Commission found there was a 'heightened' responsibility in relation to the right to health in detention (*International Pen, Constitutional Rights Project, Interights on behalf of Ken Saro-Wiwa Jr and Civil Liberties Organization v Nigeria*). Of course, the Commission has recognised the need for gradual realisation of healthcare in the economic circumstances of Africa. But it has still been able to find that in certain situations there is a duty to provide treatment. The point arose in the context of extremely inadequate provision of healthcare for those detained in a psychiatric institution (*Purohit and Moore v The Gambia*). This contrasts starkly with EU states arguing they cannot afford healthcare for migrants.

It is significant that despite only a handful of reported decisions each year, the African Commission has found time to rule favourably on the right to health. Unfortunately, the lack of an enforcement mechanism to compel African states to follow the Commission's recommendations makes it difficult to regard these decisions as enforceable rights. The African Court on Human and Peoples' Rights now has the power to make binding decisions on human rights violations in relation to the 26 African Union member states that have ratified the Protocol establishing the Court, but it is in its infancy, having been able to consider cases only since June 2008.

Although there is no specific right to health provision in the ACHR, the Inter-American Commission and Court have upheld the right in a number of their decisions,[4] although none relates specifically to migrants. They have indirectly found a right to health and to healthcare in violations of the ACHR article 4(1) (protection of the right to life), article 5(1) (the right to physical, mental and moral integrity), and article 5(2) (freedom from torture or to cruel, inhuman or degrading punishment or treatment) as in the *Cesti Hurtado Case (Peru)*. They have also underlined the right to health when finding violations of article 19, which deals with the health and welfare of children (*Children's Rehabilitation Institute v Paraguay*). In the Additional Protocol to the ACHR in the Area of Economic, Social and Cultural Rights (Protocol of San Salvador), article 10 specifically provides for a right to health, but individual complaints are outside both the Commission and the Court's jurisdiction and few member states have ratified it.

On the face of it, the ECHR is limited to the protection of civil and political rights, but it has been regularly used to extend economic, social and cultural rights, including the right to health. Because there is no specific reference to a right to health or healthcare, the gap has been filled by the right to life (article 2(1)), the prohibition of torture or inhuman and degrading treatment or punishment (article 3), and the right to respect for private and family life, home and correspondence (article 8).

In relation to the right to life, the ECtHR has recognised some healthcare-related obligations, finding that article 2(1) requires the state 'to take appropriate steps to safeguard the lives of those within its jurisdiction' (*L.C.B. v UK* para. 36). In the context of Turkey's occupation of Northern Cyprus and its ill-treatment of Greek Cypriots there, the Court found that the right to life may be violated 'where it is shown that the authorities ... put an individual's life at risk through the denial of health care which they have undertaken to make available to the population generally' (*Cyprus v Turkey* para. 219). Delay in treatment can also breach article 2, as in *Ilhan v Turkey*, where a prisoner died after a delay in sending him to hospital. In *Nitecki v Poland*, a patient with a rare and life-threatening condition complained that the Polish government would only finance 70 per cent of a life-saving drug that he could not afford. Although ECtHR found his complaint inadmissible in the particular circumstances, it reiterated that there may be a breach of the right to life where a state puts an individual's life at risk through the denial of healthcare that they have undertaken to make available to the population generally.

Where a claim succeeds under ECHR article 2 or 3, the Court's practice is not to go on to consider the merits of a potential violation of the article 8 right to respect for private life on the same facts, so article 8 decisions are relatively rare (*Musial v Poland* paras 99–101). However the Court has found that delay in providing hospital treatment can breach the right to respect for private life, if it is likely to have a serious impact on the patient's health (*Passanante v Italy*).

It is now well established that ECHR article 3 imposes an obligation on the state to protect the physical and mental wellbeing of persons deprived of their liberty by providing them with the requisite medical assistance, such as psychiatric treatment, as in *Musial v Poland* (paras 85–8). This requirement applies equally to migrants held in immigration detention.

Turning to cases that involve migrants, the ECtHR's initial approach was to find that it would amount to inhuman and degrading treatment under article 3 to deport a terminally ill migrant who could not access care in their country of origin (*D v the United Kingdom* para. 53). But in later decisions the Court has taken a more restrictive approach, finding that deporting people living with HIV/AIDS to countries where they may not be able to receive treatment does not necessarily breach ECHR article 2 or 3, if their illness has not reached an advanced stage. The effect of this approach is dramatically illustrated in the case of a Ugandan woman with HIV/AIDS whose asylum claim had been rejected by the UK. She argued that her removal to Uganda would be inhuman and degrading treatment within ECHR article 3, as well as a breach of her ECHR article 8 rights because she would not be able to access medical treatment there and faced an early death (*N v the United Kingdom*). The evidence was that there was treatment available in Uganda but she would not be able to afford it. Revisiting *D v UK*, the ECtHR rejected her complaint, deciding that the decision to remove an alien who was suffering from a serious mental or physical illness to a country where the facilities for the treatment of that illness were inferior might raise an issue under article 3, but only in a very exceptional case, where the humanitarian grounds against the removal were compelling, as in *D v UK*. In this context of a refused asylum seeker, subject to removal and global health inequalities, the Court indicated that article 3 did not place an obligation on the member state to 'alleviate such disparities through the provision of free and unlimited health care to all aliens without a right to stay within its jurisdiction' (para. 44). This decision clearly makes it harder for a migrant to demonstrate entitlement to healthcare via the ECHR, but the door is not entirely closed. More recently, the ECtHR found that Belgium's decision to return an Afghan asylum seeker to Greece violated the ECHR, since this exposed him to detention and living conditions that were in breach of article 3 (*M.S.S. v Belgium and Greece*).

As yet untested, there may be scope for a European right to health in article 35 of the EU Charter of Fundamental Rights. The Charter became a binding set of principles in all EU member countries when the Lisbon Treaty was adopted in December 2009. Significantly, the wording does not exclude migrants from access to healthcare. Although article 35 is vague, it must have persuasive value in domestic courts, which are bound by EU law, for example, when interpreting national provisions. It is also relevant to the interpretation of cases brought under the ECHR.

Migrant-specific human rights protection

In Europe, the theme that undocumented migrants may not benefit from the same health rights as citizens or those who are lawfully resident is endorsed by the European Social Charter (ESC) and the Revised ESC, which expressly exclude aliens from their scope except 'in so far as they are nationals of other Contracting parties lawfully resident or working within the territory of the Contracting Party concerned ...'. The monitoring body, the Committee of Experts, has attempted to water down this approach, warning that 'the implementation of certain provisions of the Charter could in certain specific situations require complete equality of treatment between nationals and foreigners, whether or not they are nationals of member States, Party to the Charter' (European Committee of Social Rights Conclusions 2004, 10, para. 5). When France introduced new laws making illegal immigrants with very low incomes liable to charges for medical treatment, a complaint was brought on behalf of migrants as a group, that France had violated the Revised ESC (*FIDH v France*). The complaint was partly successful; the Committee decided that France had violated the rights of children, but not adults, but the decision contains useful guidance. While ESC rights only cover foreigners who are nationals of other parties to the Charter and who are lawfully resident or lawfully working in the host state, the Committee emphasised that it must be interpreted consistently with the principles of individual human dignity and that any restrictions should consequently be read narrowly. It went on to say that 'legislation or practice which denies entitlement to medical assistance to foreign nationals, within the territory of a State party, even if they are there illegally, is contrary to the Charter', although not all the Charter rights may be extended to illegal migrants. There was no violation of the right to medical assistance (article 13), since illegal immigrants could access some forms of medical assistance after three months of residence in France, and all foreign nationals could at any time obtain treatment for emergencies and life-threatening conditions. The Committee found a violation of the right of children to protection (article 17), even though the affected children had similar access to healthcare as adults, since article 17 was more expansive than the right to medical assistance. In response to the decision, France changed its policy in relation to the provision of healthcare for migrant children.

Unfortunately, ESC complaints may only be brought on behalf of a migrant in a state that is a signatory to the protocol providing for collective complaints to the Committee, and the Charter is not directly enforceable in a number of states, including the UK. However ESC is a relevant consideration when applying the ECHR or where EU law is engaged, so it can be referred to in domestic legal cases and policy arguments.

The ILO has produced several conventions protecting the rights of all workers, including migrant workers, as well as some that specifically cover migrants. There is a right to access to appropriate medical services for authorised migrants and members of their families in Convention No. 97 of 1949 concerning Migration (article 5), but relatively few states have ratified it. Similarly the ICPRMW provides for equal access to healthcare for lawful migrant workers and their family members. It also requires that migrants with an irregular status are entitled to medical care, but it is limited to care 'to preserve life or avoid irreparable harm to their health' (article 28), so adds little to more general human rights provisions that already protect the right to life. Refugees and stateless persons are specifically excluded from this benefit (article 3 (d)).

Those who are actually recognised as refugees are covered by the UN Convention relating to the Status of Refugees 1951 (articles 23 and 24). They are entitled to the same access to public relief and assistance – which is assumed to include medical care – as citizens. This does not of course extend to those most likely to be refused healthcare, namely undocumented migrants.

Asylum applicants in the EU are entitled to 'the necessary healthcare which shall include, at least, emergency care and essential treatment of illness' (Council Directive 2003/9/EC, article 15(1)). In addition, member states must provide 'necessary medical or other assistance to applicants who have special needs'; this includes children, disabled people, elderly people, pregnant women, single parents with minor children and persons who have been subjected to serious forms of psychological, physical or sexual violence (article 17). In the context of permission to work, the UK's Supreme Court has found that this Directive also covers refused asylum seekers who have made a second asylum claim that is outstanding (*ZO (Somalia)* 2010). As a result, it can be argued at present that a refused asylum seeker with an outstanding new claim is entitled to healthcare within the terms of the Directive. However, the Directive is being renegotiated at the time of writing and the UK is threatening not to sign up to the revised version.

Domestic law as a basis for migrants' entitlement

An estimated 67.5 per cent of states have incorporated the right to health in their domestic law constitutions (Kinney and Clark, 2004: 285). The right to healthcare has been successfully litigated in the domestic law context, particularly in those countries with a constitutional or domestic law entitlement, such as Colombia and South Africa (see *Minister of Health and others v Treatment Action Campaign and others* para. 67, but cf. *Soobramoney v Minister of Health (KwaZulu-Natal)* paras 24–7). But even where there is a domestic law right to healthcare, it may be of limited benefit for a migrant who is not aware of the right, cannot access a lawyer or tribunal to implement it, and/or who fears deportation if they make their presence known to the authorities.

Many states discriminate between the rights to healthcare of documented and undocumented migrants; in the EU the latter have the least access to medical care (Mladovsky, 2007: 9). Norway, for example, has incorporated the ICESCR into its domestic law, but undocumented migrants have no rights to access healthcare services in Norway, except for emergency services (Czapka, 2009).

The case of a Palestinian man ('A') whose asylum claim had been rejected and who was then refused urgent hospital treatment in the UK demonstrates how domestic law can be used effectively to enforce access to healthcare (*R (A) v Secretary of State for Health* (2008)). 'A' had agreed to leave the UK voluntarily but could not get travel documents to enable him to return to Palestine because of Israel's travel restrictions. UK authorities could not deport him for the same reason. He developed chronic liver disease in the UK, the hospital administrators decided that he should be charged for treatment but because he could not afford to pay, treatment was withheld and his condition deteriorated. Although he succeeded at the first stage in the High Court, his human rights argument was roundly rejected by the judge:

> Article 8 of the Convention does not impose on a Convention state the
> obligation to provide medical treatment at any specific level to persons

within its territory (see *Tysiac v Poland* 5410/03, 20th March 2007, paragraph 107) ... By providing treatment to deal with life-threatening emergencies and situations in which serious injury may result if the patient is untreated, the state is fulfilling its minimum obligation under Article 8 and, if it still exists, under the law of common humanity'. (*R (on the application of A) v Secretary of State for Health* [2009])

The UK government appealed to the Court of Appeal against the High Court's decision. Allowing the appeal in part, the Court of Appeal decided that refused asylum seekers were not 'ordinarily' or 'lawfully resident' in the UK for the purposes of entitlement to treatment. However the Court found that guidelines on how hospitals should exercise their discretion to refuse treatment was unlawful because all three definitions of types of treatment ('immediately necessary', 'urgent' and 'non-urgent') failed to provide sufficiently clear guidance as to whether treatment should be withheld if a patient cannot pay and cannot reasonably be expected to return to his country of origin. The effect of the judgment in 2011 was that the UK government issued revised guidance and new legislation, so that a refused asylum seeker in A's position, receiving asylum support because they are unable to return home, is now entitled to healthcare (National Health Service (Charges to Overseas Visitors) Regulations, 2011, and Guidance on Implementing the Overseas Visitors Hospital Charging Regulations, Department of Health, 2011).

Unexpectedly, in February 2012, the UK government agreed to provide free HIV treatment to overseas visitors if they have been in the UK for six months, as an amendment to the Health Bill. This appeared to be a concession to health experts and campaigners working with people with HIV, who have long argued that refusing HIV drugs to migrants, including refused asylum seekers, was morally wrong and presented a risk to public health.

Conclusion

This chapter has highlighted both the opportunities and obstacles intrinsic in relying on international human rights law to identify a migrant's right to healthcare. In general an international human rights treaty provides an inter-state remedy, not a remedy for individuals. Where there is an enforcement mechanism for individuals, the enforcing body or court is likely to have limited powers, be under-resourced and so incapable of responding quickly to a patient in need of treatment. A treaty's content may be vague and aspirational, or the host state may not have ratified it or effectively implemented it in domestic law. Apart from the ECtHR, the regional human rights bodies have a minuscule capacity and no means of enforcing their decisions.

Because so much of international human rights law is 'soft law', there is much to be gained through grassroots work to increase awareness of these arguments, through the training and disseminating of information to health professionals, health providers, service users and third sector organisations. The needs of migrants could also be better protected by applying a human rights framework approach, rather than a purely medical approach when developing healthcare policy.

Where policy fails, and access to the law is needed, the courts in a number of countries are bound to take international human rights law into account by virtue of their constitution. Where they are not, as in the UK, judges are required to consider customary international law in decision-making. Both greater knowledge and greater courage are therefore needed by lawyers to push home the position of healthcare as a fundamental right.

With greater awareness of health as a human right, there could be an increase in the number of individual complaints to the international human rights supervisory bodies, particularly in countries with weak domestic provisions. There is also potential to promote the healthcare of migrants in the reporting mechanisms, some of which allow NGOs to respond to, and challenge, government's accounts of their human rights compliance.

While progressive attitudes towards health can be seen in the regional human rights systems of Africa and the Americas, the approach of the migration hubs of Europe and North America may have a greater impact. It is surely time for the influential ECtHR to consider the issue, hopefully implementing the European Charter of Fundamental Rights statement that *'everyone* has the right of access to healthcare'.

Despite the difficulties, there is now a large, dynamic body of international human rights cases on healthcare. Its potential for creative use to achieve policy and domestic legislative change should not be underestimated or overlooked.

Notes

1 For a more detailed review of the legal provisions see Pace (2009) and Oakshott (2005).

2 The current status of ratifications is recorded at www.un.org/

disabilities/ (last accessed 30 August 2011).

3 See also Chapter 7, this volume.

4 The Inter-American Court of

Human Rights was established in 1979 as an autonomous judicial institution of the Organization of American States (OAS) to provide advisory opinions and adjudicate disputes under the American Convention on Human Rights 1969, but not all the signatories to the Convention have accepted the Court's jurisdiction.

References

Advisory Opinion Concerning Legal Consequences of the Construction of a Wall in the Occupied Palestinian Territory, International Court of Justice (ICJ), (9 July 2004).

African Charter on Human and Peoples' Rights 1981, OAU Doc. CAB/LEG/67/3 rev. 5, entry into force 21 October 1986.

American Convention on Human Rights (1968) 1144 U.N.T.S. 123, entry into force 18 July 1978.

Buergenthal, T. (1995) *International Human Rights in a Nutshell*, West Group, St Paul, MN.

Cesti Hurtado Case (Peru), Provisional Measures, Order of the President of the Court, Inter-Am. Ct. H.R. (ser. E) (29 July 1997).

Chapman, A. R. (1997–8) 'Conceptualizing the right to health: A violations approach', *Tennessee Law Review*, 65(2): 389–418.

Charter of Fundamental Rights of the European Union (2010/C 83/02).

Children's Rehabilitation Institute v Paraguay, Judgment, Inter-Am. Ct. H.R. (ser. C) No. 112 (2 September 2004).

Committee for the Elimination of Racial Discrimination (CERD) General Recommendation XXX, Discrimination against non-citizens (2004) CERD/C/64/Misc.11/rev.3.

Committee on Economic, Social and Cultural Rights (CESCR), General Comment No. 14 (2000), The Right to the Highest Attainable Standard of Health, 33, U.N. Doc. E/C.12/2000/4 (adopted 11 August, 2000).

Convention against Torture and Cruel, Inhuman or Degrading Treatment or Punishment (1984), UNGA Res. 39/46, adopted 9 February 2000.

Convention on the Elimination of All Forms of Discrimination Against Women (1979), UNGA Res. 34/180, entry into force 3 September 1981.

Convention on the Rights of Persons with Disabilities and Optional Protocol (2006), UNGA Res. 61/106, entry into force 3 May 2008.

Convention on the Rights of the Child 1989, adopted UNGA Res. 44/25, entry into force 2 September 1990.

Council Directive 2003/9/EC of 27 January 2003 laying down minimum standards for the reception of asylum seekers.

Cyprus v Turkey [2002] 35 EHRR 30.

Czapka, E. (2009) 'Migrants' access to healthcare services in Norway', http://mighealth.net/no/index.php/Accessibility_of_health_care#Migrants.E2.80.99_access_to_health_care_services_in_Norway (accessed 31 August 2011).

D. v the United Kingdom, 24 EHRR 423 May 1997.

D. R. Congo v Burundi, Rwanda and Uganda, Communication No. 227/99, Twentieth Activity Report, 2006, Annex IV.

Directive 2011/36/EU of the European Parliament and of the Council of 5 April 2011 on preventing and combating trafficking in human beings and protecting its victims, and replacing Council Framework Decision 2002/629/JHA; Official Journal L 101, 15/04/2011 P. 0001–0011.

European Committee of Social Rights Conclusions XVII-1 Vol. 1 2004 p. 10, www.coe.int/T/E/ Human_Rights/Esc/3_Reporting_ procedure/2_Recent_Conclusions /2_By_Year/Social_Charter/ Table_of_conclusions_2004. asp#TopOfPage repeated in respect of the Revised ESC in Conclusions 2004 Volume 1, pp. 9–10, www.coe.int/T/E/Human_Rights/ Esc/3_Reporting_procedure/2_ Recent_Conclusions/2_By_Year/ Revised_Social_Charter/default. asp#TopOfPage (accessed 30 August 2011).

European Convention for the Protection of Fundamental Rights and Freedoms ('European Convention on Human Rights') (1950), ETS No. 5, entered into force 3 September 1953, as amended by Protocol No. 11 and No. 14.

European Social Charter, 529 UNTS 89, entry into force 26 February 1965.

European Social Charter Revised, ETS No. 163, entry into force 7 January 1999.

FIDH (International Federation of Human Rights Leagues) v France Complaint No. 14/2003, European Committee on Social Rights, www.coe.int/T/E/ Human_Rights/ Esc/4_Collective_ complaints/List_of_collective_ complaints/01List_%20of_ complaints.asp#TopOfPage (accessed 30 August 2011).

Gaygusz v Austria (1996) 23 EHRR 364.

Gueye et al. v France Communication No. 196/1983 U.N. Doc. Supp. No. 40 (A/44/40) (1989).

Guidance on Implementing the Overseas Visitors Hospital Charging Regulations, Department of Health, 22 December 2011, www. dh.gov.uk/prod_consum_dh/ groups_dh_digitalassets@dh/@ en/documents/digitalasset/ dh_133999.pdf.

Human Rights Committee (1986) General Comment No. 15: The Position of aliens under the Covenant adopted on 11 April 1986.

— (1989) General Comment No. 18: Non Discrimination UN Doc. HRI/Gen/1/Rev.7, adopted on 10 November 1989.

— (2004) General Comment No. 31: The Nature of the General Legal Obligations Imposed on States Parties to the Covenant adopted on 29 March 2004.

Hurtado v Switzerland, App. No. 17549/90, Eur. Comm'n H.R. Dec. & Rep. (ser. A) 280 (1994).

ILO Convention (No. 97) Concerning Migration for Employment (Revised) 120 U.N.T.S. 70, entry into force 22 January 1952.

International Convention on the Elimination of All Forms of Racial Discrimination, UNGA Res. 2106A (XX) entry into force 4 January 1969.

International Convention on the Protection of the Rights of All Migrant Workers and Members of their Families 1990 UNGA Res. 45/158, entry into force 1 July 2003.

International Covenant on Civil and Political Rights, UNGA Res. 2200A(XXI), entry into force 23 March 1976.

International Covenant on Economic, Social and Cultural Rights 1966 UNGA Res. 2200A(XXI), entry into force 3 January 1976.

International Pen, Constitutional Rights Project, Interights on behalf of Ken Saro-Wiwa Jr and Civil Liberties Organisation v Nigeria, Communications 137/94, 139/94, 154/96 and 161/97, Twelfth Activity Report 1998–1999, Annex V.

Kinney, E. and B. Clark (2004) 'Provisions for health and health care in the constitutions of the countries of the world', *Cornell International Law Journal*, 37: 285–355.

L.C.B. v the United Kingdom (1999) 27 EHRR 212.

Minister of Health and others v Treatment Action Campaign and others (2002) Constitutional Court of South Africa, Case CCT 8/02.

Mladovsky, P. (2007) 'Migrant health in the EU', *Eurohealth*, 13(1): 9–11.

M.S.S. v. Belgium and Greece, App. No. 30696/09 [2011] ECHR 108 (21 January 2011).

Musial v Poland, App. No. 24557/94, 1999-II Eur. Ct. H.R. 15.

N v the United Kingdom, App. No. 26565/05, 27 May 2008.

National Health Service (Charges to Overseas Visitors) Regulations, 2011. SI No. 1556

Nitecki v Poland, App. No. 65653/01, admissibility decision, 21 March 2002.

Oakshott, N. (2005) 'To what extent does international human rights law guarantee access to healthcare for aliens?', unpublished LLM dissertation, University of Essex, Essex.

Pace, P. (2009) *Migration and the Right to Health, A Review of International Law,* International Migration Law No. 19, IOM, Geneva.

Passanantev Italy, App. No. 32647/96, 26 Eur. H. R. Rep. 105 (1998).

Proposed Amendments to the Naturalization Provisions of the Constitution of Costa Rica. Advisory Opinion OC-4/84 of 19 January 1984 Inter-Am Ct. H.R., (ser.A) No. 4.

Purohit and Moore v The Gambia, Communication No. 241/2001, Sixteenth Activity report 2002–2003, Annex VII.

R. (on the application of A) v Secretary of State for Health [2008] EWHC 855 (Admin); [2008] H.R.L.R. 29; *Times*, 13 May 2008.

UN Human Rights Council (2007) *Report of the Special Rapporteur on the Right to Health (A/HRC/4/28/ Add.2)*, 28 February, UNHCR, Geneva www.essex.ac.uk/human _rights_centre/research/rth/docs/ sweden.pdf.

— (2010) *Report of the Special Rapporteur on the Human Rights of Migrants*, UNHRC, Geneva.

US Department of State (2008) *Observations by the United States of America on 'The Right to Health, Fact Sheet No. 31'*, 15 October, www.state.gov.documents/ organization/138850.pdf.

4 | International health worker migration: global inequality and the right to health[1]

REBECCA SHAH

Introduction

In 2006 WHO identified 57 countries with critical shortages of health workers. Most of these were in the developing world with 36 in the world's poorest sub-region: sub-Saharan Africa (WHO, 2006). Relatively speaking, rich countries have health workers in abundance. Iceland, for example, has almost 100 times as many doctors and 60 times as many nurses per head of population as Chad (WHO, 2011).

Countries experiencing critical staff shortages struggle to deliver even the basic services that are an essential part of the right to health. Unsurprisingly, critical shortages correlate with extremely poor health outcomes for the populations dependent on those services. Life expectancy in Iceland, for example, is 82 compared to Chad's 48, and under-five mortality in Iceland is less than half of 1 per cent compared to over 20 per cent in Chad (ibid.).

Against this background there is a steady directional movement of trained health workers from poor countries of greater need to rich countries of lesser need. Despite the fact that average life expectancy in OECD countries is 25 years longer than across Africa, nearly 25 per cent of all doctors trained in sub-Saharan Africa work in OECD countries (OECD, 2011; WHO, 2006, 2011). Some have estimated that more than 50 per cent of doctors from countries such as Ghana and Liberia emigrate to work in richer countries (Mullen, 2007; Physicians for Human Rights, 2004).

The result is a bizarre situation in which poor countries are investing scarce resources in training health professionals to meet the disproportionately high health needs of their populace, but instead of reaping the returns of this investment, the substantial financial and health returns are accruing to the health systems, populations and governments of richer countries, which are financially and institutionally equipped to train health workers with far greater ease. Compounding this 'perverse subsidy' (Mensah et al., 2005), rich countries have historically actively targeted recruitment drives at poor countries with the explicit intention of taking away much-needed health workers. In some cases, they still do.

These powerful concerns motivate the search for ethical solutions to the harmful migration of health workers, but when you look closely, it is not so very easy to establish exactly what the moral problem we are trying to solve is. Is it wrong for a nurse to seek better career development opportunities with a different employer? Is it wrong for a doctor to seek a better salary or to live in an area with access to better education for her children? Is it wrong for a health provider to employ a talented professional from a poor country? Is it wrong for countries to allow their citizens the freedom to leave as they so desire? The answer to each of these would seem to be no. In fact, each of these opportunities is important and morally defensible. But if we cannot answer these questions, how can we design and implement ethical policy responses?

Human rights analysis

The human rights framework provides a key tool to disambiguate the complex moral problems involved in harmful health worker migration. One way of understanding the potentially harmful impact of international health worker migration on the health systems (and hence, health outcomes) in poor 'source' countries is in terms of its contribution to the violation or under-fulfilment of the right to health.

There is legitimate debate about the degree of connectedness between health worker migration and under-fulfilment of the right to health; certainly it is not the only or perhaps even primary cause of poorly functioning health systems in poor countries. Nevertheless, the loss of even just a few health workers from a critically understaffed health system can have an enormous and detrimental impact on access to the services necessary for a minimal enjoyment of the right to health. Sufficient numbers of properly trained and resourced health workers are essential to delivering the basic healthcare and preventative measures necessary for the right to health. But the problem of harmful migration must also be understood within a broader rights context.

The former UN Special Rapporteur on the Right to Health, Paul Hunt, described the right to health 'as a right to an effective and integrated health system, encompassing health care and the underlying determinants of health' (Hunt, 2005). The underlying determinants of health include myriad social, economic and political factors including safe living and working environments, access to adequate safe and nutritious food, freedom from physical violence, freedom from harmful discrimination, access to education, fair pay for work and time to rest. In other words, the determinants of health include most other human rights. In drawing attention to the underlying determinants of health as part of the right to health, this definition reaffirms the idea that all human rights are indivisible and interdependent.

This interdependence has resonance for recognising the complexity associated with harmful health worker migration and finding ways to address it. Health workers often migrate because of the life-constraining lack of choices and under-fulfilment of their and others' rights in their home countries relative to destination countries. Inadequate pay and intolerable working conditions, insufficient infrastructure and resources necessary to perform optimally, overwhelming patient load, threats to personal safety and security, poor living conditions, including limited educational and work opportunities for their children and other relatives, are strongly motivating factors in the decision to migrate. Harmful health worker migration therefore relates to rights other than the right to health, including health workers' rights to freedom of movement and to leave their countries, and the rights to work, to free choice of employment and to just and favourable remuneration for work.

A human rights analysis allows us to understand a variety of harms and potential harms associated with health worker migration. But while this helps to clarify the complexity of the problem, it also indicates the complexity of finding a solution. It is unsurprising that the case of harmful migration has been described as a 'clash of rights' between the employment, opportunity and migratory rights of health workers and the rights to health of all members of the population left behind (e.g. Bueno de Mesquita and Gordon, 2005). Devising policies that can meet all of the rights at stake is a challenge: the human rights framework has no easy solution for how to resolve conflicts between different rights or between the rights of different groups.

What the human rights framework does provide, however, is a clear framework for responsibility. In the remainder of this chapter I consider how adequate this distribution of responsibility is to ensure that all these rights are met in the context of harmful health worker migration, focusing on the right to health in poor countries.

'Source' country governments and the right to health

The founding bases of human rights are cosmopolitan: human rights are held equally by all individuals without exception or distinction. The mechanism for their realisation, however, is distinctly state-based: states have the primary responsibility to respect, protect and fulfil the human rights of their citizens.

As the primary protectors of the right to health for their populations, developing country governments have been criticised for taking inadequate steps to ensure this right, including taking inadequate steps to resolve the human resources for health crises. For example, African heads of state pledged to allocate at least 15 per cent of national budgets to healthcare in the Abuja Declaration in 2001 (African Union, cited in Action for Global Health, 2007). In 2011, the average government expenditure on health across Africa is still below 10 per cent of overall budget expenditure and few African countries meet the 15 per cent target (WHO, 2011).

Even when poor countries assign relatively high proportions of government expenditure to health, however, the monetary value and purchasing power of that allocation remains low. For example, Germany and Rwanda both allocate similarly high proportions of total government spending to health (18 and 18.2 per cent respectively; ibid.). In Germany this spending amounts to about US$3,323 annual per capita spending on health. In Rwanda this amounts to only $22 annual per capita spending on health, or about half of 1 per cent of Germany's spending (ibid.). Even when compared in terms of purchasing power parity, Rwanda's health expenditure amounts to approximately 1.7 per cent of that in Germany.

This reveals a twin problem for poor countries seeking to protect the right to health of their citizens. First, poor countries (almost by definition) lack adequate resources. Poverty fuels the problem as it creates enormously difficult working environments and encourages people to seek better opportunities abroad, and it also hinders successful responses to the problem as resources to train more workers and improve pay and conditions are extremely limited. Second, this problem is amplified by being *relative* as well as *absolute*. No matter how much poor countries prioritise the right to health of their people, they are unlikely to be able to nullify the differences in living and working conditions, salaries, training opportunities and so on between their own and richer countries. It is precisely because living and working conditions and opportunities are so different between rich and poor countries that the current pattern of international skilled migration from poor to richer countries exists. People migrate not just because things are hard at home but also because they are better elsewhere. The international *inequality*, therefore, matters as much as the deprivation.

Poor source country governments have clear responsibilities to protect the right to health of their citizens. The human rights framework and the right to health in particular makes explicit a core range of obligations on the part of states, the implementation of which will form an essential part of approaches to address harmful migration. Poor country governments can and should strive for excellence in this, and there are certainly innovative and efficient ways of optimising health outcomes and employment conditions under extreme budgetary pressure. Examples particularly relevant to harmful migration include the explicit contracting of health workers, the training of para-health professionals and the incentivising of work placements in high need areas (see Shah, 2010b for further details). Even in best case scenarios, however, the strong and clear responsibilities of poor source countries are matched by weak capacity to fulfil them, especially when core elements of the right to health are determined by a global context that they have limited power to address. While the human rights framework is highly instructive on responsibilities for the absolute, it struggles when it needs to take into account inequality, especially inequality that exists not within countries but between them.

Caveats in the right to health

The inability of poor countries to provide health services necessary to fully realise the right to health to a level comparable to that in richer countries is, however, accommodated in understandings of state responsibility in the human right to health in three main ways.

First, beyond core obligations, the right to health is progressive. This means that states are not expected to immediately and fully realise the right to health but rather to 'move as expeditiously and effectively as possible towards the full realization' (UN CESCR, 2000, para. 31). This caveat recognises that health systems, particularly those in poor countries, need time to develop capacity and therefore prevents states from being considered to be rights violators because they cannot yet provide a full range of services. The strength of rights language, however, is partly the moral imperative it conveys; human rights do not merely denote the good or the desirable but *entitlements* and corresponding *duties*. When a human right no longer requires immediate fulfilment or the appropriate duty-bearer is incapable of protecting it, a right is stripped of some normative and legal force.

Second, the right to health is implicitly relative. This means that '[t]he notion of "the highest attainable standard of health" ... takes into account both the individual's biological and socio-economic preconditions and a *State's available resources*' (UN CESCR, 2000, para.

9; emphasis added). This caveat recognises the difference in wealth and capability between countries so that one country is not deemed a rights violator because it cannot provide all the services that its richer neighbour can. Taken literally, however, the implications of this relativity are confusing and repellent. Relativity suggests that for poor people in poor countries where poor health circumstances are the norm, poor health outcomes are less of a rights violation, less morally problematic and less legally compelling than for people with richer backgrounds or in rich countries where the local standards are higher. This seems to be saying that people with a poorer socioeconomic start in life and fewer state resources, such as those in countries where governments are incapable of resolving the human resources crisis, have or should have *lower entitlements* than well off people or people living in well resourced states.

It was obviously not the intention of the human rights regime to be read in this manner. Relativity and progressiveness were built into the right to health in order to avoid charges of rights violations being levied against poor states incapable, despite best intentions, of realising the right to health any further. It may sound practically reasonable but it is ethically most bizarre that poverty and inequality could be used to justify lower moral consideration and practical protection for the worse off.

The third acknowledgement of the limited ability of poor states to secure the right to health is that while states hold primary responsibilities with regard to their populations, *all* states share some responsibilities to respect and take steps to realise the right to health (and other rights) through international assistance and cooperation (UN CESCR, 2000). The responsibilities of states for human rights in other countries are more obscure and amorphous than those of states for their own citizens. Human rights instruments do stipulate responsibilities of foreign states but these are often interpreted as being undefined, weak, unaccountable or not legally binding. It is to these responsibilities of other states, particularly rich states that are receivers of health workers from poor countries, that I now turn. In particular, I consider three possible responsibilities of other states: responsibilities to assist, to not harm and to remedy.

Responsibilities to assist The clearest articulation of international responsibilities with regard to the right to health and harmful migration is that of international assistance and cooperation. The former UN Special Rapporteur noted this as including 'a responsibility on States to seek appropriate assistance and cooperation, and a responsibility on States in a position to assist to provide appropriate assistance and cooperation' (UNGA, 2008, para. 22). There is no clarity, however, about what this duty to assist entails and although global attention to and funding for health, particularly health in poor countries, has never been higher, this assistance is often a double-edged sword when it comes to protecting the right to health in the context of the human resources crisis.

International assistance in its manifold forms often and increasingly makes a massive contribution to health spending in poor countries. Development aid has contributed to enormous health benefits such as the global eradication of smallpox and dramatic reductions of river blindness and guinea worm in some developing world regions (Levine et al., 2004).

The plethora of current aid mechanisms for health, from direct budget support to global health partnerships, has, however, been seriously criticised for potentially undermining stable funding for health services in poor countries. Donor funding sources are often uncoordinated, leading to duplications and omissions; lack transparency and accountability to recipients; are interested in short-term results rather than long-term stability; are concerned with high-tech solutions rather than making existing low-tech solutions more widely available; and may reflect donor values and preferences rather than recipient needs (see, for example, Bloom, 2007; Brown, 2007; Buse et al., 2006; England, 2007; Lorenz, 2007). As a long-term ongoing cost, staff training and remuneration requires long-term funding stability, whereas much current aid funding for health is short-term, disease specific, unpredictable and uncoordinated (e.g. Dodd et al., 2007). Donors are usually disinclined to commit to the long-term funding necessary to address the human resources for health crisis such as in the form of salary support. Aid can sometimes even exacerbate health worker shortages by enticing health workers out of public health systems into the better funded parallel private systems of donor-endorsed organisations (Poore, 2004).

Rights-based approaches to international assistance are increasingly valued and common, and donors continue to look for ways to deliver aid in a more coherent fashion that minimises negative externalities, but even in this context the primary human rights responsibilities remain with the poor country government. It is the primary responsibility of states to ensure that external or non-state actors do not act in such a way that undermines the realisation of human rights for their citizens. The onus, therefore, is on the governments of poor countries, both to seek aid and also to ensure that any aid received does not impede the realisation of the right to health, rather than for donors to ensure that their actions do not impede the realisation of the right to health. In reality this often serves to place responsibility with the parties with the weakest international bargaining power.

High levels of external funding, which often exceed public funding for health, can swamp domestic infrastructure, prevent governments from sticking to comprehensive national health and development plans and may have a particular impact on human resources for health. Rwanda provides a clear example. The Rwandan government has seven strategic objectives for health that include human resources, but donor funding is many times higher for one sub-objective (health services for HIV/AIDS) than for all the other strategic objectives combined (Dodd et al., 2007). In fact, international funding for HIV/AIDS dwarfs Rwanda's entire domestic health budget (Shiffman, 2006). The Rwandan government may not be in a position to refuse such generosity, indeed they might be considered negligent on human rights grounds if they did, but with money comes power and they may also struggle to ensure that this generosity is compatible with their sustainable objectives for realising the right to health.

International responsibilities to assist the right to health are important but have sadly often been discharged in a manner that meets the interests of donors more than the needs and rights of recipients. Assistance that fails to attend to potential negative human rights impacts would seem to be an insufficient response to harmful migration.

Responsibilities to not harm The UN CESCR has said that: 'States parties have to respect the enjoyment of the right to health in other countries' (UN CESCR, 2000, para. 36). The legal grounds for this are unclear and some would disagree that such an obligation exists (e.g. Gibney et al., 1999). Rich countries, of course, also have responsibilities for the right to health of their own citizens and many have shortages of domestically trained health workers. They may claim that it is both morally and legally legitimate to prioritise their own obligations and their own citizens' right to health over the right to health of citizens in foreign countries, even if this means that they practise international health worker recruitment that threatens human rights abroad. This may seem reasonable on many readings of human rights responsibilities and it serves to indicate how the human rights regime struggles to accommodate international inequality, especially if the standards for rights fulfilment are considered to be locally relative. Taking the inequality in both financial and health terms between the world's poorest and richest countries into account, however, gives us reason to try to push for a better reading of the human rights regime in this regard.

Although there may not be a legally binding responsibility to not harm human rights in other countries, it may nevertheless be interpreted as a (non-legally binding) moral obligation. In the case of health worker migration, this obligation might relate to the unintended externalities of international assistance, but may also require that rich countries stop their active involvement in harming the right to health abroad by ceasing their active recruitment of health workers from countries with critical shortages of health workers.

In the past, the UK recruited large proportions of its health workforce from poor countries, but in recognising the incongruence of this behaviour with its stated international development goals it introduced an ethical code for the recruitment of international health workers (Department of Health, 2004). The code restricts active recruitment from a list of poor countries, although passive recruitment and active recruitment from countries that have specific agreements with the UK are permitted.

The idea is that the code evades the morally suspect option of specifically restricting the immigration of health workers from poor countries by instead merely removing the actively harmful role the state plays in that immigration. The code therefore plays on what moral philosophers call the 'acts and omissions doctrine', whereby it may be morally wrong to *act* to bring about a particular result but not wrong, or at least not as wrong, if the same result is brought about through a *failure* to act (the example often used is the difference between actively killing someone and allowing them to die). So, rich country governments may not be actively recruiting from poor countries, which would be wrong, but they may passively allow migration to continue on its own, which is not wrong, or at least not as wrong. Philosophers disagree, however, about whether passive allowing is really morally better than active doing. If the same result occurs regardless of active involvement, is this not equally bad?

The jury is also out as to the effectiveness of the UK's ethical code. The years since its inception have seen some decline in the number of health workers entering the UK to work from listed poor countries (Buchan et al., 2009). There is also some evidence to suggest that the ethical code simply makes migration more difficult and expensive for migrants from poor countries without reducing migration (e.g. Mensah et al., 2005), which may heighten migrants' dependence on private recruitment agencies and make them more vulnerable to exploitation and abusive conditions such as debt bondage (e.g. Anderson and Rogaly, 2005; Skrivánková, 2006). It is not possible, however, to distinguish the causal impact of the ethical code from that of other policies specifically designed to restrict skilled immigration in order to protect the domestic workforce, such as changes to the UK's immigration rules (e.g. Buchan et al., 2009; Cangiano et al., 2009). The impact of the code is therefore both practically and ethically ambiguous and reflects the complexity of taking measures to address harmful migration that do not themselves prove harmful in some other respect.

Even if the ethical code is successful, however, it seems an insufficient response as it does nothing to address the harmful consequences of continuing passive migration on health systems and the right to health in poor countries; to compensate for the harms caused by past active recruitment of health workers or to address the causal factors – the inequality – that ensure health workers continue migrating even as it becomes more arduous to do so. The following section therefore looks at whether human rights responsibilities can go further than this.

Responsibilities to remedy Human rights instruments indicate that when a rights violation is proven, the duty-bearer has an obligation not only to stop violating the right but also to provide 'effective remedy' (e.g. UNGA, 1948). The responsibility to provide remedy is therefore part of due process when states violate the rights of their own citizens, but is far beyond what is usually considered to be the responsibility of foreign states. Nevertheless, given that rich countries have played a role in the deprivation of the right to health in poor countries, some people have suggested that rich countries ought to make some form of restitution for their active role in the creation of the problem.

This approach has enormous intuitive moral appeal. Recognition of past wrongs would seem to be an essential aspect of retributive justice as well as being crucial in determining the sorts of international relations we will have in the future. There are reasons to be cautious, however, about responsibilities to remedy.

Even in the absence of significant human rights precedents, states are usually highly reluctant to admit responsibility for actions that violate or impede human rights in other states. One reason is because it presupposes that they have done something legally or morally wrong (in this case, in employing health workers from overseas), an idea that many countries will reject, even if they accept that the associated deficits in the right to health for poor populations are regrettable. Working out exactly what remedy is required and of whom will also be extremely, perhaps even prohibitively, complex, even in the fairly discrete case of health worker migration. There is a considerable risk that establishing the exact forms, content and extent of reparation, compensation or even retribution may prove a considerable drain on resources, and be contentious and divisive. It may also provide a reason for health systems in rich countries to discriminate specifically against health workers from poor countries, thereby disadvantaging them further (Mensah et al., 2005).

What concerns me more than these issues, however, is that if states should accept responsibilities for remedying their harmful acts in this instance then we should also consider claims for remedy for other acts that have had negative human rights impacts in other countries. Receiving country governments, and rich countries in general, have had starring roles in the creation of failing health services in poor countries and the wider conditions of global inequality that perpetuate the directional movement of skilled labour from poor to rich countries, even if they are not implicated in the active international recruitment of health workers. These roles ripple outwards in proximity from the current crisis. They include the championing of trade liberalisation in health services under the General Agreement on Trade in Services (GATS), which facilitates harmful health worker migration and poses serious threats to health in poor populations (Woodward, 2005). They include the imposition of structural adjustment policies that had cata-strophic effects on salaries, working conditions, staffing levels and infrastructural investment in the health sector and ultimately rolled back progress in health and other social and economic human rights (e.g. Ambrose, 2006; Daniels, 2006; Logie and Woodroffe, 1993). They include the creation of poor countries' crippling levels of debt and inability to refuse aid or loans with rights-harming conditions attached (Guissé, 2004). They extend back to colonialism itself, which deprived great proportions of the world of rights to self-determination and allowed the colonisers to reap massive benefits at the expense of the lands and lives of the colonised, and further still to the slave trade that catapulted slave-holding nations into the positions of global afflu-ence they inhabit today for the price of the lives, liberty and dignity of millions of people from what are now the world's poorest regions.

These may be matters of history but their impacts on health systems in poor countries and their legacies of global inequality are still keenly felt; these inequalities now drive, and are reinforced by, health worker migration. These roles, much like the active recruitment of health workers from poor countries, did not contravene any legal norms existing at the time but we nonetheless have reason to retrospectively find them morally problematic. If we are concerned with receiving countries' atonement for past wrongs, consistency would seem to require that we do not limit our concern to only the most obviously proximal actions when a great many others have also had a significant impact on the situation. This is especially true given that harmful migration itself is not the only or even principal cause of the human resources crisis and the wider failure to fulfil the right to health in poor countries, even if it exacerbates these problems (Dumont, 2007). The real causal factors radiate outwards into history beyond the identifiable actions of specific contemporary agents.[2] Should all these harmful acts be entered into calculations for remedy in the context of harmful migration?

I think attempts to do so would be unhelpful. Doing so may be prohibitively complex, but it would also serve to prioritise culpability for *harms* over fulfilment of *rights*. There is the danger that addressing past injustice will not match contemporary need and may even create new inequalities and inequities, for example, if there are populations suffering today that are not identifiably the victims of past incidents of injustice or who were also perpetrators. Human rights violations will be no less morally pressing in countries that were not victims of internationally harmful acts or that also perpetrated internationally harmful acts. These historic harms are of too great a magnitude to simply be ignored, but how they can be properly dealt with is a complex matter beyond the scope of this chapter.

Despite the powerful moral appeal of responsibilities to remedy, I am not convinced that it is a helpful focus for human rights responsibilities for harmful migration. It is difficult to accurately administer and it spills over into far wider-reaching and equally powerful historical claims. Nevertheless, I think consideration of responsibilities to remedy leads us towards what are more important responsibilities: those of distributive rather than retributive justice. We need to draw our attention away from the particular metrics of remedy and the particular symptom of harmful migration to the broader problem of the inequality that allows harmful migration to prosper. To a certain extent the focus on harmful migration is a red herring. There is nothing inherently wrong with the movement of people including, or even especially, the movement of people from impoverished areas seeking better opportunities elsewhere. Indeed, health workers continue in the morally praiseworthy task of saving lives whether they do so in

London or Lusaka. The real nub of the problem is that this current wave of migration takes place within a context of inequality that means it is largely directional and that benefits accrue to the richer nations at the expense of the poorer. The complexity of historical and global relationships has created an international system in which feedback loops, which perpetuate the distribution of benefits to the rich and the distribution of harms to the poor, now operate independently of specific and identifiable harmful acts.

Perhaps a first step towards a focus on the wider context is represented by the 'Global Code of Practice on the International Recruitment of Health Personnel', which was launched by the World Health Assembly in 2010 (WHO, 2010). This is the first code applicable to all countries, all health sectors and all types of employers. The code aims at achieving balance between the rights, obligations and expectations of the different parties to the process of health worker migration. It therefore promotes the rights obligations of *all* countries (source and receiving), the principle of mutual benefit with the scales being tipped in *favour* of poorer countries, and information gathering and sharing, alongside ethical recruitment practices. The balance and multiplicity of recommendations means that it touches on the specific responsibilities outlined in the sections above as well as the more general distributive principle that even when benefits and skills are being shared globally, these should accrue primarily to those in greatest need. The impact of the code is, as yet, unclear. Initial, tentative research suggests that awareness of the code remains low, and its impact to date has been limited (Edge and Hoffman, 2011). One reason for this may be that the code remains entirely voluntary, leaving countries and recruiters free to decide whether and how far they take the code on board. In a global context where many countries – both rich and poor – are feeling the pinch of a global economic downturn, a voluntary code may simply not be enough. Nevertheless, it represents a step towards an approach that can accommodate human rights but also move beyond their, at times, restrictive nature, to accommodate the inequality that drives the current situation.

Conclusion

A human rights analysis allows us to understand and disambiguate a variety of actual and potential harms associated with health worker migration. This fulfils a vital first step to help policy-makers to more accurately and fruitfully concentrate their efforts on trying to devise solutions.

The human rights framework also provides a clear model for who bears responsibility and of what kind. While bringing clarity, however, this framework also has its limitations. The direct responsibilities of source states to respect, protect and fulfil the right to health of their citizens are clear, but are often matched with limited abilities to dispatch these responsibilities. This problem is compounded by the fact that it is the inequalities between states that implicitly drive harmful migration. The human rights framework has a limited capacity to accommodate these problems of global inequality. The responsibilities of other states, including rich countries that receive migrant health workers, are more limited and less clear. Other states have obligations to assist, but current experience suggests that the enormous influx on spending for health may not always make it easier for poor states to implement sustainable long-term objectives on the right to health. They may have obligations to desist from activities that actively violate the right to health in other countries, but even measures to avoid this active role (such as ethical recruitment policies) can render ethically ambiguous results. They are not usually held to have obligations to remedy under human rights law, but even if they were to be, I have argued that it may not be appropriate, helpful or even fair to focus on responsibility to remedy.

What the human rights framework does not do is identify any easy solutions for addressing the complex problems causing and caused by the international migration of health workers. Successful policy approaches will require a mixed set of measures on the part of all parties involved, but it will also require going beyond this. Specific measures by individual countries (whether sending or receiving) need also to be accompanied by more general commitments from all parties to modifying the global rules of the game that allow the inequality that fuels health worker migration to flourish.[3]

Notes

1 This chapter is adapted from Shah, R. S. (2010a), with extracts reproduced here with the permission of Palgrave MacMillan.

2 These causal factors of course also include actions of the leaders and the people in some poor countries themselves, ranging from benign mismanagement of services to corruption, conflict and tyranni-cal dictatorships that have committed gross human rights violations and contributed to the long-term impoverishment of their countries. The human rights responsibilities of states for their own populations are not in doubt, even if they are not always observed.

3 See Shah (2010a) for a more detailed discussion of how the

human rights framework can better accommodate distributive justice concerns about the global inequality that drives and reinforces harmful health worker migration.

References

Action for Global Health (2007) *Health Warning: Why Europe Must Act Now to Rescue the Health Millennium Development Goals*, Action for Global Health, Brussels.

Ambrose, S. (2006) 'Preserving disorder: IMF policies and Kenya's healthcare crisis', *Pambazuka News*, 257: Special Issue on Trade and Justice, www.pambazuka.org/ (accessed 2 June 2006).

Anderson, B. and B. Rogaly (2005) *Forced Labour and Migration*, TUC, London.

Bloom, D. E. (2007) 'Governing global health', *Finance and Development*, 44(4): 31–5.

Brown, H. (2007) 'Great expectations', *British Medical Journal*, 334: 874–6.

Buchan, J., B. McPake, K. Mensah and G. Rae (2009) 'Does a code make a difference: Assessing the English Code of Practice on International Recruitment', *Human Resources for Health*, 7: 33–40.

Bueno de Mesquita, J. and M. Gordon (2005) *The International Migration of Health Workers: A Human Rights Analysis*, Medact, London.

Buse, K., M. Sidibe, D. Whyms, I. Huijts and S. Jensen (2006) *Scaling-Up the HIV/AIDS Response: From Alignment and Harmonisation to Mutual Accountability*, Overseas Development Institute Briefing Paper 9, ODI, London.

Cangiano, A., I. Shutes, S. Spencer and G. Leeson (2009) *Migrant Care Workers in Ageing Societies: Research Findings in the United Kingdom*, COMPAS, Oxford.

Daniels, N. (2006) 'Equity and population health: Towards a broader bioethics agenda', *Hastings Center Report*, 36(4): 22–35.

Department of Health (2004) *Code of Practice for the International Recruitment of Healthcare Professionals*, www.dh.gov.uk/ prod_consum_dh/groups/ dh_digitalassets/@dh/@en/documents/digitalasset/dh_4097734. pdf (accessed 30 December 2009).

Dodd, R., G. Schieber, A. Cassels, L. Fleisher and P. Gottret (2007) *Aid Effectiveness and Health*, Making Health Systems Work: Working Paper No. 9, WHO/HSS/healthsystems/2007.2, WHO, Geneva.

Dumont, J. C. (2007) 'International Migration of Health Professionals: New Evidence and Recent Trends', presented to the Workshop on Human Resources for Health and Migration: Mobility, Training and the Global Supply of Health Workers, Sussex University, 16–17 May 2007.

Edge, J. S. and S. J. Hoffman (2011) 'Empirical Impact Evaluation of the WHO Global Code of Practice on the International Recruitment of Health Personnel (2010) on Government, Civil Society and Private Sectors in Australia, Canada, United Kingdom and United States of America', presented at the 2011 American Political Science Association Conference and posted to SSRN, http://papers.ssrn.com/sol3/ papers.cfm?abstract_id=1900293 (accessed 20 October 2011).

England, R. (2007) 'Are we spending too much on HIV?', *British Medical Journal*, 334: 344.

Gibney, M., K. Tomaševski and J. Vedsted-Hansen (1999) 'Transnational state responsibility for violations of human rights', *Harvard Human Rights Journal*, 12: 267–95.

Guissé, E. H. (2004) *Effects of Debt on Human Rights*, Economic and Social Council of the United Nations, E/CN.4/Sub.2/2004/27, 1 July 2004.

Hunt, P. (2005) *Statement by Paul Hunt, Special Rapporteur on the Right of Everyone to the Enjoyment of the Highest Attainable Standard of Physical and Mental Health*, UN General Assembly, Third Committee, 28 October 2005, www. essex.ac.uk/human_rights_centre/research/rth/docs/General_Assembly_Third_Committee_ Oral_Remarks.doc (accessed 1 December 2009).

Levine, R., M. Kinder and the What Works Working Group (2004) *Millions Saved: Proven Successes in Global Health*, Peterson Institute for International Economics, Washington DC.

Logie, D. E. and J. Woodroffe (1993) 'Structural adjustment: The wrong prescription for Africa?', *British Medical Journal*, 301: 41–4.

Lorenz, N. (2007) 'Effectiveness of global health partnerships: Will the past repeat itself?', *Bulletin of the World Health Organisation*, 85(7): 501–68.

Mensah, K., M. Mackintosh and L. Henry (2005) *The 'Skills Drain' of Health Professionals from the Developing World: A Framework for Policy Formulation*, Medact, London.

Mullen, F. (2007) 'Doctors and soccer players – African professionals on the move', *New England Journal of Medicine*, 356(5): 440–3.

OECD (Organisation for Economic Co-operation and Development) (2011) *OECD Health Data 2011*, www.oecd.org/document/30/0, 3746, en_2649_37407_12968 734_1_1_1_37407,00.html (accessed 27 October 2011).

Physicians for Human Rights (2004) *An Action Plan to Prevent Brain Drain: Building Equitable Health Systems in Africa*, Physicians for Human Rights, Boston.

Poore, P. (2004) 'Opinion piece: The Global Fund to fight Aids, Tuberculosis and Malaria (GFATM)', *Health Policy and Planning*, 19(1): 52–3.

Shah, R. S. (2010a) 'The right to health, state responsibility and global justice', in R. S. Shah (ed.) (2010) *The International Migration of Health Workers: Ethics, Rights and Justice*, Palgrave Macmillan, Basingstoke.

— (ed.) (2010b) *The International Migration of Health Workers: Ethics, Rights and Justice*, Palgrave Macmillan, Basingstoke.

Shiffman, J. (2006) 'HIV/AIDS and the rest of the global health agenda', *Bulletin of the World Health Organization*, 84(12): 923.

Skrivánková, K. (2006) *Trafficking for Forced Labour: UK Country Report*, Anti-Slavery International, London.

UN CESR (United Nations Committee on Economic, Social and Cultural Rights) (2000) *E/C.12/2000/4. General Comment No. 14, The Right to the Highest Attainable Standard of Health (Article 12 of the International Covenant on Economic, Social and Cultural Rights)*, 11 August 2000, United Nations, Geneva.

UNGA (United Nations General Assembly) (1948) *Universal*

Declaration of Human Rights, Resolution 217 A (III), UNGA, Paris.

— (2008) *Addendum to the Report of the Special Rapporteur on the Right of Everyone to the Enjoyment of the Highest Attainable Standard of Physical and Mental Health, Paul Hunt, to the Human Rights Council, Seventh Session*, A/HRC/7/11/ Add.2, UNGA, Paris.

WHO (World Health Organization) (2006) *World Health Report 2006: Working Together for Health*, WHO, Geneva.

— (2010) *Global Code of Practice on the International Recruitment of Health Personnel*, WHO, Geneva.

— (2011) *World Health Statistics 2011*, WHO, Geneva.

Woodward, D. (2005) 'The GATS and trade in health services: Implications for healthcare in developing countries', *Review of International Political Economy*, 12(3): 511–34.

5 | Socioeconomic vulnerability and access to healthcare among immigrants in Chile

BÁLTICA CABIESES AND HELENA TUNSTALL

Introduction

Recent data describing immigration to Chile suggest that immigrants now comprise approximately 1.6–1.8 per cent of the Chilean population, equal to 258,350 persons. Over 50 per cent of these immigrants have arrived in Chile since 1996 (Departamento de Extranjería y Migración, 2007). The characteristics of migration to Chile are closely related to changes in economic and political circumstances in the country and the region (UNESCO, 1999). In recent years there has been growing migration *within* the Latin American region; with Chile's social stability and rapid economic growth over the past decade attracting growing immigration from other Latin American countries (Departamento de Extranjería y Migración, 2007).

However, relatively little health and social research has so far considered international migrants moving between middle income countries. The purpose of this chapter is to contribute to the current understanding of inequalities in access to healthcare among international immigrants in Chile. Inequalities – such as health inequalities – have been defined as the systematic, structural difference in any given outcome between and within social groups. In the social epidemiology field, health inequalities refer to the multiple influences upon health status, including socioeconomic status, diet, education, employment, housing, income and others, which affect to different extents the wellbeing of every population (Marmot, 1999, 2010; Marmot and Wilkinson, 1999). In this chapter, we consider inequalities in socioeconomic conditions and healthcare provision entitlement as a relevant measure of vulnerability among international immigrants in Chile. Vulnerability has been defined as the risk that some future event will negatively affect the wellbeing of people in a given place (Shorrocks, 2009).

The chapter has three objectives. The first is to outline the recent flows of migration to Chile. We then use new data from the Chilean CASEN (National Socioeconomic Characterization) (Caracterización Socio-Económica Nacional) survey from 2006 and 2009 (Mideplan, 2006,

2009) to provide the first national analysis of the socioeconomic profile of immigrants living in Chile and its association with their health-care provision entitlement. Lastly, the chapter aims to highlight and discuss the existence of vulnerability and social disadvantage within the immigrant population and compare this to the local Chilean-born population.

The Republic of Chile and the Chilean healthcare system

Chile is a middle income country with an intermediate level of development, currently experiencing a shift from infectious diseases to chronic health conditions, the so-called epidemiological transition (Arteaga et al., 2002a). It has a population of just over 16 million in-habitants. The country is divided into 15 regions; 40 per cent of the population live in the Metropolitan Region of Santiago, and 85 per cent in total in urban areas.

The Chilean national healthcare system has experienced significant changes over time. A public integrated system called FONASA (Fondo Nacional de Salud or National Health Fund) was first introduced in 1952; this lasted until the dictatorship period. During the 1980s, the military government took a series of measures to stimulate growth in the membership of the private healthcare system ISAPREs (in-stituciónes de salud previsionales or health insurance institutions). As a consequence the Chilean healthcare system is now a mixed sys-tem characterised by segmentation. The public FONASA and private ISAPRE sectors coexist with little interaction between them in terms of either insurance or provision. The private system covers about 25 per cent of the population and the public sector around 60 per cent of the population. The rest of the population is either part of the army healthcare system (around 4 per cent) or have no healthcare coverage at all (around 10 per cent) (Arteaga et al., 2002b; Oyarzo, 2000). The public system is divided between 100 per cent free of charge care (called type A or indigent card), available to those living in poverty as based upon a means test, and public with co-payment care with fees based upon household earnings (types B, C or D). Around a quarter of the population entitled to the public system has a type A card and the rest pay proportionally to their earnings. With the exception of the public free of charge provision that is given to the poorest in the country, people can choose between a huge range of health insurances, with over 150 different public and private schemes available.

Chile faces significant difficulties as a developing country trying to improve health and reduce social and health inequalities. Waiting lists and barriers to access the healthcare system remain (Mardones, 2004). Consequently, public opinion polls in Chile have revealed that the populations in both the public and private healthcare subsystems feel insecure and unhappy with their healthcare because of access difficulties and because, in some circumstances, costs may not be covered by health insurance (UN, 2006).

The Chilean health reform implemented in 2003 was intended to have a significant impact on population health (Arrau, 2002). This reform was based on three fundamental values: 1) equity in access to healthcare; 2) effectiveness in interventions designed to promote, preserve and restore health; and 3) efficient use of available resources. While this reform demonstrates the increasing prominence of the reduction of social and health inequalities within social policy in Chile, much more needs to be done in order to transform Chilean society into a more egalitarian one, more respectful of health as a social value. Stronger research evidence is also needed especially regarding those in socioeconomic vulnerability, that is the lower socioeconomic status and those without access to healthcare (Cabieses et al., 2010). Moreover, Chile's growing proportion of international immigrants adds further complexity to the picture. Little is known about the circumstances of these immigrants in Chile. It has been presumed, however, that a significant proportion of this group live in vulnerable circumstances, experiencing absolute poverty, lack of health insurance and are at risk of poor health (Amador, 2010; IOM and MINSAL, 2008a, 2008b; Nuñez-Carrasco, 2008). Before presenting data on healthcare provision entitlement among immigrants in Chile, the following section briefly introduces the general characteristics of the immigration flow to Chile in recent years.

Immigration patterns in Chile

Chile is still primarily a migrant issuer country. There is a ratio of three to one Chileans living outside the country to immigrants in Chile (Departamento de Extranjería y Migración, 2007). Chile has, however, become an increasingly attractive destination to international immigrants in recent years. As migration to Chile has increased, the characteristics of migrants have changed. Until 1982, immigration to Chile was mainly from Europe, the Arab states and East Asia (Pizarro, 2002; Stefoni, 2001). During the last two decades, however, immigration rates from South American and other Asian countries have increased (Departamento de Extranjería y Migración, 2007). The latest governmental figures indicate that Chile is currently experiencing a 'new immigration' pattern, with the majority of immigrants coming from

Latin America seeking labour opportunities. According to the latest Census in 2002, 67.8 per cent of total immigrants currently living in Chile come from South America (ibid.). Despite this recent evidence, relatively little is known about their socioeconomic characteristics or access to healthcare provision in Chile. The following section of this chapter draws on new analysis of the Chilean CASEN survey 2006 and 2009 undertaken by the authors, which provides the first national analysis of the relationship between socioeconomic characteristics and access to healthcare among immigrants living in Chile.

Legal rights to healthcare and policies to support access among immigrants in Chile

Healthcare provision available in Chile is dependent on migrant status. Some public services are available to selected groups of immigrants. Legally documented immigrants, with a valid temporary or permanent visa permit, have the same right to access primary healthcare as those who are Chilean-born: either free (if living in poverty) or with some co-payment (depending on earnings). In addition, immigrants can receive prenatal care, childcare, emergency care and the universal child vaccination scheme irrespective of their legal status.

Some recent efforts have been made to improve the access to healthcare of immigrants in Chile and have been motivated in part by a wish to reduce health inequalities in Chile. These policies have focused upon vulnerable groups, in particular, pregnant women and children, irrespective of their legal status. Immigration policies have also resulted from a desire to promote positive relationships with other Latin American countries. In particular, some policies have been developed to support healthcare among some groups of potentially disadvantaged legal and illegal immigrants from Peru, the most common country of origin among immigrants in Chile.

To date, the following healthcare and social policies have been developed to support immigrants in Chile:

1 Programme for pregnant immigrant women. Supported by the Social Organizations Directorate, the Chilean Ministry of Health and the Department of Immigration and Migration, the programme enables migrant women who are pregnant and have no current legal documentation to attend the primary clinic nearest their home. This entitles them to access the health system and receive documentation to approach the Department of Immigration and obtain a temporary visa for one year.

2 Programme for immigrants under 18 years old. This is a collaborative agreement between the Chilean Ministry of Health and the Ministry of the Interior to regularise migration for immigrants who are under 18 years old. Immigrants who are under 18 and socially vulnerable (for example, exposed to higher risks of violence and/or drugs) can receive healthcare in the public health network, on an equal basis and regardless of their immigration status and that of their parents (Resolution No. 1914 of 13 March 2008 and REGULAR 14 Number 3 229, of 11 June 2008).

3 Free medical care for Peruvians with precarious resources. Since late August 2002, the General Consulate of Peru in Santiago has had an agreement with the Chilean Red Cross, with additional voluntary support of the Peruvian community physicians. This is a free medical clinic serving Peruvians, whether documented or not, who for economic or other reasons are unable to access these services from other government or private institutions. The clinic provides a primary care service (Consulado General del Perú en Santiago de Chile, 2009).

4 Social security agreement between the Republic of Peru and the Republic of Chile. This is a Convention concerning the right of Peruvian pensioners to receive benefits equivalent to those of their country of residence, such as retirement pensions and social benefits due to disability (ibid.).

Despite these policy initiatives important limitations regarding the accessibility of healthcare to immigrants still exist in Chile, particularly among economically marginalised immigrants and those who are undocumented. These groups, who experience socioeconomic vulnerability, are discussed in more detail below, later with reference to access to the Chilean healthcare system.

Demographic characteristics of international immigrants in Chile

As mentioned, most immigrants currently living in Chile come from other Latin American countries. Recent data from the 2006 CASEN survey suggest the most common countries of origin are Peru (27.8 per cent), Argentina (26.1 per cent), Bolivia (5.8 per cent) and Ecuador (5.0 per cent). Other Latin American and Caribbean countries account for 12.2 per cent of immigrants, the most significant being Colombia, Brazil, Costa Rica, Mexico and El Salvador. Around 19 per cent of immigrants are from parts of Europe or the US, while just under

4 per cent of immigrants are from a miscellaneous group of countries including China, Japan and Mozambique.

The majority of immigrants living in Chile are of working ages (79 per cent in 2006) and concentrated in urban areas in the central area of the country, reflecting job opportunities. Over 60 per cent of immigrants live in the capital of Chile, Santiago, while around 7 per cent are in Valparaiso and around 5 per cent are in Tarapacá (the frontier region with Peru). The length of time immigrants have spent in Chile varies according to country of origin. Argentineans are most established, having lived in Chile for an average of 16.4 years. In contrast those from Peru and Ecuador are predominantly recent arrivals and have lived in Chile between four and six years.

Just over half of immigrants currently living in Chile are women. A greater proportion of more recent arrivals are women (among immigrants living less than a year in Chile 56.7 per cent are female) pointing to the increasing feminisation of migration to Chile. The gender of migrants also varies significantly, however, by country of origin. The majority of immigrants from Peru, Argentina and Bolivia are female. This reflects the significance of low skilled and domestic labour to the new intra-regional migration patterns in South America and seems to be closely related to underlying social and economic factors affecting Latin American women in the region (Cerrutti, 2009). As a reflection of this, Mora and Piper (2011) recently identified that Peruvian immigrants differ from other immigrant groups in Chile due to their well known extensive social networks in both Peru and Chile. Most of them tend to live in particular boroughs in downtown Santiago and face great challenges in the Chilean labour market, mostly due to prejudice and stereotypes held by employers and wider society. Of interest is the fact that Peruvian immigrant women are being largely recruited to work in domestic services, in conditions that do not improve their economic and social marginalisation, but that still improve their living conditions compared to their country of origin (ibid.).

Additional variation in gender patterns of immigrants in Chile depending on the country of origin should be considered. The proportion of male and female immigrants from Ecuador and the group of other Latin American and Caribbean countries are approximately equal. In contrast, a much greater proportion of immigrants from countries in Europe and the US and the other miscellaneous group of countries are men, with a male over female ratio of 1.4 in 2006 and 1.7 in 2009, respectively (CASEN surveys 2006 and 2009).

Socioeconomic conditions of international immigrants in Chile

Analysis of the CASEN survey demonstrates that the socioeconomic status of the immigrant population in Chile is highly polarised. The gap that exists between the poorest income quintile and the wealthiest income quintile immigrants in Chile (the 20 per cent top to 20 per cent bottom ratio) is much wider than the gap observed within the Chilean-born population. There is a 23 times difference in the mean household income per capita per month between immigrants living in the richest and the poorest quintiles in 2006; this grew to 24.5 times in 2009. This difference among the Chilean-born population in comparison was thirteenfold in 2006 and twelvefold in 2009 (CASEN surveys).

Among immigrants in Chile in the richest income quintile, over a third have university level education compared to only 15 per cent of immigrants in the bottom income quintile (CASEN, 2006). Immigrants in the poorest income quintile are comparatively more likely to be female (54.1 per cent), children and from an ethnic minority background (10.2 per cent versus 4.1 per cent in the wealthiest group). Virtually all immigrant women working in domestic service in Chile belong to the poorest income quintile. In addition, there are also differences in the socioeconomic status of international immigrants by country of origin. Ecuadorian immigrants, and to a lesser extent Bolivian immigrants, are distinguished by their low income in comparison to both the Chilean-born people and immigrants coming from other Latin American countries.

The most recently available data describing immigrants in Chile from CASEN 2009 suggest that the inequalities between immigrants may be increasing over time. Between 2006 and 2009 there was a small increase in the rate of immigrants with only primary school education level (21.1 per cent in 2006 and 23.1 per cent in 2009) and simultaneously a large increase in the rate of immigrants with university level education (27.3 per cent in 2006 and 35.7 per cent in 2009). Overall, measures of socioeconomic status, such as education and income, all suggest that immigrants in Chile are a highly polarised group in terms of their socioeconomic status and are becoming a more polarised group over time.

These results also suggest the existence of a growing vulnerable and marginalised group of immigrants in Chile. The negative consequences of vulnerability and marginalisation among some groups of immigrants in Chile could be devastating, since socioeconomic deprivation from mainstream society is enhanced by labour conditions and different forms of social stratification in the country (Mora and Piper, 2011). Immigrants living in socioeconomic deprivation not only face everyday barriers to safe and fair work, but also the barriers of absolute poverty, discrimination and social segregation. Specific strategies to promote the social protection of groups of immigrants living in social vulnerability should be developed beyond those broad measures described earlier in this chapter. An extension of these analyses is discussed in the following section, looking at the association between socioeconomic status and access to healthcare.

Healthcare provision among international immigrants and its association with socioeconomic status

Recent data from CASEN surveys 2006 and 2009 allow patterns of healthcare provision among immigrants in Chile to be assessed and compared to people born in Chile. Unfortunately this survey data cannot distinguish the legal status of immigrants and no other national level data in Chile describe healthcare use among this group. However, the data can provide the first broad national level comparison of the types of healthcare provision among immigrants and the Chilean-born and how these patterns vary between socio-demographic groups.

Public with co-payment healthcare was the most common type of care among both immigrants and the Chilean-born in 2006 and 2009. Immigrants are, however, significantly less likely than the Chilean-born to report that they are entitled to either public healthcare with co-payment or free public healthcare. In contrast immigrants were more likely to report that they were not entitled to any healthcare provision or did not know their entitlement to healthcare in 2006 and 2009.

Provision entitlement varied significantly among immigrants by country of origin and years lived in the country. In 2006 those coming from Peru and Ecuador most commonly reported access to public with co-payment, followed by no provision. Immigrants from Argentina and Bolivia also reported public healthcare with co-payment most commonly, but public care free of charge was the next most common healthcare type. Strikingly, over 50 per cent of Ecuadorian immigrants reported no healthcare provision. No health provision was most common among recent arrivals to Chile and became less common as time living in the country increased. Most immigrants who reported private provision were also recent arrivals and had lived for less than a year in Chile (Cabieses, 2011).

The factors that may underlie low levels of healthcare provision as considered in the research literature include understanding of the healthcare system, contractual and legal status, health status, stigma and discrimination (Allin, 2008; Días et al., 2008; Dunlop et al., 2000; Gushulak and MacPherson, 2006; Sousa et al., 2010; Porthe et al., 2009, 2010; Virtanen et al., 2005). Where universal healthcare programmes are available for everyone living in Chile, immigrants might not be aware of their existence (e.g. free of charge pap smear, contraception or antenatal care) (Cabieses, 2011). Undocumented immigrants might also not access healthcare services as a result of administrative obstacles or fear of being reported to the police (Carta et al., 2005).

When the characteristics of immigrants with no entitlement to healthcare or unsure of their entitlement are compared to the Chilean-born in the CASEN survey, interesting results emerge. Among the Chilean-born without healthcare, 64.0 per cent were educated up to high school only. In contrast, among immigrants reporting no healthcare provision entitlement at all, 55.6 per cent had only high school education (similar to the Chilean-born), but 41.7 per cent had university level education (significantly higher than the Chilean-born population).

These results do not support the positive association (gradient) between level of education attainment and access and use of health-care that has commonly been reported among immigrants in the international literature. While immigrants working in lower positions than would be expected from their educational skills have been well documented in the international literature (Buchan, 2007; De Jong and Gordon, 1999; Ritsilä and Ovaskainen, 2001; Tseng, 2001), the relatively poor access to healthcare among highly educated immigrants found in this chapter has not previously been widely considered. However, a study of immigrants in Portugal found those with more than ten years of school education or born in Eastern European or South American countries were less likely to use health services (Días et al., 2008). This lower access and use of healthcare services by highly educated immigrants might reflect lack of knowledge, fear, perception of discrimination and racism. It could also be the case that well educated immigrants consider themselves healthy enough to dismiss the need for healthcare insurance or are confident they will be able to pay out of pocket for private healthcare if required. It could also be that recent immigrants return to their home countries for healthcare when needed and, therefore, report no healthcare provision need in the destination country. Beyond possible explanations of these findings, further qualitative analyses might shed some light on the causes, consequences and potential solutions.

The impact of socioeconomic status upon immigrants' healthcare provision can be explored further by comparing immigrants by income group. When stratifying by income, those immigrants in the poorest income quintile are most likely to have access to public free of charge healthcare provision (60 per cent), followed by public with co-payment (33 per cent). The middle three income quintiles have public with co-payment care and public free of charge care as the most prevalent form of healthcare (55 per cent and 35 per cent, respectively), whereas the wealthiest income quintile among immigrants shows public care with co-payment and the private system as the most common forms of care (45 per cent and 35 per cent, respectively).

Healthcare provision among some potentially vulnerable groups of immigrants can also be considered in data from CASEN 2009. Results indicate that just over half of immigrant children (up to 16 years old) were entitled to the public with co-payment provision, followed by a third entitled to the public free of charge type of healthcare. Among immigrant children, 8 per cent had no healthcare provision at all. Similar patterns are observed among older immigrants. Around 14 per cent of immigrant women reported that that they had no healthcare provision, a similar proportion to immigrant men. A third of women were entitled to the public free of charge provision compared to around 16 per cent of immigrant men, reflecting the higher prevalence of poverty among women.

Even though immigrants as a whole might appear to be better off than the Chilean-born (e.g. with regards to their global mean income compared to Chilean-born people), there are potential vulnerable groups living in socioeconomic deprivation within this population that need to be disentangled and further explored. The relationship between socioeconomic status and access to healthcare (as measured by healthcare provision entitlement in Chile) among immigrants is complex and not as linear as it has been previously reported by other authors. Income and education are significant dimensions that affect the reported healthcare entitlement among both immigrants and the Chilean-born, but other dimensions need to be added to this analysis for better understanding of the nature and characteristics of these patterns. Social position is a multidimensional construct and it is shaped by one's occupation, self-perceived value and contribution to society, integration into society (especially if living in a foreign country), perceived stigma and discrimination, among many other factors.

Previous qualitative studies conducted in Chile have already discussed the existence of Peruvian and other immigrant groups living in poor socioeconomic conditions, with poor understanding of the healthcare system and in fear of prejudice from the host population (Amador, 2010; Mora and Piper, 2011; Nuñez-Carrasco, 2008). Further qualitative and mixed methods studies on the living conditions of immigrants in Chile could provide broader patterns to help understand different groups of immigrants, particularly those in socioeconomic deprivation, including children and women. To this end, this chapter adds to our understanding of the complexity of this phenomenon by addressing the relationship between migration status, socioeconomic status and access to healthcare in Chile at a population scale.

Are international immigrants in Chile a vulnerable group and why?

In this chapter, we consider inequalities in socioeconomic conditions and healthcare provision entitlement as a relevant measure of vulnerability among international immigrants in Chile. This first comprehensive national analysis of the characteristics of immigrants to Chile based on the CASEN surveys of 2006 and 2009 clearly indicates their diversity and suggests that they are changing over time. There is no simple story to tell about a heterogeneous population of immigrants in Chile, and within this great variability lies their vulnerability. There is a significant group of highly educated and wealthy immigrants now living in Chile but there are also vulnerable subgroups within the total immigrant population. Subgroups of immigrants experiencing poverty, discrimination and isolation from the healthcare system could be lost within the average. Further research needs to be conducted in order to understand the causes of such great variations in socioeconomic conditions and access to the Chilean healthcare system. Both quantitative and qualitative research approaches may play a crucial role in disentangling these complex patterns and providing meaningful findings with direct policy implications for Chile.

Immigrants appear to be polarised in their living conditions and provision entitlement, and this seems to be largely determined by their socioeconomic position. Low socioeconomic status reinforces the marginalisation of vulnerable immigrant groups in Chile. As the analysis presented demonstrates, in Chile immigrants in the lowest income quintile are more likely to be women and children and to belong to an ethnic minority group when compared to those with higher incomes.

Supporting the health and healthcare needs of vulnerable immigrants may require policies to improve their working conditions and reduce employment discrimination. In addition, comparison between low income immigrants and Chilean-born people in this analysis suggests the vulnerability of all low socioeconomic status people in Chile and the need to continue to develop policies to tackle broader socioeconomic health inequalities in the country. In other words, two types of health policies could be advocated in Chile, one related to reducing inequalities in health that are explained by absolute poverty and are shared by all people living in the country, and a second particularly focused on reducing inequalities in health that are explained by immigration status, which, in addition to poverty often also correlates with lack of opportunities, discrimination, lack of understanding of Chilean culture and the healthcare system and its available resources, fear of prosecution when undocumented, and many other factors.

Vulnerable immigrant groups identified in this analysis include immigrants with low income and education, those with minority ethnic backgrounds, female immigrants in domestic and service industries and those coming from Ecuador and Bolivia. Additional evidence from qualitative studies on international immigrants provides further understanding of the potential vulnerabilities of some of these groups. It has been reported by Nuñez-Carrasco (2008) and Amador (2010) in their studies of Afro-Columbian and Peruvian immigrants in Chile that these immigrant groups perceive significant amounts of discrimination from the local population. Their vulnerability results from stigmatisation for their migration status, lack of understanding of the healthcare system and lack of labour opportunities that could provide economic stability for them and their families over time.

As international immigration to Chile has grown in the past decade, the country has not been adequately prepared to address this phenomenon. Broad policies for social and health protection among immigrants in Chile might not fully address the wide range of needs of this very heterogeneous group. Immigrants should therefore be recognised as a complex group, or a collection of multiple subgroups with different cultural backgrounds, histories and migratory experiences. Tailored interventions to protect immigrants' living conditions and health status should be developed from robust evidence and understanding of their needs, in addition to the current policies focused upon pregnant women, children and Peruvian immigrants.

Results from this study also suggest that there is a complex relationship between migration, socioeconomic status and access to healthcare among immigrants in Chile. In addition, it indicates the existence of further specific vulnerable groups of immigrants in this country, given the association between gender, poverty and ethnicity. For example, immigrants from Ecuador and Bolivia are more likely to be female, minority ethnic status and poor. Different types of vulnerabilities may reinforce each other to limit access to healthcare, and potentially increase the perception of barriers limiting their understanding and willingness to use the Chilean healthcare system. Finally, patterns of migration within the Latin American region and to Chile have changed in recent years and will continue to evolve. This chapter has drawn on the first national analysis of immigrants to Chile to describe their patterns of healthcare provision. Further quantitative and qualitative data will be needed to fully understand their vulnerabilities and the reasons for their poor access to healthcare.

References

Allin, A. (2008) 'Does equity in healthcare use vary across Canadian provinces?', *Healthcare Policy*, 3(4): 83–99.

Amador, M. (2010) 'Forced migration to emerging countries. Case: Chilean society receiving Afro-Colombian asylum seekers', The 2010 Conference, British Society for Population Studies, University of Exeter, www2.lse.ac.uk/socialPolicy/BSPS/annual-Conference/2010/2010%20Exeter.aspx#generated-subheading1 (accessed 1 October 2010).

Arrau, F. (2002) 'Conceptualización del plan AUGE en salud. Eje de la actual reforma en salud. Estudios de anticipación', Biblioteca del Congreso Nacional de Chile, www.bcn.cl/carpeta_temas/temas_portada.2005-10-27.7644862447/documentos_pdf.2005-10-28.2320771530 (accessed 1 July 2009).

Arteaga, O., S. Thollaug, A. C. Nogueira and C. Darras (2002a) 'Información para la equidad en salud en Chile', *Pan American Journal of Public Health*, 11(5/6): 374–85.

Arteaga, O., I. Astorga and A. M.

Pinto (2002b) 'Inequalities in public healthcare provision in Chile', *Cadernos Saúde Pública*, 18(4): 1053–66.

Buchan, J. (2007) 'Health worker migration in Europe: Assessing the policy options. Migration and Health', *Eurohealth*, 13(1): 6–8.

Cabieses, B. (2011) 'The living conditions and health status of international immigrants in Chile: A comparison within this group and between them and the Chilean-born', unpublished PhD thesis, University of York, http://etheses.whiterose.ac.uk/1935/

Cabieses, B., H. Tunstall and K. E. Pickett (2010) 'Social determinants of disability among the immigrant population in Chile', *Journal of Epidemiology and Community Health*, 64 (S1): A58.

Carta, M. G., M. Bernal, M. C. Hardoy and J. M. Haro-Abad (2005) 'Migration and mental health in Europe (the state of the mental health in Europe working group: appendix 1)', *Clinical Practice and Epidemiology in Mental Health*, 1: 13.

Cerrutti, M. (2009) *Gender and Intra-regional Migration in South*

America, Research paper 12, Human Development Reports, United Nations Development Programme, New York.

Consulado General del Perú en Santiago de Chile (2009) 'Derecho a la salud, como acceder a la salud en Chile', Consulado General del Perú en Santiago de Chile, Santiago, www.conpersantiago.cl/?q=node/46 (accessed 1 July 2010).

De Jong, G. and F. Gordon (1999) 'Choice processes in migration behaviour', in K. Pandit and S. Withers (eds) *Migration and Restructuring in the US*, Rowman and Littlefield Publishers Inc., New York: 273–92.

Departamento de Extranjería y Migración (2007) 'Desarrollo del fenómeno de las migraciones en Chile. Evolución de la gestión gubernamental desde 1990', Subsecretaria del Interior, Ministerio del Interior, Santiago de Chile, www.extranjeria.gov.cl/filesapp/migraciones.pdf (accessed 1 November 2008).

Días, S., M. Severo and H. Barros (2008) 'Determinants of health-care utilization by immigrants in Portugal', *BMC Health Services Research*, 8: 207.

Dunlop, S., P. Coyte and W. McIsaac (2000) 'Socio-economic status and the utilisation of physicians' services: Results from the Canadian National Population Health Survey', *Social Science & Medicine*, 51: 123–33.

Gushulak, B. D. and D. W. MacPherson (2006) 'The basic principles of migration health: Population mobility and gaps in disease prevalence', *Emerging Themes in Epidemiology*, 3: 3.

IOM (International Organization for Migration) and MINSAL (Ministerio de Salud de Chile) (2008a) 'Migración y salud en Chile. Estudio de Salud Global en poblacion immigrante en Chile', IOM and MINSAL, www.oimconosur.org/notas/buscador.php?nota=716 (accessed 1 March 2009).

— (2008b) 'Migración y salud en Chile. Estudio de Salud Mental en poblacion immigrante en la comuna de Independencia', IOM and MINSAL, www.oimconosur.org/notas/buscador.php?nota=716 (accessed 1 March 2009).

Mardones F. (2004) 'Algunos antecedents sobre la inequidad en la situación del adulto mayor en Chile', *Revista Médica de Chile*, 132: 865–72.

Marmot, M. (1999) 'Multi-level approaches to understanding social determinants', in L. Berkman and L. Kawachi (eds) *Social Epidemiology*, Oxford University Press, Oxford: 349–67.

— (2010) *Fair Society, Healthy Lives. The Marmot Review*, www.marmotreview.org (accessed 1 August 2010).

Marmot, M. and R. Wilkinson (1999) *Social Determinants of Health*, Oxford University Press, New York: 16–91.

Mideplan (Ministry of Planning in Chile) (2006) 'Encuesta de caracterizacion socioeconomica 2006. Resultados generales de pobreza e indigencia', www.mideplan.gob.cl/casen2009/RESULTADOS_CASEN_2006.pd (accessed 1 November 2010).

— (2009) 'Encuesta de caracterizacion socioeconomica 2009. Resultados generales de pobreza e indigencia', www.mideplan.gob.cl/casen2009/RESULTA-

DOS_CASEN_2009.pd (accessed 1 November 2010).

Mora, C. and N. Piper (2011) 'Notions of rights and entitlements among Peruvian female workers in Chile', *Diversities*, 13(1): 4–18.

Nuñez-Carrasco, L. (2008) 'Living on the margins: Illness and health care among Peruvian migrants in Chile', unpublished PhD Thesis, Leiden University Medical Centre, Leiden.

Oyarzo C. (2000) 'La descentralización financiera en Chile en la década de los noventa', *Revista Panamericana de la Salud*, 8: 72–82.

Pizarro J. (2002) *Exigencias y posibilidades para políticas de población y migración internacional. El contexto latinoamericano y el caso de Chile*, Serie Población y Desarrollo, Centro Latinoamericano y Caribeño de Demografía (CELADE), División de Población, Santiago de Chile.

Porthe, V., F. G. Benavides, M. L. Vasquez, L. Ruiz-Frutos, A. M. Garcia, E. Ahonen, A. A. Agudelo-Suarez and J. Benach (2009) 'La precariedad laboral en inmigrantes en situacion irregular en Espana y su relacion con la salud', *Gac Sanit*, 23(Supl 1): 107–14.

Porthe, V., E. Ahonen, M. L. Vasquez, C. Pope, A. A. Agudelo-Suarez, A. M. Garcia, M. Amable, N. Benavides and J. Benach (2010) 'Extending a model of precarious employment: A qualitative study of immigrant workers in Spain', *American Journal of Industrial Medicine*, 53: 417–24.

Ritsilä, J. and M. Ovaskainen (2001) 'Migration and regional centralization of human capital', *Applied Economics*, 33: 317–25.

Shorrocks, A. (2009) 'Foreword', in W. Naude, A. L. Santos-Paulino and M. McGillivray (eds) *Vulnerability in Developing Countries*, United Nations University Press, Japan: 18.

Sousa, E., E. Agudelo-Suarez, F. Benavides, M. Schenker, M. Garcia, J. Benach, C. Delclos, M. J. Lopez-Jacob, C. Ruiz-Frutos, E. Ronda-Perez and V. Porthe (2010) 'Immigration, work and health in Spain: The influence of legal status and employment contract on reported health indicators', *International Journal of Public Health*, 55: 443–51.

Stefoni C. (2001) *Representaciones culturales y estereotipos de la migración Peruana en Chile*, http://bibliotecavirtual.clacso.org.ar/ar/libros/becas/2000/stefoni.pdf (accessed 1 November 2008).

Tseng, W. S. (2001) *The Handbook of Cultural Psychiatry*, Academic Press, San Diego.

UN (United Nations) (2006) *Informe Desarrollo Humano en Chile. Las Paradojas de la Modernización*, Programa de las Naciones Unidas para el Desarrollo, Santiago de Chile, www.desarrollohumano.cl/informe.../informe-2006-COMPLETO.pdf (accessed 1 November 2011).

UNESCO (United Nations Educational, Scientific and Cultural Organization) (1999) *Globalisation and International Migration in Latin America and the Caribbean: Trends and Prospectus for the 21st Century*, http://unesdoc.unesco.org/images/0011/001185/118565Eo.pdf (accessed February 2009).

Virtanen, M., M. Kivimäki, M. Joensuu, P. Virtanen, M. Elovainio and J. Vahtera (2005) 'Temporary employment and health: A review', *International Journal of Epidemiology*, 34: 610–22.

6 | Unaccompanied young asylum seekers in the UK: mental health and rights

ELAINE CHASE

Introduction

This chapter considers the relevance of the concept of a sense of security to contemporary debates surrounding health and rights and poses the question as to whether we can conceptualise a right to having and executing a life plan as a basis of a right to health. Drawing on examples of how unaccompanied young people seeking asylum in the UK describe the importance of having a clear sense of their future prospects as essential to their sense of wellbeing, it suggests that such security offers an important missing link within current health, rights and inequalities discourses. A focus on these dimensions of wellbeing implies a shift from purely medical approaches to the treatment of mental health issues towards a consideration of the wider factors that play an equally important role in determining wellbeing: factors such as social status, identity and most importantly a sense of predictability for the future. Yet for people to nurture these dimensions to their lives requires a combination of resources including certain rights, resources to which young people seeking asylum alone have limited access, particularly as they make the transition to adulthood.

Ontological security

Recognising the insecurity emanating from the uncertainty of modern day life, Giddens (1984, 1991) offers the notion of *ontological security* – a sense of order, stability, routine and predictability that in turn give life meaning. Such security helps foster a robust autonomous identity, enabling us to socially interact with others without having that identity threatened. Laing (1965: 44) relates this *autonomous identity* to the ability to sustain a '*biographical narrative*', essentially having a degree of confidence in who we are, where we have come from and where we are going in life. The opposite of such a sense of security is one of *ontological insecurity* – a state typified by being overwhelmed by generalised anxieties, a loss of trust in one's own capabilities and the inability to maintain a coherent life story.

While chaos, turmoil and disruption threaten security, create a state of anxiety and erode any trust in the predictability of life, ontological security has the opposite effect and opportunities to nurture it ultimately bring about a sense of wellbeing. Yet such notions of security and coherence are contingent on the availability of a combination of biological, material, economic, psychosocial and political resources such as rights. The ability to establish and sustain a core sense of security as a basis of wellbeing arguably therefore becomes a contestable ground when those striving for it have limited recourse, by nature of their lack of citizenship, to the fundamental rights that underpin such security. The remainder of this chapter provides an illustrative example of how such inequalities play out in practice and the impact that they have on the emotional and mental health of young people seeking asylum alone.

Unaccompanied young people seeking asylum in the UK

Some 44 per cent of the world's refugees and asylum seekers are under the age of 18 years (UNHCR, 2009a) and at the beginning of 2008, there were an estimated 1.6 million separated or unaccompanied children and young people of concern to UNHCR (2009b), although only a very small proportion of these claimed asylum (11,300 in 2007). Central to young people's existence as 'asylum seekers' is the need to establish grounds for asylum or protection as enshrined in Article 1A (2) of the Refugee Convention (1951, and amended in 1967) that defines a refugee as someone who:

> owing to a well-founded fear of being persecuted for reasons of race, religion, nationality, membership of a particular social group or political opinion is outside the country of his nationality and is unable, or, owing to such fear, is unwilling to avail himself of the protection of that country.

Every year, several thousand children and young people arrive in the UK to seek asylum without the care or support of parents or other family members, more so than anywhere else in Europe (UNHCR, 2009c). In 2009, 2,990 (just over 12 per cent of all asylum applications registered in the UK) were from unaccompanied asylum seeking children and young people claiming to be under the age of 18 (Home Office, 2010). Of these only 11 per cent were granted asylum. Less than 1 per cent (only 20 applicants) were granted humanitarian protection, 16 per cent were refused and the remainder (73 per cent) were awarded discretionary leave, mostly until they reached the age of 17 years and 6 months[1] (ibid.). Hence, the majority of young people arriving unaccompanied into the UK are judged not to meet the criteria of 'persecution' and consequently have no clear sense of how long they will be able to remain here. In the current research (described below), only 6 of the 54 young people (four male and two female) who participated in the in-depth interviews were considered to meet the criteria for persecution and hence granted indefinite leave to remain (ILR) in the UK. The majority of young people enter a proverbial limbo within the asylum and immigration system where uncertainty about the future becomes a central part of their narrative. This uncertainty, as is argued later in the chapter, can have a profoundly detrimental impact on the mental health and wellbeing of young people, yet to date appears to have received limited attention when compared to other factors associated with young people seeking asylum, such as trauma and the stresses of migration.

Rights as instruments or moral claims

As they enter the asylum process, young people come into contact with a plethora of international and national human rights instruments and frameworks that govern what rights and entitlements they are eligible to. Broadly speaking, such tools consider their rights as refugees; their rights as children; their rights as looked after children and young people (and subsequently care leavers); their rights as non-citizens with legitimate temporary status in the UK; and their rights as humans.

Yet such frameworks fail to fully acknowledge young people's actual experiences of attempting to secure their rights throughout the asylum process, nor do they allow a discourse of rights that has value and meaning for those seeking asylum to emerge. For this, we need to turn to a sociological discourse of rights. While the legal discourse of rights is concerned with the letter of the law and the arbitration through the courts of who has access to what, a sociological analysis of rights applies an inherently moral lens. It asks questions such as whether rights and privileges are just and whether they are fairly administered, how rights come into social being and how they operate in social practice; it considers whose purpose they serve, what interests they protect and whether they are guaranteed or constrained by law (see for example Benton, 2006; Douzinas, 2000, 2009a, 2009b, 20009c; Landman, 2006; Morris, 2006, 2009; Turner, 1993; Woodiwiss, 2005).

Turner (1993: 489), offered the first outline of a sociology of rights around three analytical props: 'ontological frailty', 'social precariousness', and '*moral sympathy*'. For Turner, ontological, or embodied, frailty is not located within the individual but is a human universal condition, compounded by the risky and precarious nature of social institutions. Such vulnerability can therefore be mitigated by an institution of rights that protects human beings from ontological uncertainty. The efficacy of such an institution, however, is contingent on a '*collective sympathy*' and therefore has an intrinsically moral character – people have an awareness of their own frailty and so the strong can empathise with the weak (ibid.: 504). The ability of young people seeking asylum to access the support, services and resources they require to maintain their mental health rests, therefore, not only on rights frameworks per se but on the strength of the collective sympathy shared by professionals within the institutions, organisations and services they come into contact with. And it is for this very reason that the space for inequalities in access to such support and services emerges.

Methodology

This chapter draws on a combination of data gathered through 1) a Department of Health-funded research study into the factors affecting the emotional wellbeing of children and young people seeking asylum on their own in the UK (see Chase et al., 2008); and 2) a qualitative analysis of legal case files of unaccompanied young people seeking asylum in the UK. A combined analysis of both sets of data centred on the following questions:

- What are the rights and entitlements of young people seeking asylum alone?
- How do young people seeking asylum alone experience asylum, immigration and support systems over time and particularly as they make the transition to 'adulthood'?
- What factors determine whether young people seeking asylum alone feel ontologically secure or insecure and how might this impact on their emotional and mental health and wellbeing?

The qualitative interviews were carried out between January and July 2007 with 54 unaccompanied children and young people accommodated by local authorities in London (for a fuller description of methods see ibid.). Although the analysis of a purposive sample (see Patton, 1990) of 46 legal case files took place earlier, over a period of seven months during 2005, the emergent themes proved to be highly salient to the experiences of young people drawn from the later qualitative interviews.

An inductive methodology based on the grounded theory approach (Glaser and Strauss, 1967; Neuman, 2003; Strauss and Corbin, 2008) was adopted for both components of the research. Throughout the in-depth interviews, this allowed young people to talk openly about their lives and wellbeing in an integrated way (see for example Aggleton et al., 1998), while foregrounding those aspects of their experiences that they felt most able to share. A topic guide was used to draw out key aspects of young people's lives and experiences and helped to ensure that comparative data were generated. Examination of legal case files involved a process of submersion in the data contained within each file and included an analysis of demographic data; geographical trajectories, statement of evidence forms (SEFs) (which constitute the basis of the asylum claim) and all relevant correspondence between the young person seeking asylum and the range of institutions and professionals with which they came into contact.

Once all data from the research interviews had been transcribed and relevant notes of case file analysis had been compiled, inductive thematic analysis was conducted (Bowen, 2006; Glaser and Strauss, 1967; Patton, 1990). Constant comparison (Merriam, 2002; Seale, 2002) was then used as an analytic tool to compare empirical indicators such as actions and events, observed, recorded or described (whether in documents or in the words of interviewees) and to identify similarities and differences in the data. Emerging themes were then compared with further empirical indicators to test for 'negative instances', or examples that contradicted these themes, prior to their inclusion in the findings.

Threats to ontological security

The stories[2] documented by young people in the legal case files and shared through the in-depth interviews showed that, prior to their departure from their countries of origin (or the countries in which they were residing), they had directly experienced, witnessed or were at risk of being subjected to events that would jeopardise their safety. Varying degrees of violence underpinned young people's narratives. Many had been beaten or tortured themselves, others had witnessed others being beaten, tortured or killed. However the specific circumstances surrounding each of the statements were unique. Even when young people had fled the same conflict – as in the case of those who came from Eritrea or Afghanistan – the circumstances surrounding their departure, the traumas and the events that they had witnessed and experienced were highly individual. Despite these differences, there were some general patterns in the narratives. Younger children, for instance, tended to describe events in less detail than older young people and there were indications that, on many occasions, they had been removed from danger before they had actually witnessed or experienced it firsthand. Older young people (in their mid to late teens), however, frequently described some of the most extreme forms of violence. The types of brutality witnessed and/or endured were to some extent gendered. Young women, for example, were more likely than young men to describe being subjected to various forms of sexual violence including rape (sometimes resulting in pregnancy), trafficking and exploitation through forced prostitution. By contrast, while some young men talked of being persecuted because of their ethnic minority status, religion or political affiliation, many others described situations where they were the target of reprisals for actions by their fathers or other family members and hence were caught up in blood feuds between families. They were also more likely than young women to report being tortured and imprisoned.

And the trauma and upheaval continued as children and young people subsequently became separated from families, friends and communities, endured arduous journeys that took them across the globe and catapulted them into worlds that were profoundly unfamiliar. Fundamentally, all the young people experienced a unique trail of events, most of which they had no control over, which irreversibly transformed their worlds and sent them off into the unknown in a quest for safety and security. This lack of control combined with varying degrees of loss, trauma and upheaval all worked to fundamentally undermine young people's *ontological security*.

The nature and impact of these events are difficult to capture here but they affected young people in specific and distinct ways (see Chase et al., 2008). Young people talked of experiencing emotional health difficulties that spanned a wide spectrum, from sleeping problems, nightmares and anxieties, through to acute and chronic depression, attempted suicide and in some cases periods of severe mental illness requiring hospitalisation.

Yet importantly, young people described how threats to their sense of security, in terms of who they were and what they might become, emanated from many other sources beyond the trauma and upheaval they had experienced. The label of 'asylum seeker' carried an inherent stigma that was ubiquitous in many young people's accounts of their lives in the UK and their relationships with others. They commonly spoke of how they could not be open about who they were, the fact that they were seeking asylum or about their past experiences. Such stigma was pervasive (see for example Hopkins and Hill, 2010; McDonald and Billings, 2007; Lynn and Lea, 2003; Morris, 2009) and young people selected the content of their narratives to suit the particular circumstances they were in (Chase, 2010). The inability to sustain a biographical narrative of their lives in keeping with their true experiences, and hence sustain a sense of ontological security (Giddens, 1991), for many young people was inextricably linked to the perceptions that others had of them.

Equally young people were concerned with how they were treated within the various systems they came into contact with, particularly via social care services that provided the gateway to other services such as education, housing and care placements. The variable quality of support and assistance they received appeared to depend largely on individual social care workers, their personal feelings towards young people and whether or not they considered them 'deserving' of support (Chase, 2010). Social care workers, for example, impacted both positively and negatively on important aspects of young people's sense of being (their ontological security). Not being believed, age disputes (experienced by about 25 per cent of young people participating in interviews) and being made to feel unworthy of support on the one hand, and consistency of care and support on the other hand, were two sides of the same coin. Social workers were thus variably portrayed as guardian angels – going out of their way to do anything possible to support young people – and agents of the state, more concerned with their duties towards the asylum and immigration system than to young people themselves (Chambon et al., 1999; Humphries 2004a, 2004b, Lovelock et al., 2004; Parton, 1999).

The examples of differentiated and 'unfair' treatment, which were many considering the size of the sample of young people, are illustrative of how the exercise of rights and entitlements are dependent on notions of sympathy and judgements of merit and worth by professionals who have the power to accord or withhold such rights. Where young people's denial of rights and entitlements was contested, it was through the mitigation of others with sway or influence holding a different moral position with respect to the young person, such as foster carers, residential care workers, solicitors, doctors, teachers and independent advocacy services.

Yet the overwhelming factor that destabilised young people's sense of security was the proverbial limbo they found themselves in and the consequent uncertainties about the future. These anxieties were most pronounced for young people reaching the end of their discretionary leave to remain in the UK (around the age of 17 years and 6 months). As the threat of dispersal, detention (prior to deportation) or deportation itself looms, young men and women are faced with fundamental questions about who they are, where they belong and what will become of them. Irrespective of what they have achieved in the UK during the time they are here, aspirations, dreams and life plans can all be curtailed by a decision from the Home Office that means that they must leave. Faith, aged 17 from Nigeria commented, 'I'm afraid, my papers are nearly finished. Before they gave me two years but it finishes in June. I don't want to go back to my country … I think about it every day.'

And where young people had suffered extreme trauma and consequent mental health problems, there was little doubt about the connection between uncertainty about the future and a deterioration in their mental health. At the time of the research, Innocent, aged 20, who had arrived from Nigeria four years earlier, continued to see a counsellor on a weekly basis and struggled with his mental health. He had attempted suicide on a number of occasions, had constant nightmares and slept, he said, for just four hours a night despite taking more than twice the recommended dose of sleeping tablets every day. Innocent spoke of how changes in his asylum situation largely accounted for the deterioration in his mental health. While he had the security of discretionary leave for two years, he was thriving. Rather than going to college he decided to take an apprenticeship with a large supermarket chain. The training programme, he said, kept him busy, gave him new opportunities and helped to keep him well. When his discretionary leave ended, however, and he was waiting for a response from the Home Office about his application for further leave to remain, life started to unravel. The distress of a court appearance led to a mental health crisis that culminated in him being sectioned under the Mental Health Act (1983). His allusion to a threatened sense of security is evident in his narrative:

> But last year January, it was too much for me, you know? With the Home Office as well. I was doing well, but when the papers ran out and I started going to the Home Office, I didn't know what to do … my plans collapsed. After all I have experienced, I feel like I'm 50 years old. I don't feel like I'm 20. I don't have the heart to carry lots of things more. You don't know when you're going to have your freedom [status]. I don't believe in anything now, 'cos tomorrow they can say you go back.

And a number of other young people like Ibrahim and Rakeb had reached a similar juncture in their asylum claim. Rakeb, aged 21 from Eritrea, was having to consider the imminent prospect of deportation. Living in a hostel with her young son and surviving on vouchers for food, she reflected how she had no clear sense of belonging or family ties anywhere:

> I have no husband, no food, no benefits, no status, no job. I can't see any light in front of me. I feel that everything is just blank. Sometimes I don't know what to do even. I tried to suicide lots of times. My baby stops me. I am fighting too much to make my baby and myself happy. Otherwise, the feelings just come in front of me, killing all the feelings of being happy. But this status thing gets in the way, it affects everything. I feel like it is a big mountain in front of me and I can't shift it ... it stops me from being myself.

And Ibrahim captured the inextricable link between a lack of insecurity about the future and his state of mental health. Having been refused asylum and forced to report to the Home Office every month and with the constant threat of deportation hanging over him, he commented on the impact it had:

> I can't do anything. I'm not allowed to work. I'm not allowed to do anything because three years have finished and I am still ... I go to the doctor and he gives me tablets and I have depression. The Home Office don't listen. I went to the them and said, 'you know my problem ... I don't understand. I have been coming here every month for three years' ... this is not freedom, it's like I'm in jail.

The limitations of a clinical response

There is an extensive literature on the trauma and upheaval that many people seeking asylum have experienced before fleeing their home countries, during flight or after they arrive in host countries and the effects of these life events on their emotional wellbeing and mental health (Fazel and Stein, 2002; Hopkins and Hill, 2008; Huegler, 2005; Kohli, 2006; Rutter, 2003; Thomas et al., 2004). In particular, symptoms of post-traumatic stress disorder (PTSD) observed among refugee children and young people have generated important research (Dyregov and Yule, 2006; Ehntholt and Yule, 2006; Hodes, 2002a, 2002b; Hodes et al. 2008; Hodes and Tolmac, 2005; Salmon and Bryant, 2002). And so too have there been studies indicating how the uncertainties of the asylum process disorientate and destabilise young people, leaving them anxious and depressed (Cemlyn and Briskman, 2003; Fazel and Stein, 2002; Hepinstall et al., 2004; Kralj and Goldberg, 2005; Sourander, 2003; Steel et al., 2004; Warwick et al., 2006). The particular stresses on unaccompanied asylum seeking young people as they approach the end of their discretionary leave to remain in the UK have also been documented, albeit to a lesser extent (Chase et al., 2008; ILPA, 2004; Refugee Council, 2005; Wade et al., 2005).

Understandably, a common, and logical response to symptoms of trauma and upheaval is clinical support, including drug therapies, counselling and, in the extreme, hospitalisation. Many young people in the current study spoke of such interventions. While some recognised their benefits, many were highly sceptical of approaches to mental health promotion, and in particular those that encouraged a revisiting of the past. There was a common resistance to counselling and talk therapies combined with a perceived overuse of medication. Mahlet from Ethiopia commented:

> I think the counsellor thinks that if you are speaking it, it just goes away but it doesn't ... it's not in your mouth and like you took it out – it's inside in your heart ... so you can't take it out. I just told you now but it's still inside me ... I got it in here [Mahlet motions to her heart] it doesn't go out.

The notion that past trauma and upset was in the heart – rather than something that could be addressed through working through the mind, was a theme reiterated in different forms by many young people. Mahamat from Chad spoke of his confusion as to why he was offered anti-depressant medication when he was experiencing 'a sickness of the heart, not of the mind'.

For many young people it was only through bracketing past events that they could focus on the future and retain a clear sense of what it might bring. Alban, from Albania, explained:

> I'm trying to leave the past. If I'm going to think about the past, there's no point. There are bad things in the past – I can't think about it. I just have to let it go. The past is the past and you have to leave it to the past and look to the future ... What's gone is gone.

And Nanu from Eritrea, who had arrived at the age of 16 and six months pregnant as a result of being raped, talked like so many others of the importance of her education – an opportunity to focus, look forward and forget about the past. Her description neatly captures the importance of routine, predictability and order as core to a strong feeling of security:

For me, the better things that helped me is that I go to college ... that helped me a lot. I used to concentrate on my study and I forget everything. I just want to be someone for me and my son. I don't want to live this life every year [i.e. not knowing about status]. When I stay at home, all the things I think about is family, myself and what I have been through with these problems. But now I have college, I think, 'what am I going to do next year? What is my progress now?'

Many others too talked of the importance of keeping busy and 'not thinking too much' since this distracted them from being able to cope with the present. Keeping busy came about through establishing strong friendships, playing sports, regularly attending church, mosque or temple and participating in church-based activities. But more than anything, the majority of young people bore testimony to the fact that educational opportunities offered a reprieve from thinking, afforded meaning to their existence, made the more difficult aspects of their lives (such as trauma and upheaval) more manageable, and in a variety of ways facilitated the comprehensibility of their new environments and new circumstances. It offered a degree of ontological security through establishing a sense of continuity of events, a routinisation of their day-to-day lives, predictability for the future and opportunities to devise goals and aspirations.

Many young people framed their current experiences of education as the first rung on a ladder leading to opportunities at 'A' level, up to vocational or higher education at university, and on to clearly defined careers – 'doctor', 'scientist', 'engineer', 'lawyer', 'pharmacist', 'nurse', 'cook' – which would in turn offer a 'good life' for themselves. Yet the continuity of the privileges of education for older young people and the realisation of the aspirations engendered through earlier experiences of learning were contingent on many other factors. On reaching the age of majority, young people's rights to education became less clear and they faced difficulties on a number of levels with respect to accessing and sustaining educational opportunities. Maryam, from Iran, summed up how her hopes and aspirations for the future were tied up with her immigration status:

It's really, really stressful. I ask, 'what I am doing this for?' Two months before I graduate, they might ask me to leave the country. You just don't know. It's really horrible. There are two different sides of your life – on the one side you are trying to build it up and find wide experiences and do this and that so your CV will look good and you will get a job and build up your future. And on the other side, you don't know if you'll be able to live here the day after tomorrow. I don't enjoy thinking about the future at the moment. I just want to take it step by step. Not knowing doesn't make me feel more motivated – it actually puts me off. You think 'Why?' They don't even have to kick me out of the country: it's enough to get an interview just before my finals ... I just don't want to think about it.

Discussion

Current discourses concerned with the wellbeing of separated young people seeking asylum alone predominantly centre on notions of vulnerability and protection. Understandably, there has been a great deal of attention paid to the mental health of young refugees and the need to mitigate past trauma through clinical and therapeutic interventions. While the importance of culturally sensitive psychosocial and clinical support is not questioned here, this research demonstrates that such interventions fall short of addressing young people's fundamental need to health through security.

Throughout their narratives, young people alluded to the different ways in which previous and current experiences threatened their sense of security and belonging and undermined any feelings of continuity with respect to their biographical narrative. Young people were variably dogged by the traumas of the past and consequent mental health problems; by an invasive immigration and asylum system that ultimately dictated their futures; and by the uncertainties about where they would go and where they would belong if they were unable to remain in the UK. Being without status or in effect 'stateless', variably invoked fear, anxiety, indignation and frustration, it stopped them *becoming* and brought into question the very nature of their being.

Health and wellbeing is undeniably nested within ontological security – a sense that life has some routine, predictability and enables one to project into the future. While clinical intervention, appropriately targeted, may help alleviate the individual symptoms of poor mental health, the more holistic feeling of 'security' for which young people seeking asylum invariably strive cannot be provided without engaging with the wider factors that dictate how they can or cannot access it.

As unaccompanied children and young people pass through the immigration and asylum system, their access to the diverse rights frameworks outlined earlier varies depending on where they are situated geographically, legally, politically and socially at any point in time. The rules and regulations that govern their access are both objective (such as entitlements according to age) but also highly subjective and arbitrary. The rights of young people seeking asylum alone become further stratified by the fact that they enter the asylum process as children but reach the age of majority before their asylum status is determined. What they subsequently experience is a gradual stripping away of potential rights and entitlements as they make the transition to the category of adult. The majority of them, we have seen, do not meet the criteria for refugee status under the Refugee Convention (1951). Consequently, at the age of 18, they face the potential end to discretionary leave (granted according to their status as 'children'); have commonly exhausted the appeals process; no longer meet the criteria of '*children*' with respect to international frameworks such as the UNCRC; and frequently face substantially fewer rights as care leavers compared to their looked after peers who are British citizens. As they become non-citizen adults, therefore, opportunities for accessing or contesting their denial of rights diminish.

As young asylum seekers enter the status of 'adulthood', they are constantly at risk of floating in a proverbial rights no-man's land. In the most extreme cases, such as with Rakeb, Innocent, Ibrahim and others, they are left with a single sphere of rights, 'human' rights. Yet not having any attachment to structures to uphold their rights as human beings – no longer children, no longer looked after young people, not citizens – even on a temporary basis – and not accepted as refugees, they risk being right-less (Arendt, 1951). The impact on their health as a result of the gradual erosion of these rights and entitlements can be profound.

Evident from their narratives, however, were many examples of how some young people's threatened loss of rights was mitigated by the actions of other individuals who recognise the injustice of their situation and come to their support vis-à-vis the asylum process. For Alban, it was his foster carer who rallied the support of those with power to intervene when he was detained and threatened with deportation; in Mahamat's case it was his colleagues within the nursery where he worked who achieved the same outcome. The situations for these young people changed because of the '*collective sympathy*' (Turner, 1993: 506) of others who were willing to make public their plight. These serendipitous outcomes are unsettling, yet they add further weight to the argument that rights are essentially socially constructed and that the power to mediate their access is widely dispersed.

Conclusion

There is no question of the importance of offering appropriate assessment, diagnosis and intervention to alleviate systems of poor mental health as a result of significant distress, or indeed of the potential effectiveness of such interventions. However, I suggest that to date there has been limited exploration of the evidence that, irrespective of previous trauma, one of the primary objectives for young people seeking asylum alone is to establish and retain ontological security, a fundamental sense that there is some routine and predictability to their lives that enables them to look forward to the future and move on from the past. Indeed, it could be suggested that a greater focus on these concerns may potentially offer as much or even more therapeutic benefit than medical assessment and clinical involvement.

Since ontological security is arguably an essential prerequisite to health, then a sociological discourse of rights needs to continue to question what should be the key constituents of a body of fundamental rights that has relevance to those on the margins of society. Douzinas (2000: 142) presents the 'refugee' as the ultimate challenge for a universal discourse of rights, stating that:

> Unable to speak our language, having left her community and with no community, the refugee is the absolute other. She represents in an extreme way the trauma that marks the genesis of state and self and puts to the test the claims of universalisation of human rights.

As we consider the questions of health, rights and inequalities concerning the many millions of people migrating across the globe, we might think about the questions arising from the narratives of young people contained here and their profound relevance to these debates. Should there be a right to ontological security? A right not to be in limbo? A right to become rather than just to be? If the answer is yes, then how should we operationalise such aspirations? For the answers to such questions, we perhaps need to return to Turner's (1993) notion of *collective sympathy* – that shared human understanding of our universal frailty – and think about its implications for individual and communal action. In order to ensure that rights become more than serendipitous privileges, we might begin by making all practitioners and professionals cognisant of their profound role in mediating access to rights, a discourse within training and professional development that to date has received limited attention. After all, as Douzinas (2009b) also argues, 'human rights do not belong to humans: they help construct who and how one becomes human'.

Notes

1 Prior to the introduction of the New Asylum Model (2007), discretionary leave was normally awarded for three years or until the young person reached 18 years.

2 The word 'story' was used repeatedly by young people participating in the research to denote the combination of events that had taken place in their lives prior to discussing them in the research context.

References

Aggleton, P., G. Whitty, A. Knight, D. Prayle, I. Warwick and K. Rivers (1998) 'Promoting young people's health: The health concerns and needs of young people', *Health Education*, 98(6): 213–19.

Antonovsky, A. (1987) *Unravelling the Mystery of Health*, Jossey-Bass, San Francisco.

Arendt, H. (1951) *The Origins of Totalitarianism*, Harcourt Brace, New York.

Benton, T. (2006) 'Do we need rights? If so, what sort?', in L. Morris (ed.) *Rights: Sociological Perspectives*, Routledge, Abingdon: 21–37.

Bowen, G. (2006) 'Grounded theory and sensitising concepts', *Journal of Qualitative Methods*, 5: 3, www.ualberta.ca/~iiqm/backissues/5_3/PDF/bowen.pdf (accessed 6 October 2009).

Cemlyn, S. and L. Briskman (2003) 'Asylum, children's rights and social work', *Child and Family Social Work*, 8: 163–78.

Chambon, A., A. Irving and L. Epstein (eds) (1999) *Reading Foucault of Social Work*, Columbia University Press, New York.

Chase, E. (2010) 'Agency and silence: Young people seeking asylum alone in the UK', *British Journal of Social Work*, 40(7): 2050–68.

Chase, E., A. Knight and J. Statham (2008) *The Emotional Wellbeing of Unaccompanied Young People Seeking Asylum in the UK*, BAAF, London.

Douzinas, C. (2000) *The End of Human Rights: Critical Legal Thought at the Turn of the Century*, Hart Publishing, Oxford.

— (2009a) 'Are rights universal?', *Guardian*, 11 March.

— (2009b) 'What are human rights?', *Guardian*, 18 March, www.guardian.co.uk/commentisfree/libertycentral/2009/mar/18/human-rights-asylum (accessed 18 January 2012).

— (2009c) 'Who counts as human?', *Guardian*, 1 April.

Dyregov, A. and W. Yule (2006) 'A review of PTSD in children', *Child and Adolescent Mental Health*, 11(4): 176–84.

Ehntholt, K. and W. Yule (2006) 'Practitioner review: Assessment and treatment of refugee children and adolescents who have experienced war-related trauma', *Journal of Child Psychology and Psychiatry*, 47(12): 1197–210.

Fazel, M. and A. Stein (2002) 'The mental health of refugee children', *Archives of Disease in Children*, 87: 366–70.

Giddens, A. (1984) *The Constitution of Society*, Polity Press, Cambridge.

— (1991) *Modernity and Self-Identity: Self and Society in the Late Modern Age*, Polity Press, Cambridge.

Glaser, B. and A. Strauss (1967) *The Discovery of Grounded Theory: Strategies for Qualitative Research*, Aldine Publishing Company, Chicago.

Hepinstall, E., V. Sethna and

E. Taylor (2004) 'PTSD and depression in refugee children: Associations with pre-migration trauma and post-migration stress', *European Child and Adolescent Psychiatry*, 13(6): 373–80.

Hodes, M. (2002a) 'Implications for psychiatric services of chronic civilian strife: Young refugees in the UK', *Advances in Psychiatric Treatment*, 8: 366–74.

— (2002b) 'Three key issues for young refugees' mental health', *Transcultural Psychiatry*, 39(2): 196–213.

Hodes, M. and J. Tolmac (2005) 'Severely impaired young refugees', *Clinical Child Psychology and Psychiatry*, 10(2): 251–61.

Hodes, M., D. Jagdev, N. Chandra and A.Cunniff (2008) 'Risk and resilience for psychological distress amongst unaccompanied asylum seeking adolescents', *Journal of Child Psychology and Psychiatry*, 48(7): 723–32.

Home Office (2010) *Quarterly Statistical Supplementary Tables*, October–December, Home office, London.

Hopkins, P. and Hill, M. (2008) 'Pre-flight experiences and migration stories: The accounts of unaccompanied asylum-seeking children', *Children's Geographies*, 6(3): 257–68.

— (2010) 'Contested bodies of asylum-seeking children', in K. Hörschelmann and R. Colls (eds) (2010) *Contested Bodies of Childhood and Youth*, Palgrave Macmillan, Basingstoke: 136–47.

Huegler, N. (2005) *Care and Support for Young Separated Refugees Aged 16 and 17 in Germany and the United Kingdom*, BASW, Birmingham.

Humphries, B (2004a) 'An unacceptable role for social work: Implementing immigration policy', *British Journal of Social Work*, 34: 93–107.

— (2004b) 'Taking sides: Social work research as a moral and political activity', in R. Lovelock, K. Lyons and J. Powell (eds) *Reflecting on Social Work: Discipline and Profession*, Ashgate, Surrey: 113–29.

ILPA (Immigration Law Practitioners' Association) (2004) *Working with Children and Young People Subject to Immigration Control: Guidelines for Best Practice*, ILPA, London.

Kohli, R. (2006) 'The sound of silence: Listening to what unaccompanied asylum-seeking children say and do not say', *British Journal of Social Work*, 36(5): 707–21.

Kralj, L. and D. Goldberg (2005) 'UK government policy and unaccompanied adolescents seeking asylum', *Child and Adolescent Mental Health*, 10(4): 202–5.

Laing, R. D. (1965) *The Divided Self*, Penguin, Harmondsworth.

Landman, T. (2006) *Studying Human Rights*, Routledge, London.

Lovelock, R., K. Lyons and J. Powell (2004) *Reflecting on Social Work: Discipline and Profession*, Ashgate, Surrey.

Lynn, N. and S. Lea (2003) 'A phantom menace and the new apartheid: The social construction of asylum-seekers in the United Kingdom', *Discourse and Society*, 14(4): 425–52.

McDonald, I. and P. Billings (2007) 'The treatment of asylum seekers in the UK', *Journal of Social Welfare and Family Law*, 29(1): 49–65.

Merriam, S. B. (2002) 'Assessing and evaluating qualitative research', in S. B. Merriam (ed.) *Qualitative*

Research in Practice: Examples for Discussion and Analysis, Jossey-Bass, San Francisco: 18–37.

Morris, L. (ed.) (2006) *Rights: Socio-logical Perspectives*, Routledge, Abingdon.

— (2009) 'Civic stratification and the cosmopolitan ideal', *European Societies*, 11(4): 603–24.

Neuman, W. L. (2003) *Social Research Methods: Qualitative and Quantitative Approaches*, Allyn and Bacon Fifth Edition, London.

Parton, N. (1999) 'Reconfiguring child welfare practices: Risk, advanced liberalism and the government of freedom', in L. Chambon, A. Irving and L. Epstein (eds) *Reading Foucault for Social Work*, Columbia University Press, New York: 101–31.

Patton, M. Q. (1990) *Qualitative Evaluation and Research Methods*, 2nd edn, Sage Publications Inc., Newbury Park, CA.

Refugee Council (2005) *Ringing the Changes: The Impact of Guidance on the Use of Sections 17 and 20 of the Children Act 1989 to Support Unaccompanied Asylum-Seeking Children*, Refugee Council, London.

Rutter, J. (2003) *Supporting Refugee Children in 21st Century Britain: A Compendium of Essential Information*, OUP, London.

Salmon, K. and B. Bryant (2002) 'Posttraumatic stress disorder in children. The influence of developmental factors', *Clinical Psychological Review*, 22: 163–88.

Seale, C. (2002) 'Quality issues in qualitative inquiry', *Qualitative Social Work*, 1: 97–110.

Sourander, A. (2003) 'Refugee families during asylum seeking', *Nordic Journal of Psychiatry*, 57(3): 203–7.

Steel, Z., N. Frommer and D. Silove (2004) 'Part 1 – the mental health impacts of migration: The law and its effects. Failing to understand: Refugee determination and the traumatized applicant', *International Journal of Law and Psychiatry*, 27(6): 511–28.

Strauss, A. and J. Corbin (1990) *Basics of Qualitative Research: Grounded Theory Procedures and Techniques*, Sage Publications Inc., Newbury Park, CA.

Thomas, S., B. Nafees and D. Bhugra (2004) '"I was running away from death" – the pre-flight experiences of unaccompanied asylum-seeking children in the UK', *Child Care Health and Development*, 30(2): 113–22.

Turner, B. (1993) 'Outline of a theory of human rights', *Sociology*, 27(3): 489–512.

UNHCR (United Nations High Commission for Refugees) (1951) *Convention and Protocol Relating to the Status of Refugees*, UNHCR, Geneva.

— (2009a) *2008 Global Trends: Refugees, Asylum Seekers, Returnees, Internally Displaced and Stateless Persons*, UNHCR, Geneva.

— (2009b) *Unaccompanied Minors in the European Union Member States*, Panel Discussion (Vienna Migration Group and European Migration Network) Vienna, 8 June, www.emn.at/modules/typetool/pnincludes/uploads/Einzenberger_UNHCR_BE.pdf (accessed 4 April 2010).

— (2009c) *Unaccompanied Minors in the European Union Member States*, UNHCR, Geneva.

Wade, J., F. Mitchell and G. Baylis (2005) *Unaccompanied Asylum*

Seeking Children. The Response of Social Work Services, BAAF, London.

Warwick, I., R. Neville and K. Smith (2006) 'My life in Huddersfield: Supporting young asylum seekers and refugees to record their experiences of living in Huddersfield', *Social Work Education*, 25(2): 128–37.

Woodiwiss, A. (2005) *Human Rights*, Routledge, London.

7 | Healthcare for trafficked migrants: UK policy 2000–10 and consequences for access

SIÂN ORAM

Introduction

Human trafficking is recognised as a serious crime and a violation of human rights (UNHCR, 2002; UNODC, 2008). It was defined by the international community in the Optional Protocol to Prevent, Suppress and Punish Trafficking in Persons, Especially Women and Children (the Palermo Protocol) as:

> the recruitment, transportation, transfer, harbouring or receipt of persons by means of threat or use of force or other forms of coercion, of abduction, of fraud, of deception, of the abuse of power, or of a position of vulnerability or of the giving or receiving of payments or benefits to achieve the consent of a person having control over another person, for the purpose of exploitation. (United Nations, 2000, article 3)

Although the trafficking of women and girls for sexual exploitation has received the greatest attention to date, trafficked people may be exploited in a diverse array of other settings, including agriculture, construction, factories and in catering and hospitality. Trafficked people may also be exploited in domestic servitude or through enforced participation in criminal activities such as selling counterfeit DVDs, petty theft, tending cannabis farms, begging and benefit fraud (Anderson and Rogaly, 2005; ASI, 2001, 2006; ILO, 2005; Wijers and Lap-Chew, 1997).

Many trafficked people endure high levels of violence, abuse and neglect and may consequently suffer from a range of poor physical, mental and sexual and reproductive health outcomes. A European multi-country study of women trafficked for sexual exploitation found, for example, that 76 per cent of women reported experiencing physical violence while trafficked and that 63 per cent of women reported suffering from ten or more concurrent physical symptoms 0–14 days after entering into post-trafficking support services (Zimmerman et al., 2006, 2008). In particular, women suffered from headaches, dizziness, memory loss, back pain and stomach pain. Other surveys of women trafficked for sexual exploitation in Europe have suggested that the majority of trafficked women are denied access to healthcare services to remedy these and other problems while they are trafficked (Di Tommaso et al., 2009). Studies from India and Nepal have reported that women trafficked for sexual exploitation are also vulnerable to HIV infection. The risk of infection varies significantly with the local prevalence of disease, but increases with longer duration of exploitation (Silverman et al., 2006, 2007). High levels of mental disorder have also been reported in studies of women who have been trafficked for sexual exploitation. Research with women receiving post-trafficking support in Moldova, for example, found that 88 per cent of women had clinically diagnosable psychiatric illnesses one to five days after registering for support, including PTSD (48 per cent) and mood disorder (7 per cent) (Ostrovschi et al., 2011).

The health-related harms associated with human trafficking, and the need for governments to respond to them, are recognised by international anti-trafficking instruments. The Palermo Protocol, for example, requires signatory states to 'consider implementing measures to provide for the physical, psychological and social recovery' of trafficked people, including through the provision of 'medical psychological and material assistance' (United Nations, 2000, article 6). The 2005 Council of Europe Convention on Action against Trafficking in Human Beings (ECAT) goes further by requiring governments to ensure that 'emergency medical treatment' is provided to all persons who are suspected of, or identified as, having been trafficked. Furthermore, the ECAT obliges signatory governments to provide necessary non-emergency healthcare to trafficked people who are lawfully resident, without adequate resources and in need (Council of Europe, 2005, article 12). The UK is bound by these requirements, having signed and ratified the Palermo Protocol in 2000 and 2006, respectively, and the ECAT in 2007 and 2008.

International data suggest that traffickers often limit their victims' access to healthcare and that when trafficked people are able to receive care, they are inhibited from disclosing their abuse and exploitation by the continued physical proximity of their traffickers during appointments, language barriers, shame and fear of authorities (Baldwin et al., 2011; Di Tommaso et al., 2009; Family Violence Prevention Fund, 2005). Data on the barriers and opportunities for people's access to healthcare after leaving their traffickers are limited. The healthcare needs and experiences of trafficked people may overlap with those of asylum seekers (discussed in detail elsewhere in this volume), people who have experienced other forms of violence and abuse, and migrant labourers and sex workers (Zimmerman et al., 2003). This chapter presents data and analysis from a qualitative study that examined how concerns for the health of trafficked people were incorporated into the UK policy and service response to human trafficking between 2000 and 2010. It describes the regulations that governed trafficked people's access to National Health Service (NHS) care, how these regulations were amended following the ratification of ECAT in 2008, and the impact of the regulations on trafficked people's access to NHS care.

Ethics approval for the research was provided by the ethics committees of the London School of Hygiene and Tropical Medicine and the NHS National Research Ethics Service. Semi-structured, qualitative interviews were conducted with 46 representatives of 43 organizations: healthcare providers (n=7), non-governmental post-trafficking support providers (n=7), NGO advocates (n=10), enforcement officials (n=7), lawyers (n=5) and civil servants (n=7). Participants provided written informed consent to take part in the interviews, which were digitally recorded and transcribed in full. In 2009, 43 interviews were conducted between January and September, coinciding with the entry of ECAT into force in the UK. A further three follow-up interviews were conducted with post-trafficking support providers one year after ECAT had entered into force. No interviews were conducted with trafficked people. It was clear at the start of the research that trafficked people had not been invited to participate in the development of the UK response to trafficking and the participation of this vulnerable population in research interviews could therefore not be ethically justified (Zimmerman and Watts, 2003). Interviews were, however, conducted with post-trafficking support providers, NGO advocates, enforcement officials and lawyers who had extensive professional experience working with and on behalf of trafficked people. Data were also collected using participant observation and document collection. Anonymised field notes were made during 41 policy relevant meetings and events between September 2007 and July 2010. Documents (e.g. government consultations, parliamentary committee reports and testimonies, impact assessments and meeting minutes) were collected and analysed to provide context for the research and as a supplementary data source. Data analysis followed the principles of framework analysis and was conducted using the software package NVivo8 (Ritchie and Spencer, 1994).

Trafficked migrants' access to NHS care: policy environment 2000–10

In the UK, NHS medical care is provided free to people who are considered to be 'ordinarily resident'.[1] Particular categories of overseas visitors, named within the NHS (Charges to Overseas Visitors) Regulations 1989 (the NHS charging regulations), are also entitled to access free NHS care (NHS, 1989). Included within these categories are asylum seekers and refugees and people who have been living lawfully within the UK for the preceding 12 months. The charging regulations also state that certain categories of treatment should be provided free of charge regardless of a person's immigration status. Services provided within emergency departments are exempt from charge on this basis, as are sexual healthcare, family planning services, compulsory psychiatric treatment and treatment for specified infectious diseases. Under the charging regulations, GPs are not required to refuse to treat irregular migrants and are legally required to treat anyone in immediate need of treatment.

Trafficked people were not included within the list of overseas visitors who were entitled to free medical care until the NHS charging regulations were amended following the ratification of ECAT in 2008 (NHS, 2008). Thus, trafficked people's entitlement to access to primary and hospital level care varied according to whether they – or the type of healthcare they needed – fell within the existing exemptions. Trafficked people were entitled to free NHS care if they were EU citizens with the right to reside in the UK, or if they had claimed or had been granted asylum or another form of leave to remain in the UK. Trafficked people who were EU citizens with no right to reside in the UK, non-EU citizens who were unlawfully in the UK and who had not made a claim for asylum, and refused asylum seekers, however, were not exempt from charges for NHS care. Although this latter group could access some basic services without charge, they were not entitled to free HIV treatment, maternity care, or abortion services.

As part of the legislative changes that accompanied the UK's ratification of ECAT, the NHS charging regulations were amended to exempt trafficked people from charges for NHS care.[2] In order to qualify for this exemption, people claiming to have been trafficked were required, first, to enter into the newly created National Referral Mechanism (NRM) (a system that was introduced in order to satisfy the UK's obligations under ECAT to identify trafficked people and provide them with a temporary period of protection from deportation) (Home Office and BIA, 2008).

People who were suspected of having been trafficked could be referred into the UK NRM, with their consent, by police officers, immigration officials, local authorities and named NGOs. These 'first responder' agencies would complete referral forms for claimants within 48 hours of contact, marking which indicators of human trafficking the claimant met and providing supplementary information to support the claim. Referral forms would then be sent to NRM caseworkers for assessment. Within five working days of a referral, caseworkers were to make an initial, low-threshold decision about whether there were 'reasonable grounds' to believe that the claimant had been trafficked. Claimants who received a positive reasonable grounds decision were automatically given a 45 day 'recovery and reflection' period, extendable according to personal circumstances, during which time they were eligible for post-trafficking support services in the UK and were protected from immigration removal. During this time, the caseworkers also made a second, higher threshold decision about whether they believed, 'on the balance of possibilities', that the claimant had been trafficked. A positive 'conclusive grounds' decision entitled the trafficked person to apply for a one year permit to remain in the UK, either to participate in criminal proceedings against their trafficker or on humanitarian grounds, during which time they could continue to access support. Although it was possible to judicially review refusals, the UK NRM did not include an appeals process.

Entry into the NRM was in itself, however, insufficient to secure free NHS care for people claiming to have been trafficked (NHS, 2008). Claimants were instead required to wait for a positive 'reasonable grounds' decision about their case to be made. A positive decision entitled the person to free NHS care for the duration of the 45 day recovery and reflection period. If, following the recovery and reflection period, the claimant also received a positive 'conclusive grounds' decision *and* was granted a temporary residence permit, they could continue to receive NHS care without charge. People who did not enter into the NRM, or whose claims were rejected, could not make use of the exemption and, unless they were exempt from charges on other grounds (e.g. because they are pursuing an asylum claim) could access only the basic array of NHS services that were free to all. The NRM became operational on 1 April 2009. Over the following 12 months, 527 adults and 179 children applied to be recognised as trafficked under this new system, of which 316 applications pertained to trafficking for sexual exploitation, 133 to domestic servitude and 193 to trafficking for labour exploitation (UKHTC, 2010). As of 31 March 2010, half had been granted a positive decision at the initial 'reasonable grounds' stage, nearly 30 per cent had been refused, and a further 17 per cent were still awaiting a decision. Second stage 'conclusive grounds' decisions had been issued to 361 of the applicants, just over a third had received a positive decision, while around a fifth had been refused (ibid.).

Primary care During interviews conducted prior to the implementation of ECAT and the changes to the NHS charging regulations, post-trafficking support providers, NGO advocates and lawyers reported that their clients often faced difficulties accessing primary and secondary medical care and discussed the strategies they used to overcome this.

Post-trafficking support providers and NGO advocates reported that difficulties within primary care settings tended to emerge first in relation to GPs' requirements that prospective patients provided identification documents in order to register, and second as a consequence of their inability, or reluctance, to arrange interpreters for trafficked people who had registered.

The requirement of many GP practices that patients provided proof of identification in order to register with their service posed particular challenges for trafficked migrants, as revealed by a support provider:

> When we took service users to register with a GP for instance it was 'no, you haven't got this, you haven't got that, and how long have you been in the country? Can you give us your old address?' And all of these things that they would ask for, which obviously women could not provide. So they could not register with GPs. In some cases they could not even register with emergency appointments.

As another NGO advocate explained, not only did trafficked migrants not have a permanent address, most were also not in possession of their personal documents:

> We fall down at the first hurdle; the person doesn't have the documents that they need. Because they live in precarious accommodation they don't have bills or tenancy agreements or things, official documentation in their name. And then obviously there's this issue with status documentation. They don't have their passport anymore … it's very rare that trafficked people have that status documentation.

Many trafficked people have their passports confiscated by their traffickers in order to prevent their escape. Indeed, the confiscation or withholding of passports and other identity documents confiscated is recognised as an indicator of trafficking by the ILO and, in the UK, by the UK Border Agency (ILO, 2009; UKBA, 2010). Without their passport, however, trafficked migrants were often left unable to prove either their identity or their immigration status in the UK.

In order to overcome this difficulty, post-trafficking support providers reported that in addition to relying upon 'sympathetic GPs', they had worked to build relationships with healthcare providers with practices within the vicinity of post-trafficking shelter accommodation. A key aspect of building these relationships was explaining why trafficked persons would often be unable to provide the required documentation:

> With GPs ... we would go there and explain who we are and why certain pieces of information they need like passports for instance, or proof of ID would not be, could not be provided. And then when they see [our] address they know that that is one of our service users and based on that can register them without the necessary documentation that they would ask for from other people.

Support providers felt that this strategy had worked well for their clients and also employed it in relation to sexual health clinics and sexual assault referral centres:

> We've build up really good relationships with GPs. [Our clients] get quick access to GP surgery support, and equally we've got relationships with sexual health clinics. We can do quick access to sexual health clinics as well. The house managers have gone and spoken to the practice manager within the GP surgery, spoken to the managers of the sexual health clinics, built those relationships, explained what we were looking for.

Many trafficked migrants, having registered with a GP practice, need interpreters to be present during their appointments. Post-trafficking support providers, NGO advocates and lawyers reported that this created an additional barrier to care. One post-trafficking support provider who reported such difficulties highlighted the limited availability of interpreters in some areas, particularly for unusual dialects:

> Sometimes it [can] be difficult when English is not their first language or if they speak only a little English – [GPs] find it hard to find appropriate interpreters. Some languages – for instance, it's hard to find a specific dialect from Nigeria, Edo language. It's just one interpreter in the whole of [the city], and it's a man. So it's a male interpreter. So things can be quite tricky, interpreting issues.

Another post-trafficking support provider reported that primary care practices were reluctant to book interpreters for their clients:

> Where we do have difficulties locally is on interpreting. The [GP practice], have a budget for providing interpreters, but at the end of the

day the receptionists making the appointments invariably don't know anything about that, don't know how to go about finding an interpreter ... It's 'well, you will bring an interpreter, won't you? When you bring the client?'

Post-trafficking support providers claimed that they would sometimes organise their own interpreters in order to facilitate their clients' access to medical care, but also stated that doing so was costly and unsustainable. Although a few post-trafficking support providers reported having set up service level agreements with local healthcare providers regarding the provision of interpreters, for many, securing interpreters for clients was problematic.

Secondary care Interviewees' reports of trafficked migrants' ability to access secondary (hospital level) care were mixed. Some NGO advocates reported that many migrants who attempted to access secondary care, particularly maternity and HIV/AIDS care, were aggressively interviewed and pursued by hospital overseas payment officers:[3]

> They will just say 'why can't you pay? You need to start paying now ... we need addresses for back home so we can trace the debt back to you, overseas, if you decide to go you may not be allowed back into the country if you haven't paid this debt.' There's lots of tactics they use. Some of them will, once they have your contact details, constantly write letters, constantly call.

Yet, most post-trafficking support providers reported that their clients had not faced difficulties in accessing free secondary care:

> We haven't had problems with hospital care ... they haven't been charged for that. You know, there have been instances where asylum seekers have been landed with a bill ... But our [trafficked women] haven't, they've just gone through.

The differences in interviewees' experiences appeared to be attributable to two factors: variation in the rigour with which the NHS charging regulations were applied and the presence or absence of NGO key workers at trafficked migrants' appointments. Several researchers and clinicians have noted doctors' unease with recent restrictions on migrants' access to NHS care and their decision, therefore, not to ask about the immigration status of their patients (Borman, 2004; Rohan, 2009; Williams, 2004; Yates et al., 2007). Consistent with this, several NGO advocates and lawyers interviewed for this research suggested that accessing hospital level NHS care without charge was less challenging in some areas than in others:

> I have to say certain boroughs are more difficult than others. A large number of the trafficked people that we've seen have actually been from a borough for which it's quite easy to get someone access. So we've been quite fortunate. But every so often, we will see trafficked people from other boroughs, say in North West London and it becomes a lot more difficult.

Post-trafficking support providers also reported that they accompanied their clients to their hospital appointments. They spoke about the value of this support for their clients, whose injuries and medical conditions had typically arisen as a result of the abuse and neglect they endured while trafficked, who were most often without family and friends in the UK and for whom the NHS system was foreign and difficult to navigate. They also believed, however, that their presence at the hospital made it less likely that trafficked migrants' access to care would be challenged:

> Maybe that's staff presence, because we're always there. We're always there. So there's always that extra person to deal with. We would always give them details of the office, that we're the contact people, we're the key worker. And I think half the time they confuse us with social workers when we say key workers. And I think that probably has helped.

Implications of NHS access policies 2008–10

The 2008 amendment to the NHS charging regulations appears to have had little impact on trafficked migrants' access to health. Post-trafficking support providers, NGO advocates and lawyers argued that linking access to NHS care with the NRM decision-making process was problematic for several reasons: there was no provision for people who claimed to have been trafficked but decided against entering into the NRM, NRM timescales delayed trafficked migrants' entitlement to free care, and few healthcare providers were aware of trafficked people's new entitlements to care under the NHS charging regulations.

First responders were not permitted to refer adults whom they suspected of having been trafficking into the NRM unless the person gave their consent – and many would not. The Anti-Trafficking Monitoring Group,[4] for example, reported that between 1 April 2009 and 1 April 2010 there were more than 130 potentially trafficked individuals who were in contact with first responders and support organisations but were not referred into the NRM. Non-referral was primarily because the trafficked people 'did not see the benefit of being referred or were afraid that it would have adverse impact on them because of their immigration status' (ATMG, 2010: 9). Consistent with this, during interviews for this research several post-trafficking support providers, NGO advocates and lawyers claimed that many people whom they believed to have been trafficked refused to be referred into the NRM. They explained that this was because entry into the NRM alerted the immigration authorities to a person's presence in the UK and, because the mechanism did not include an appeals process, could hasten their removal from the country:

> You get [your healthcare] free. I mean that's great, but really, how many people are going through the National Referral Mechanism? You've alerted people to yourself and that if you're not accepted then you would be removed much quicker than you necessarily would have been.

For many trafficked people (e.g., those who had not made a claim for asylum, had not been living lawfully in the UK for 12 months or who were not EU nationals with a right to reside in the UK), refusal to enter into the NRM meant, consequently, that they were not entitled to access the full range of NHS services without charge.

Interviewees also criticised the government's decision to link the entitlement to free medical care to the 'reasonable grounds' decision rather than to a person's entry into the NRM. According to a lawyer interviewed:

> Healthcare interventions are needed fairly early on in the process – having to wait for [NRM] assessments to be undertaken and [approval] letters to be sent out means delays in care.

Although asylum seekers are entitled to access free primary and secondary NHS care from the point of registering their claim in the UK, people who claimed to have been trafficked were not entitled to free healthcare until they had been positively identified as such by NRM caseworkers (NHS, 2008). In 2009, the Department of Health (DH) recommended that patients who had entered into the NRM were 'not asked to pay in advance for any treatment they might need before [caseworkers] confirm them as a suspected victim (five days)' and that trusts should not 'pursue charges for any treatment given within the five day referral period' (DH, 2009: 3). It could be argued, therefore, that creating a link between the NRM and the NHS charging regulations should have had no impact on trafficked migrants' access to NHS care.

The DH also recommended, however, that the debts of patients whose claims were rejected by the NRM should be pursued 'in the usual way' (ibid.). Thus, migrants whose claims to have been trafficked were rejected by NRM caseworkers could be charged for healthcare they had received while awaiting their 'reasonable grounds' decision. Furthermore, for many claimants, these interim decisions were not issued within the five day target. Indeed by mid-2010, two post-trafficking support provider interviewees reported that their clients were waiting an average of 40 and 70 days for decisions to be made.

Over half of the applicants to the NRM between April 2009 and March 2010 were approved (UKHTC, 2010). The DH guidance advises that trafficked people who have been approved by the NRM 'will have been given a letter, either from the UKHTC or the UKBA stating that there are reasonable grounds to believe that they have been trafficked ... [or] concluding that the person is, in fact, a victim of trafficking' (DH, 2009: 1). During interviews, however, post-trafficking support providers reported that NHS staff lacked awareness of the NRM and the changes to the NHS charging regulations:

> There have been occasions where [trafficked people] perhaps haven't taken their NRM letters and they've still been able to access [healthcare]. Or, sometimes they've been questioned and we've confirmed that they are under the NRM as a victim of trafficking. And the [staff] may well have absolutely no knowledge at all about what we're talking about and never heard of anything such as the NRM.

They therefore reported that, despite the legislative changes, it continued to be necessary to advocate on their clients' behalf even after they had received a positive 'reasonable grounds' decision through the NRM.

Conclusion

Between 2000 and 2010, trafficked people's access to NHS healthcare varied according to their immigration status, the rigour with which the NHS charging regulations were implemented, and the extent to which NHS staff were aware of human trafficking. Despite this variation, post-trafficking support providers and NGO advocates found that barriers to access at the primary and secondary level could usually be overcome by building relationships with local providers and accompanying trafficked migrants to register with services and to their medical appointments. This required NGOs to invest resources into health advocacy work, however, and did not address the situation of trafficked migrants who were not in contact with post-trafficking support providers or other NGO advocates.

Despite legislative changes in 2008 that formalised trafficked migrants' rights to free NHS care, their access remains variable and continues to be dependent on the local awareness and enforcement of the NHS charging regulations and on the local activities of post-trafficking support providers and NGOs. As has been found for asylum seekers, legislative provisions for entitlements to free NHS services do not ensure trafficked migrants' access to healthcare. Some of the barriers to access that were reported to be experienced by trafficked people, such as the poor availability of interpreters and unfamiliarity of the NHS, are similar to those faced by asylum seekers. The UK's decision to make trafficked migrants' healthcare entitlements contingent not only on being referred into the NRM but also being positively identified within this system as having been trafficked has created an additional, structural barrier to care for this vulnerable population.

Notes

1 Ordinary residence is a common law concept, the established meaning of which is that a person is ordinarily residing in the UK, apart from temporary or occasional absences, and that their residence has been adopted voluntarily for settled purposes as part of the regular order of their life for the time being.

2 The exemption was created in a 2008 amendment to the NHS charging regulations, but the conditions of the amendment meant that the exemption could not be claimed until 1 April 2009, when the NRM became operational.

3 Overseas payment officers are the hospital staff responsible for implementing the NHS charging regulations.

4 The Anti-Trafficking Monitoring Group was a coalition of nine UK NGOs (Amnesty International UK, Anti-Slavery International, ECPAT UK, Helen Bamber Foundation, the Immigration Law Practitioners' Association (ILPA), Kalayaan, Poppy Project, the Trafficking Awareness Raising Alliance (TARA) and the United Nations Children's Fund (UNICEF) UK) who monitored the UK's implementation of the Council of Europe ECAT between 2009 and 2010.

References

Anderson, B. and B. Rogaly (2005) *Forced Labour and Migration to the UK*, COMPAS in collaboration with the TUC, 68, London.

ASI (Anti-Slavery International) (2001) *Forced Labour in the 21st Century*, Anti-Slavery International, London.

— (2006) *Trafficking for Forced Labour in Europe*, Anti-Slavery International, London.

ATMG (Anti-Slavery Monitoring Group) (2010) *Wrong Kind of Victim? One Year On: An Analysis of UK Measures to Protect Trafficked Persons*, Anti-Slavery International for the Anti-Trafficking Monitoring Group, London.

Baldwin, S. B., D. P. Eisenman, J. Sayles, G. Ryan and K. Chuang (2011) 'Identification of human trafficking victims in healthcare settings', *Health and Human Rights* 13(1), www.hhrjournal. org/index.php/hhr/article/view/ 409/636 (accessed 4 January 2012).

Borman, E. (2004) 'Health tourism: Where healthcare, ethics and the state collide', *British Medical Journal*, 328: 60–1.

Council of Europe (2005) *Council of Europe Convention on Action Against Trafficking in Human Beings*, 16 May, CETS 197, www.unhcr.org/refworld/ docid/43fded544.html (accessed 6 January).

DH (Department of Health) (2009) *Victims of Human Trafficking – Advice for Overseas Visitors Managers*, Department of Health, London.

Di Tommaso, M. L., I. Shima, S. Strøm and F. Bettio (2009) 'As bad as it gets: Well-being deprivation of sexually exploited trafficked women', *European Journal of Political Economy*, 25(2): 143–62.

Family Violence Prevention Fund (2005) *Turning Pain into Power: Trafficking Survivors' Perspectives on Early Intervention Strategies*, Family Violence Prevention Fund, in partnership with the World Childhood Foundation, San Francisco, CA.

Home Office and BIA (Border Immigration Agency) (2008) *Impact Assessment of the Ratification of the Council of Europe Convention on Action against Trafficking in Human Beings*, Home Office, London.

ILO (International Labour Organization) (2005) *A Global Alliance Against Forced Labour*, International Labour Organization, Geneva.

— (2009) *Operational Indicators of Trafficking in Human Beings: Results from a Delphi Survey Implemented by the ILO and the European Commission*, ILO, Geneva.

NHS (National Health Service) (1989) 'S.I.1989/306 Charges to Overseas Visitors Regulations 1989', NHS, London.

— (2008) 'S.I.2008/2251 Charges to Overseas Visitors (Amendment) Regulations 2008', NHS, London.

Ostrovschi, N. V., M. J. Prince, C. Zimmerman, M. A. Hotineanu, L. T. Gorceag, I. Viorel, V. I. Gorceag, C. Flach and M. A. Abas (2011) 'Women in post-trafficking services in Moldova: Diagnostic interviews over two time periods to assess returning women's mental health', *BMC Public Health*, 11(232).

Ritchie, J. and L. Spencer (1994) 'Qualitative data analysis for applied policy research', in A. Bryman and R. Burgess (eds) *Analysing Qualitative Data*, Routledge, London: 173–94.

Rohan, H. (2009) 'Zimbabwean women and HIV care access: Analysis of UK immigration and health policies', unpublished PhD thesis, London School of Hygiene and Tropical Medicine, London.

Silverman, J. G., M. R. Decker, J. Gupta, A. Maheshwari, V. Patel and A. Raj (2006) 'HIV prevalence and predictors among rescued sex-trafficked women and girls in Mumbai, India', *Journal of Acquired Immune Deficiency Syndromes*, 43(5): 588–93.

Silverman, J. G., M. R. Decker, J. Gupta, A. Maheshwari, B. M.

Willis and A. Raj (2007) 'HIV prevalence and predictors of infection in sex-trafficked Nepalese girls and women', *Journal of the American Medical Association*, 298(5): 536–42.

UKBA (United Kingdom Border Agency) (2010) *Asylum Process Guidance: Victims of Trafficking*, UKBA, London.

UKHTC (United Kingdom Human Trafficking Centre) (2010) *NRM Statistical Data 1st April 2009–31st March 2010*, UK Human Trafficking Centre, Sheffield.

UNHCR (United Nations High Commission for Refugees) (2002) *Principles and Guidelines on Human Rights and Trafficking*, United Nations High Commissioner for Human Rights, Geneva.

United Nations (2000) *UN Convention against Transnational Organized Crime, and optional Protocol to Prevent, Suppress and Punish Trafficking in Persons, Especially Women and Children, Supplementing the United Nations Convention Against Transnational Organized Crime*, UN, Geneva.

UNODC (United Nations Office on Drugs and Crime) (2008) *An Introduction to Human Trafficking: Vulnerability, Impact and Action: Background Paper*, United Nations Office on Drugs and Crime, New York.

Wijers, M. and L. Lap-Chew (1997) *Trafficking in Women, Forced Labour, and Slavery-like Practices in Marriage, Domestic Labour and Prostitution*, STV, Utrecht.

Williams, P. (2004) 'Why failed asylum seekers must not be denied access to the NHS', *British Medical Journal*, 329: 298.

Yates, T., R. Crane and A. Burnett (2007) 'Rights and the reality of healthcare charging in the United Kingdom', *Medicine Conflict and Survival*, 23(4): 297–304.

Zimmerman, C. and C. Watts (2003) *WHO Ethical and Safety Recommendations for Interviewing Trafficked Women*, London School of Hygiene and Tropical Medicine/World Health Organization, London.

Zimmerman, C., K. Yun, I. Shvab, C. Watts, L. Trappolin, M. Treppete, F. Bimbi, B. Adams, S. Jiraporn, L. Beci, M. Albrecht, J. Bindel and L. Regan (2003) *The Health Risks and Consequences of Trafficking in Women and Adolescents: Findings from a European Study*, London School of Hygiene and Tropical Medicine, London.

Zimmerman, C., M. Hossain, K. Yun, B. Roche, L. Morison and C. Watts (2006) *Stolen Smiles: The Physical and Psychological Health Consequences of Women and Adolescents Trafficked in Europe*, London School of Hygiene and Tropical Medicine, London.

Zimmerman, C., M. Hossain, K. Yun, V. Gajdadziev, N. Guzun, M. Tchomarova, R. A. Ciarrocchi, A. Johansson, A. Kefurtova, S. Scodanibbio, M. N. Motus, B. Roche, L. Morison and C. Watts (2008) 'The health of trafficked women: A survey of women entering post-trafficking services in Europe', *American Journal of Public Health*, 98(1): 55–9.

8 | Vulnerable migrant women and charging for maternity care in the UK: advocating change

ROSALIND BRAGG

Introduction

This chapter draws upon the experiences of Maternity Action, a UK charity working on maternity and equalities. Maternity Action sees some of the harsh effects on pregnant migrant women of the charging practices of the NHS and this chapter is therefore written from an activist perspective. While the vast majority of the population receives healthcare free of charge, many of the most vulnerable migrant women are asked to pay for care, with bills commonly in excess of £3,000. Maternity care is one area where restrictions on entitlement to free NHS care impacts most heavily on women. Advocating for change at national level has had mixed results and we have refocused our advocacy work on improving practice within individual maternity services.

Charging for maternity care

In the UK, the NHS provides a comprehensive health service that is free of charge at the point of delivery for most UK residents. Charging applies to foreign nationals and a small number of UK citizens who do not meet the residency requirements. Different charging rules apply to primary care, which is predominantly provided by GPs, and to secondary care. Maternity care is classed as secondary care. However, women commonly access maternity care after receiving a referral from their GP. There are some differences in the rules applying in England, Scotland and Wales.

Secondary care, including maternity care, is chargeable for individuals who are not considered to be 'ordinarily resident' in the UK (Department of Health, 2011). To be 'ordinarily resident', a person must be lawfully in the country and 'settled' in the UK. The Department of Health generally interprets 'settled' as requiring six months' residence in the UK, although this is not an explicit requirement. In addition to this rule, there are a number of groups that are specifically exempt from charging. Maternity care is classed as 'immediately necessary' treatment, which means that maternity care must not be refused or delayed because of an inability to pay in advance. This is because of the severe health risks associated with conditions such as eclampsia and pre-eclampsia.

Women subject to charging include women who have overstayed their visas or who entered the country without permission. Asylum seekers are entitled to free care. Refused asylum seekers are entitled to free care in Scotland and Wales but are only entitled to free care in England if they are in receipt of support from the UK Border Agency. Women who are students are entitled to free care if their courses are longer than six months or are substantially funded by the UK government. Women who arrive in the UK on a work visa or as the dependant of an individual with a work visa are entitled to free care if they are in work or about to commence a specific job, but not if they are still looking for work.

The rules on entitlement to secondary care are extremely complex. The Department of Health guidance document amounts to 89 pages. Applying the rules requires a good understanding of the immigration system as well as the charging regulations and guidance. It is unsurprising therefore that midwives report confusion about the rules on entitlement to care. Awareness within the voluntary and community sector is variable and the Maternity Action information sheet on entitlement to maternity care appears to be the only available leaflet on this issue (Maternity Action, 2011).

Feedback from voluntary organisations and midwives indicates significant problems in the administration of the charging regulations. There are examples of breaches of the guidance, failure to fully inform women about their entitlements, and practices that are likely to deter women from engaging in maternity services. These include: overseas visitor managers failing to use interpreters when meeting with women with little or no English; letters to women that demand immediate payment without mentioning the entitlement to care irrespective of ability to pay; overseas visitor managers attending initial appointments with midwives, which is highly intrusive; and invoices issued after each appointment or scan, without mentioning the entitlement to care irrespective of ability to pay.

To access most secondary care, an individual requires a referral from their GP. Maternity care is an exception. In theory, pregnant women are entitled to contact their maternity service directly and gain an appointment without a referral letter. This has not been consistently implemented across the UK and the levels of community awareness are also variable. Because of the 'gatekeeper' role of GPs, many women believe that they require a referral from their GP in order to commence maternity care. As a result, charging practices within primary care also affect vulnerable women's engagement with maternity services.

At the time of writing, there are no formal restrictions on access to primary care for anyone in the UK. A GP has the discretion to provide care free of charge to anyone, irrespective of their immigration status. Increasingly, GPs are under pressure not to provide care to individuals who are not entitled to free NHS secondary care. GPs report receiving letters from primary care trusts instructing them not to register these patients, or to remove them from their lists. A review of entitlement to primary care is planned for 2012 and this may result in the formal introduction of charging for primary care.

In October 2011 new rules on unpaid healthcare bills were introduced. The new rules state that individuals with an outstanding NHS debt in excess of £1,000 may be refused permission to enter the UK or to extend their stay, such as by renewing a visa (House of Lords, 2011). The costs of standard, uncomplicated maternity care are in excess of this threshold figure. At the time of writing, it was too soon to observe how the rules would be applied or the impact on vulnerable migrant women.

Access to maternity care

Antenatal appointments enable clinicians to identify and treat conditions that impact on the health of the mother or baby. These include conditions such as eclampsia and pre-eclampsia, which are potentially fatal and which present with few symptoms. Some pre-existing conditions, such as cardiovascular disease or diabetes, require careful management during pregnancy. Early and ongoing treatment of HIV/AIDS during pregnancy reduces the risk of transmission to the baby. In addition to clinical care, antenatal appointments also provide an opportunity for women to seek help with circumstances that impact on their health, including domestic violence, homelessness and destitution.

Standard maternity care in the UK commences with a 'booking' appointment between the eighth and twelfth week of pregnancy. In uncomplicated pregnancies, there are seven to ten antenatal appointments during the pregnancy. In complicated pregnancies, the number of appointments can be considerably higher. Commencing antenatal care after 20 weeks ('late booking') or missing four or more regulation appointments ('non-attendance') are associated with a higher risk of maternal death (Lewis, 2007, 2011).

Charging rules and practices affect engagement with maternity services by vulnerable migrant women. Two case studies of calls to Maternity Action illustrate the problems:

Maternity Action received a call from an overseas student who was studying in the UK. His wife had come to join him and had become pregnant. When they went to the maternity service, he was asked to sign a document saying that he would pay for her care as she wasn't entitled to free care. When they worked out what the costs were, they decided that they couldn't afford the care and didn't go. When they rang Maternity Action, the woman was eight months pregnant and had received no maternity care of any kind. Maternity Action outlined their rights and encouraged them to attend for care even though they could not pay.

A woman contacted Maternity Action asking what to do when she went into labour. She was waiting for the UK Border Agency to assess her application for indefinite leave to remain in the UK and while this was being assessed she was not entitled to free NHS care. She was eight months pregnant and had received no maternity care. She had tried to register with a GP but had been refused because of her immigration status. She did not contact the maternity service directly because she didn't know that she could. Instead, she waited until she was in the late stages of pregnancy and rang around until she found someone who could help her. Maternity Action encouraged her to contact her maternity service directly, which she did, and they found that she had very high blood pressure. She had an emergency caesarean and she and her baby were well. She rang Maternity Action the day after the caesarean because the overseas visitor manager was coming to see her and she was terrified about what would happen, because she couldn't afford to pay. Maternity Action outlined her rights and encouraged her to call back if she needed further help.

Both of these case studies relate to women and men who speak fluent English and were able to advocate for themselves. They were able to discuss their situation with the overseas visitor manager and their local general practice, and yet were unable to access care until very late in their pregnancy. In one case the woman could not access care from the GP. The second case involved the mistaken, though understandable, belief that they were not entitled to care if they couldn't pay. These are individuals with the skills to search the internet to find advice and to discuss their situation with an adviser. Many of the women who are subject to charging do not have these skills and resources.

Widespread confusion about the rules means that some women

who are not subject to charging are also cautious about engaging with maternity services. There are numerous ways in which women seek to avoid or minimise charging. Some women attend maternity services or A&E only when there is a problem during pregnancy. Some women attend maternity services early in pregnancy but disappear when they receive an invoice or are asked about their immigration status. There are worrying reports of women obtaining scans from unlicensed health providers rather than approaching NHS maternity services. A commonly reported story is women attending maternity services when in labour, having received no antenatal care. There are also reports of women who attend hospital after giving birth at home.

No formal research into the impacts of charging on engagement with maternity services at national level or at local level has been released, although the issue is occasionally mentioned in local and regional reports. Instead, Maternity Action has historically relied on information gathered anecdotally from individual women, individual midwives, migrant women's services and advice services. Further research in this area is urgently needed, but resources to support this are difficult to find.

In 2011 Maternity Action conducted a survey of midwives and overseas visitor managers in London (Bragg, forthcoming). The research asked midwives and overseas visitor managers about the charging practices within their trusts, including whether or not women were asked about their immigration status and length of time in the UK; who asked the questions and when; whether or not a woman would receive an appointment before her chargeability was resolved; mechanisms for follow-up for women who do not attend appointments; information provided to women on charging for care; and how unpaid invoices are followed up. Midwives were also asked if they thought that charging practices had any impact on access to maternity services by vulnerable migrant women.

The survey found that practices are very diverse. Some trusts demonstrated non-compliance with the charging regulations and guidance and others showed a high level of sensitivity to the impact of charging on vulnerable women.

Midwives were divided on the question about perceived impact on access by vulnerable migrant women. A small number of midwives responded that they were not aware that charging practices had any impact on access by these women in their trusts. In some cases, the midwives were very clear that they lacked evidence to draw any conclusions – 'difficult to answer as I don't know if they are choosing not to access services'. In other cases, midwives felt that this was not a problem at their trust.

By contrast, several midwives stated that charging practices had a significant impact on access to maternity care. Common reports were of women not attending for appointments, commencing care late in their pregnancy or receiving no antenatal care. Some midwives provided specific examples of impacts on maternity care:

> The maternity service recommended that a woman have a caesarean section due to a medical condition which had an impact on the baby. She was subject to charging. Instead of attending for the caesarean, she gave birth at home and came into the maternity service after having done so.

Poor health outcomes

The impact of charging on vulnerable migrant women's engagement with maternity services is particularly worrying given the poor maternal health outcomes for this group of women. The UK publishes a series of triennial reports on maternal deaths in the UK. The reports for 2003–05 (Lewis, 2007) and for 2006–08 (Lewis, 2011) provide a useful source of data. The 2006–08 review found that black African women are 2.4 times more likely to die during maternity than white women and the figure for black Caribbean women is 2.5 (Lewis, 2011).

There are limited data on maternal mortality according to immigration status. During the years 2003–05, refugee and asylum seeking women made up 12 per cent of all maternal deaths, despite constituting less than 0.5 per cent of the total population (Lewis, 2007). Lack of data on the total number of pregnancies or births to this group prevents calculation of comparative maternal mortality rates; however, the raw figures suggests that this would be significantly higher for this group. This is consistent with international data on maternal health outcomes for refugee and asylum seeking women. Recent research from the Netherlands found that asylum seeking women had a five times higher risk of severe acute maternal morbidity than the rest of the population (Van Hanegam et al., 2011).

While the later triennial report on maternal deaths in the UK provides no further figures based on immigration status, there are numerous case studies in the reports of deaths to vulnerable migrant women. The 2003–05 report included the following comment:

> As the global safe motherhood movement has long pointed out, the underlying root causes of maternal deaths are often underlying social

and other non-clinical factors. The link[s] between adverse pregnancy outcomes and vulnerability and social exclusion are nowhere more starkly demonstrated than by this Enquiry. (Lewis, 2007: 44)

The triennial reports found an association between ethnicity, recent migration and risk factors for poor maternal health outcomes. The 2003–05 triennial review commented on the poor general overall health of some recent migrants and flagged the risks of illnesses that have largely disappeared from the UK, such as TB and rheumatic heart disease. Recent migrants from some countries and ethnic groups are at higher risk of HIV, which requires early treatment to minimise risks to mother and baby. The report recommended that migrant women receive a full general medical examination (ibid.).

The triennial reports found that women from black and minority ethnic (BME) groups who died during maternity were disproportionately likely to have commenced maternity care after 20 weeks or missed four or more regular appointments. Suboptimal care was experienced by 35 per cent of women who did not speak English, 40 per cent of black African women, 57 per cent of black Caribbean women and 25 per cent of Middle Eastern women, compared to 17 per cent of white women (ibid.).

There were several examples of unsatisfactory interpreting arrangements. Of the 295 women who died during 2003–05, 34 spoke little or no English, and very few had access to translation services. Five women who were murdered by their partners had the abusive partner as their interpreter. In one case, diagnosis of tuberculous meningitis was delayed as the husband was acting as the interpreter. A young son translated for an asylum seeking woman who died from a complex set of conditions (ibid.).

Some migrant groups have a higher prevalence of female genital mutilation (FGM), which requires early engagement with maternity services to minimise risks during birth. The 2007 triennial review included one death to a woman who had undergone an avoidable caesarean section as a result of late identification of her FGM (ibid.).

Political environment

There is an ongoing tension between the NHS charging policies and the broader health policy objectives of reducing maternal and infant health inequalities. A key strategy for reducing health inequalities in infant mortality is ensuring pregnant women engage early with maternity services. This is encapsulated in a high level public service target of increasing the number of women who have their initial ('booking') appointment with a midwife by 13 weeks of pregnancy. While arguments about addressing health inequalities are highly persuasive in the policy debate, the fears of 'opening the flood gates' to 'health tourists' appear more powerful.

Media articles have claimed that women are coming to the UK with the specific intention of using maternity services without paying for them, often termed 'health tourism' (see for example Beckford, 2011). There is a view within the government that exempting maternity from charges would exacerbate this problem. Policy-makers have, however, been unable to point to any specific research to support this. A 2007 Home Office document, *Enforcing the Rules: A Strategy to Ensure and Enforce Compliance with our Immigration Laws* made a similar claim. It states:

> There is evidence of small-scale but very deliberate abuse of the NHS. For example, a sampling exercise last year at one airport suggested that health tourists were being detected at the rate of about 15 per month. This primarily involved heavily pregnant women arriving in the UK with an intention of using NHS maternity services. (Home Office, 2007: 14)

A request under the Freedom of Information Act about this sampling exercise found that no sampling exercise had taken place (Home Office, 2008). Instead, the figures were drawn from statistics routinely collected at Gatwick Airport over the course of a year. No figures were provided on the number of pregnancies among those designated as 'health tourists'. The criteria for identifying individuals as 'health tourists' were drawn from the Immigration Rules; however, the onus was on passengers to prove that they were not 'health tourists', rather than the reverse.

This is the sole piece of research on this issue that has been reported by the UK Border Agency. Publicly available information on the data collection is very limited and there are significant questions about the quality of the research and the conclusions that may reasonably be drawn from it. This is a very poor evidence base to support the policy positions taken by the Department of Health. It would seem that populist views of abuse of the NHS by foreigners are playing a significant role in the policy development process.

Advocating for change

Advocating for changes in the charging policies has proven extremely difficult. A loose group of voluntary and professional organisations has been working since 2004 to minimise the impacts of charging on secondary care and to prevent the formal introduction of charging into primary care. During development of the 2011 regulations and guidance there was coordinated lobbying for maternity care to be exempt from charging. This was unsuccessful.

An ongoing strand of advocacy work has focused on the implementation of the regulations and guidance within individual maternity services. Within the health system, failure to apply policy and guidance in particular cases is commonly dealt with through the complaints handling system. Conversations with Department of Health staff who have an oversight role have focused on this approach to the problem with implementing the charging regulations. This is not a satisfactory solution in this case, as vulnerable migrant women are unlikely to complain themselves or to give consent to advice and support agencies complaining on their behalf. As a result, advocacy has been based on anecdotal evidence and it has proven difficult to get this issue on the agenda for health services.

The administration of the charging regulations and guidance sits primarily with the overseas visitor managers. These are staff who are located within the finance or administrative strand of the trust, rather than any of the clinical strands. There are a few examples of joint working between overseas visitor managers and midwifery staff to ensure access for vulnerable women is taken into account in administration of the charging regulations. However these are the exception. More commonly, there is little or no midwifery involvement in developing the policies and practices that guide the work of the overseas visitor managers in individual trusts. Feedback from midwives indicates widespread confusion about the charging rules and uncertainty about the role that they are able to play in this process.

Advocacy during development of the 2011 charging regulations and guidance resulted in a useful reference point in addressing this problem. The revised guidance contained a clear, prominent statement that all maternity care must be treated as being immediately necessary and must not be denied or delayed due to charging issues. The guidance also included very specific requirements on provision of information:

> Although she should be informed if charges apply to her treatment, in doing so, she should not be discouraged from receiving the remainder of her maternity treatment. OVMs [overseas visitor managers] and clinicians should be especially careful to inform pregnant patients that further maternity care will not be withheld, regardless of their ability to pay. (Department of Health, 2011: 44)

The guidance is useful in formally flagging the problem of discouraging women from attending maternity treatment. Importantly, the guidance referred to both the overseas visitor manager and the clinician as having a role in informing patients about their entitlement. This gives a clear mandate for midwives to engage with the charging process. Further advocacy will be required to turn this policy statement into changes in practice at local level.

Maternity Action has incorporated material on charging practices in its training for midwives to improve maternity care for refugee and asylum seeking women. The training is accredited by the Royal College of Midwives and is delivered to midwives across the UK. The project is not funded by the NHS and is instead supported by the philanthropic trust, Comic Relief, as part of its stream of work on women and asylum. Maternity Action has sought to embed this training in maternity services as one means of addressing the poor maternal health outcomes for this group of women.

One of the frustrations of advocacy on this issue is the difficulty of ensuring women's voices are heard in the policy development process. Maternity services have formal processes for engaging with their local communities, but rarely involve vulnerable migrant women in these processes. Those women most likely to experience problems as a consequence of charging commonly have insecure immigration status, and so are less likely to participate in any formal engagement process. Advice agencies consistently report that vulnerable migrant women are not prepared to lodge formal complaints about charging for maternity care. It is left to the migrant women's organisations and advice agencies that support the women to collect the women's stories and communicate them to those who need to hear them.

References

Beckford, M. (2011) 'Health tourism: Why the NHS has become popular destination', *The Telegraph*, www.telegraph.co.uk/news/uknews/immigration/8391274/Health-tourism-why-the-NHS-became-popular-destination.html (accessed 30 November 2011).

Bragg, R. (forthcoming) *Charging Vulnerable Migrant Women for NHS Maternity Care: A Survey of London Maternity Services*, Maternity Action, London.

Department of Health (2011) *Guidance on Implementing the Overseas Visitor Hospital Charging Regulations*, Department of Health, London.

Home Office (2007) *Enforcing the Rules: A Strategy to Ensure and Enforce Compliance with our Immigration Laws*, Home Office, London.

— (2008) *Handling of Suspected 'Health Tourists'*, Home Office, London, www.homeoffice.gov.uk/

about-us/freedom-of-information/
released-information1/foi-
archive-immigration/9707_detec-
tion_health_tourism?view=Html
(accessed 28 November 2011).

House of Lords (2011) *Merits of
Statutory Instruments Committee
– Fortieth Report*, UK Parliament,
London.

Lewis, G. (2007) *Saving Mothers'
Lives: Reviewing Maternal Deaths
to Make Motherhood Safer: 2003–5*,
Confidential Enquiry into Maternal and Child Health, London.

— (2011) 'Saving mothers' lives: Reviewing maternal deaths to make
motherhood safer: 2006–2008',
*British Journal of Obstetrics and
Gynaecology*, 118, Supplement 1:
1–203.

Maternity Action (2011) *Entitlement
to Free NHS Maternity Care
for Women from Abroad*, www.
maternityaction.org.uk/site-
buildercontent/sitebuilderfiles/
entitlementtonhscareinfo.pdf
(accessed 28 November 2011).

Van Hanegam, N., A. S. Mittenburg,
J. J. Zwart, K. W. M. Bloemen-
kamp and J. Van Roosmalen
(2011) 'Severe acute maternal
morbidity in asylum seekers: A
two year nationwide cohort study
in the Netherlands', *Acta Obstetri-
cian et Gynecologica Scandinavia*,
90(9): 1010–16.

9 | Multiple medicaments: looking beyond structural inequalities in migrant healthcare

FELICITY THOMAS

Introduction

The past decade has witnessed a disproportionate share of HIV infection among black African migrant communities in the UK. It is now well recognised that HIV-related stigma, immigration constraints and unfamiliarity with health services can negatively influence the health outcomes of HIV positive migrants, and present particular treatment and healthcare inequalities when compared to British-born citizens. However, the majority of studies reporting such findings have, to date, been underpinned by frameworks of understanding that incorporate biomedical assumptions regarding what it means to be healthy, and make suppositions concerning 'appropriate' and 'responsible' ways for individuals to manage and to treat ill-health via the use of biomedical pharmaceuticals.

While not in any way seeking to undermine the undeniable importance of anti-retroviral treatments, this chapter argues that to more fully understand the health-related experiences of HIV positive migrants, and in particular the issues that they may confront in accessing and effectively utilising healthcare services in the UK, it is helpful to take a more holistic approach that, in addition to recognising structural constraints to healthcare, also acknowledges the different understandings that people within migrant communities may hold regarding ill-health and the meanings and values that people invest in different treatment options. Particular focus in this chapter is placed upon the use of 'traditional' and 'African' treatments and therapies, the role of transnational health networks in facilitating and upholding their use, and the implications of such treatment use for individual and public health.

HIV in the UK

Recent figures from the Health Protection Agency suggest that over 33 per cent of all new HIV diagnosis in 2009 were among black Africans and that 66 per cent of all heterosexual HIV transmission in the UK is within this population group. Of those black Africans newly diagnosed in 2009 where the location of infection was known, 16 per cent contracted HIV in the UK (a substantial increase from 4 per cent in 1999) and 84 per cent were infected abroad (HPA, 2010). Late HIV diagnosis (i.e. diagnosis after the time at which treatment should have begun) remains high, with 42 per cent of black Africans diagnosed in 2007 presenting late for treatment and care (HPA, 2008). Such a situation in turn has serious implications: individual health is affected via the limited therapy options available and the significantly raised risk and rapidity of death, while public health is also adversely impacted through the increased risk of onward HIV transmission.

Because HIV-related ill-health can manifest in a variety of forms, effective treatment requires patients to follow a strict drug taking regime that is personalised to the needs of the individual. Failure to follow such a regime can reduce and even reverse drug effectiveness, leading to an increased viral load, a weakened immune system and resistance to anti-retroviral therapy (ART). At the same time, the use of certain herbal treatments in combination with ART has also been found to result in adverse health outcomes (Mills et al., 2005; Schumaker and Bond, 2008). As such, NHS practitioners strongly encourage HIV patients to divulge their use of 'alternative', non-biomedical treatments so that any potentially harmful treatment interactions can be avoided. Sustained and personalised healthcare and support is therefore considered vital in ensuring that HIV patients adhere correctly to their treatment regimes.

Studies have, however, found that a number of factors hinder migrants from optimising their access to this kind of HIV treatment and care. These factors include structural barriers to accessing healthcare, for example language and financial constraints, insecure immigration status and associated fear of detention and deportation (Körner, 2007), a lack of familiarity with healthcare services and confusion over entitlements (experienced by both migrants and service providers) (Thomas et al., 2010a) and high levels of AIDS-related stigma and associated fear of rejection from community support networks (Doyal and Anderson, 2005).

Over the past decade, a range of policy changes relating to healthcare entitlements for foreign nationals have been put in place in the UK (cf. Kelley and Stevenson, 2006; Thomas et al., 2010a; Yates et al., 2007). While recent policy changes have, in theory, been targeted at limiting healthcare options for those with particularly insecure immigration status, for example refused asylum seekers and undocumented migrants, the frequency of the policy changes and a lack of clarity surrounding the universality of their implementation have resulted in widespread confusion. This has in turn created a situation in which many of those seeking healthcare are unclear about their entitlements (and thus fail to access them), and many of those providing healthcare are unclear about who is entitled to what (and thus fail to deliver).

While it is generally accepted that this situation is impacting adversely on particular migrant groups, relatively little is known about the implications of such confusion on the health seeking options that *are* perceived to be available among migrants. This chapter argues that in seeking to understand these options, it is important to also consider the different ways in which migrants from diverse backgrounds may interpret and seek to respond to their ill-health not only via the NHS but also *outside* the bounds of biomedical healthcare services.

Thinking beyond the biomedical

For the last two decades, sexual health promotion and HIV prevention in the UK have, in the main, been premised on the assumption that a biomedical interpretation of ill-health forms the framework within which treatment seeking decisions are made (Johnson et al., 2006). Within this framework, assumptions about health and wellbeing are incorporated that presuppose that people will act to maximise their opportunities for securing effective biomedical treatment, while at the same time, giving little recognition to the broader social, cultural and economic context within which treatment seeking and adherence decisions are made (Kesby et al., 2003; Thomas et al., 2010b).

A growing literature within medical anthropology and sociology has demonstrated the importance of exploring 'indigenous', 'popular' or 'lay' constructions of illness aetiology and treatment seeking, particularly when explanatory models of health and treatment differ markedly from dominant biomedical paradigms (Del Casino, 2004; Helman, 2007; Mogensen, 2005; Thomas, 2008). Within this literature, a small group of researchers working primarily in developing country contexts (Farmer, 1992; Mogensen, 1997; Thomas, 2008) has focused on exploring the variety of non-biomedical paradigms that are used to enable people to interpret HIV-related illness within their own cognitive and epistemological frameworks of understanding. Much of this research has focused on the role of 'illness narratives' (Garro and Mattingly, 2000; Kleinman, 1988) that reflect shared socio-cultural understandings and values and through which people can obtain or assert particular social identities, communicate what is significant in their lives, make sense of illness through a narrative structure or 'plot'

(Mattingly, 1994) and re-establish some degree of order and continuity to the 'biographical disruption' caused by illness (Bury, 1982). Many of these narratives (e.g. those emphasising shame, magic, witchcraft, pollution and taboo) have highlighted the ways in which people's understandings of health and illness are infused with socio-cultural, symbolic and contextual meanings that often contradict and elude the reductionist boundaries of biomedical models, and are seen to require 'traditional' or 'alternative' methods of treatment to those available in the mainstream health sector.

Despite increasing attention being given to the use of complementary and alternative medicines within the UK, mass produced biomedical drugs continue to dominate health discourse and practice within formal health services. In turn, the use of 'alternative' or non-biomedical treatments and therapies is commonly viewed by the mainstream health sector as irrational and as behaviour that requires supervision and management from within the biomedical sector (Broom and Adams, 2009; Cant and Sharma, 1999; Cohen et al., 2001). Yet among some migrant groups, the hegemony of biomedicine is not axiomatic in every situation of ill-health; instead, people may rely on the existence and use of a plurality of medical approaches to address their health concerns. For people living in parts of southern Africa for example, 70–80 per cent of the population have been reported to use multiple medical practices and a range of treatments from different sources, often concurrently (Peltzer et al., 2008; Stekelenburg et al., 2005). This may include the use of 'modern' biomedical pharmaceuticals alongside plant or animal-based treatments, spiritual healing and prayer, among other things. How widely such treatments are used can be influenced by a range of factors. These may include the perceived illness aetiology, (cost and resource) accessibility of treatments, pragmatic need, socio-cultural expectation and personal belief and preference regarding the meanings and values of different treatments.

The data used in this chapter were collected as part of a larger study on treatment seeking and treatment management among migrants from southern Africa living in London. Ethical approval for the study was obtained from the East London and The City Research Ethics Committee and the Institute of Education, University of London, and informed consent was obtained from all informants prior to participation. Eleven focus groups with 70 participants from Zimbabwe (n=39), South Africa (n=21) and Zambia (n=10) living in London were undertaken between October 2008 and May 2009. These discussions elicited detailed information regarding culturally influenced interpretations of ill-health and decisions over treatment sought, both while participants had lived in southern Africa and since their arrival as migrants in the UK. Although respondents were selected on their age (over 18), country of origin and their residence in London, the majority were accessed via HIV support groups, and as such, living with HIV tended to frame the discussion in most cases. Repeat interviews were also undertaken with 20 HIV positive migrants from Zimbabwe (n=10), South Africa (n=2) and Zambia (n=8) who were accessing HIV support services via a London hospital. The aim of these interviews was to gain an insight into the ways that research participants had interpreted any ill-health experienced prior to their HIV positive diagnosis and how their diagnosis had then impacted upon their understanding of their health and on their treatment seeking strategies.

Immigration status can limit people's ability to travel, with those seeking asylum in the UK often facing restrictions on visits to their home country. The majority of the Zimbabwean respondents who had arrived in the UK in the past decade were asylum seekers or refugees. Most of those who had arrived in previous decades, as well as the majority of the Zambian and South African participants, had come to the UK on student or work visas, and a significant number had later applied for leave to remain on compassionate (usually health-related) grounds. Although immigration status may constrict people's treatment seeking strategies, all of those involved in the study maintained some, usually regular, contact with family and friends in southern Africa and were able to access health and treatment networks there via telephone, email, postal and/or freighting services (for a more detailed discussion see Thomas, 2010).

Interpreting and responding to ill-health

Focus group discussions revealed that in many cases of ill-health, the type of treatment and therapy that was sought depended to a large extent on its perceived aetiology. The UK NHS was perceived as providing a vital source of healthcare and treatment and the majority of those participating in the study had sought out the services of a GP at times when they had experienced ill-health. The availability of biomedicines via health services and pharmacies in the UK was greatly appreciated by all study participants, many of whom had come from areas of southern Africa where such 'modern' and 'advanced' treatments were unobtainable or prohibitively expensive.

At the same time however, certain types of ill-health were widely regarded to require more 'traditional' forms of treatment or therapy.

This was particularly evident among the Zimbabwean and South African participants, the majority of whom came from areas of southern Africa where many forms of traditional treatments are highly valued.[1] Mental and sexual health issues in particular were seen to require these more traditional approaches, as was unexplained and prolonged ill-health. Several focus group participants from South Africa explained that they would rather go home for treatment in such cases than receive what they perceived to be inappropriate and unhelpful support from the NHS. In such cases, it was reported that people 'saved up' these health problems and tried to ensure that they got them all sorted out via what were deemed to be more appropriate methods on their annual trip home to South Africa.

The questioning of NHS methods was also a commonly raised theme among those who believed strongly in the value of more holistic approaches to healthcare. While the concept of 'healing' was considered to be particularly important in enabling an individual to restore their overall wellbeing, certain NHS approaches were considered by participants, such as Jacob, to not only provide just a partial solution to the issue, but to also risk jeopardising long term physical and mental health:

> Their interpretation [in Zimbabwe] is different from here. They believe in healing, we [in the UK] believe in chopping and removing, so if you have something wrong they will chop it and take it out. Here the whole concept is chop and take it out – not actually to heal ... We treat you, we don't heal you, there is a difference ... What I mean by chopping is taking out bits that are infected or giving you a new limb – whereas healing you are trying to put something in our body which will help your body to fight. It's more like cleansing. (Jacob, Zimbabwe)

A very commonly raised issue among all participants in focus groups and interviews related to beliefs in ill-health caused by witchcraft. Almost without exception, participants agreed that such beliefs were strongly embedded across much of southern Africa, and that despite a tendency for some people to deny it, they remained in existence among migrant groups from southern Africa living in the UK. The Zimbabwean community in particular felt that such beliefs were ongoing, most obviously among newly arrived migrants in the UK, and that they continued to impact upon people's daily wellbeing and the way that they responded to ill-health, especially when more formal biomedical services had failed to explain or solve the problem.

As has been well documented (cf. Ashforth, 2005; Thomas, 2006; Yamba, 1997) witchcraft is widely believed among southern African communities to result from jealousy. A large number of focus group participants explained that they were vulnerable to this jealousy-induced witchcraft both from those who remained in southern Africa and were jealous of the opportunities that were assumed to be available to them as migrants, and from community members in the UK. Zimbabwean women in particular commented that a shortage of Zimbabwean men in the UK had led to tensions and accusations of witchcraft among women competing to secure relationships. A minority of focus group participants claimed to have personally experienced the impacts of witchcraft. Most people though claimed to be aware of cases where it had taken place and/or to have seen evidence of witchcraft being practised by community members. Focus group discussions revealed that such beliefs could impact on people's interpretations of ill-health as well as the treatments and therapies that they sought to alleviate the perceived problem.

A similar finding emerged among several of those participating in interviews. Although most of the women interviewed had found out their HIV positive status before they suffered from serious ill-health,[2] many of the men interviewed had found themselves in a situation in which a deterioration in their health had meant that they were faced with important decisions over healthcare and treatment seeking options. In such cases, self treatment via the local pharmacy was cited as a common first step. When this failed to work, some participants sought advice from their GP, and from there, were referred for blood tests at the hospital. However, in nine (45 per cent) cases people interviewed reported that they had not undertaken an HIV test until their ill-health was in an advanced state. Not being able to access a GP to get a referral to the hospital was cited as one key explanatory factor. However, culturally influenced understandings of the illness aetiology also played a significant role in explaining late HIV testing. Most obviously, the extreme stigma associated with HIV was found to remain deeply embedded within the migrant communities concerned, resulting in denial and the repeated delaying of an HIV test. At the same time though, several respondents reported that they had also been influenced by their and their relatives' beliefs in 'alternative', non-biomedical aetiologies. Jacob, for example, reported how he and his relatives had spent several years explaining his bouts of ill-health as a result of family tensions, witchcraft and the upsetting of the ancestors:

> My sister said I should not have trusted that uncle of mine, that I
> shouldn't have eaten the food that that man had, not worn his jumper.

She said I shouldn't have done that and she strongly believed in that. And one of my close friends – he said that the reason I was so ill was because I hadn't been to visit my mother's grave, that is why you are so ill. He spent a long time telling me this ... For some time I really believed that it was my uncle who had done this. (Jacob, Zimbabwe)

Similarly, Paul reported how he and his relatives had blamed his very poor health on witchcraft when he had become ill soon after arriving in the UK. He explained how a number of men in his tenement block in Zambia had died after being witched by a neighbour. Paul had himself argued with this neighbour, and described how the man had become jealous of his comparatively high living standards. To Paul and his family, blaming this man for Paul's ill-health was deemed a feasible explanation and one which influenced his decision to delay seeking support from formal healthcare services in the UK.

Thus rather than assuming that inequalities in healthcare access result solely from the structural issues associated with immigrant status, such examples point to the need to also consider the role of culturally influenced narratives of ill-health and the meanings and values that people invest in different treatment options.

Treatment seeking following an HIV positive diagnosis

While culturally influenced interpretations of ill-health were found to play a role in delaying health seeking from the NHS, they also continued to have an impact on some people after they had received an HIV positive diagnosis. Of those participating in interviews, 45 per cent reported using some form of non-biomedical treatment or therapy before they had started taking their ART (and/or in combination with it). This had taken the form of herbal treatments and immunity boosters, spiritual healing, prayer and/or fasting. Treatments were usually acquired via relatives and friends in southern Africa and were either obtained on visits home to southern Africa or were sent via freighting companies. Spiritual healing was usually undertaken with healers (most commonly in Zimbabwe) over the telephone, or via relatives who consulted them on the patient's behalf. Although a minority of those interviewed were adamant that they had not and would not use any other treatments alongside their ART, 75 per cent of interviewees reported that they would use non-biomedical treatments either in combination with, or as alternatives to anti-retrovirals if they were able to access them.

A common assertion among those who had used these non-biomedical treatments and therapies was that they were safer than pharmaceutical drugs. As Luke explained, this was widely deemed to be because of their herbal and thus 'natural' composition, and the claim that they did not result in adverse side effects:

> A lot of the western medicines we take they control the condition that you have – but in most cases they will just create a new condition that you did not have before in the form of side effects. Some of the side effects are even worse ... with herbal medicines there are no side effects. (Luke, Zimbabwe)

Receiving treatments and therapies via trusted and well known sources such as relatives and family healers was also considered by many to be a safer option than the less familiar and more daunting environment of the NHS. In several focus groups, respondents cited cases in which they perceived that malpractice and negligence had occurred within the NHS, leading to the worsening health or even deaths of community members.

Despite the positive light in which many non-biomedical treatments and therapies were held, it was clear that their use could also have adverse consequences on an individual's health, particularly if they interfered with personalised, and necessarily precise, ART regimes. In such cases, the informants concerned explained that they had sought a range of treatments that they had used alongside or instead of their ART, thus putting themselves at risk of treatment resistance and/or the impacts of adverse treatment interactions. While they had generally done this because they believed in the healing qualities of these other treatments, most of those concerned also admitted that they were willing to try anything in a desperate bid to try to cure themselves of the HIV virus. Holly, for example, explained how stopping her ART to try fasting, prayer and traditional medicines had resulted in her becoming resistant to two types of HIV treatment:

> I heard about this church where they tell you not to take medications, but to believe in God, he is the Creator and will heal you. So I went to this church and I fasted and I stopped the [ART] medications. I fasted seven days, no eating, nothing, just praying. Then I went to the hospital to see if I could have a test that would come back [HIV] negative. And you know, when it came back the doctor said to me that I had not been taking my medication. So I said, 'It's not gone then?' And she said, 'What do you mean, not gone? Where are you getting treatment from?' I told her and I was very upset because I felt I had just wasted my time. But I saw that it wasn't working, and instead you develop resistance

– and I have now got resistance to two – Nevirapine and Combavir – those tablets don't work with me any more. There is a witchcraft voodoo man who gave me herbs to boil and drink and some solution to rub on your body but that didn't work. Then I went to another one who gave me a medicine that is very bitter, but I can't take it as I just throw up. I've gone to a lot of traditional healers, even Chinese healers, but nothing seems to work. (Holly, South Africa)

Susan relayed a similar treatment seeking narrative. Diagnosed HIV positive during routine antenatal testing, she began intense prayer and long periods of fasting over the course of a year. When her ill-health escalated and she continued to test positive for HIV she turned to African herbal medicines, sent to her by her relatives in Zimbabwe. As she hadn't told her relatives of her HIV status, her family suspected that she had been bewitched so sent treatments that they thought would help with this. Susan then consulted a spiritual healer in Zimbabwe who sent her further treatments. When this did not work, she went to an African healer in the UK who took her to the coast to cleanse her in the sea. By this time, her immune system was very much weakened and she finally started adhering to her ART. However, when interviewed, Susan was also in the process of trying to acquire other herbal medicines from social networks in the UK and Africa to take alongside the ART.

Interviews revealed that few informants had told their HIV clinicians about their use, or intended use of these other treatments and therapies (for a more detailed discussion of these issues see Thomas et al., 2010b). Three key reasons were given for this: first, informants explained that their doctors had not asked them about it or had only done so at their first appointment. As such, they either did not consider that it would matter or did not feel comfortable 'wasting' the doctor's time with such information. Second, informants reported that they were embarrassed about using these treatments as they felt that their HIV practitioners would consider them irresponsible and foolish both for using treatments that they would deem inferior to more advanced biomedical treatments and, at the same time, risking the effectiveness of the ART. Third, several patients reported that they did not want to discuss these non-biomedical treatments in case their doctor advised them to stop using them. It was explained that such a situation would pose a dilemma to a patient who did not want to upset their doctor, yet at the same time, was not willing to give up the treatments that they had placed considerable faith in. In all such cases, therefore, the difficulties that people felt that they faced discussing their treatment with their doctors put them in a position where their health outcomes risked being compromised.

Conclusion

It is now widely recognised that structural inequalities associated with a person's immigration status can adversely impact on a migrant's ability to access healthcare and support. However, this chapter has argued that in order to more fully understand the healthcare issues affecting migrants, it is important to also consider the different ways in which migrants from diverse backgrounds may interpret and seek to respond to their ill-health within their own cognitive and epistemological frameworks of understanding. Doing this in turn involves recognition that some migrants may *choose* to opt out of formal healthcare services, and seek support from alternative sources that lie outside the bounds of biomedical healthcare. This study found that many of those using non-biomedical treatments and therapies held them in high esteem, and that their familiarity, their perceived safety and their origins with well known and trusted sources could provide a level of comfort and reassurance that they had not found – or did not feel that they would be able to find – via the NHS.

At the same time, however, the study also found that the use of such treatments and therapies could also have potentially adverse consequences on individual and public health, particularly if they interfered with personalised and necessarily precise ART regimes. A major issue raised was the reluctance of respondents to divulge their use of such treatments to formal healthcare practitioners for fear of being deemed irresponsible, foolish and ungrateful, and the possibility of having the treatments taken away from them.

Such a situation raises important issues regarding the assumed hegemony of biomedicine and points clearly to the need for healthcare practitioners and service providers to acknowledge the existence of wider interpretations of health and wellbeing, and to ensure that patients feel able to discuss their use of 'alternative' treatments without fear of criticism or rebuke.

Notes

1 Most Zimbabwean participants came from Matabeleland, and most South Africans from KwaZulu Natal.

2 In most cases this happened when women underwent routine HIV testing while pregnant or while trying to get pregnant.

References

Ashforth, A. (2005) *Witchcraft, Violence, and Democracy in South Africa*, University of Chicago Press, Chicago.

Broom, A. and J. Adams (2009) 'Oncology clinicians' accounts of discussing complementary and alternative medicine with their patients', *Health*, 13: 317–36.

Bury, M. (1982) 'Chronic illness as biographical disruption', *Sociology of Health and Illness*, 4(2): 167–82.

Cant, S. and U. Sharma (1999) *A New Medical Pluralism? Alternative Medicine, Doctors, Patients and the State*, Routledge, London.

Cohen, D., M. McCubbin, J. Collin and G. Pérodeau (2001) 'Medications as social phenomena', *Health*, 5: 441–69.

Del Casino, V. J. (2004) '(Re)placing health and health care: Mapping the competing discourses and practices of "traditional" and "modern" Thai medicine', *Health and Place*, 10: 59–73.

Doyal, L. and J. Anderson (2005) '"My fear is to fall in love again…" How HIV-positive African women survive in London', *Social Science and Medicine*, 60: 1729–38.

Farmer, P. (1992) *AIDS and Accusation: Haiti and the Geography of Blame*, University of California Press, Berkeley.

Garro, L. C. and C. Mattingly (2000) 'Narrative as construct and construction', in C. Mattingly and L. C. Garro (eds) *Narrative and the Cultural Construction of Illness and Healing*, University of California Press, Berkeley: 1–49.

Helman, C. G. (2007) *Culture, Health and Illness*, Hodder Arnold, London.

HPA (Health Protection Agency) (2008) *Sexually Transmitted Infections in Black African and Black Caribbean Communities in the UK: 2008 Report*, HPA, London.

— (2010) *HIV in the United Kingdom: 2010 Report*, Health Protection Report, 4(47), 26 November, HPA, London.

Johnson, A. M., C. H. Mercer and J. A. Cassell (2006) 'Social determinants, sexual behaviour, and sexual health', in M. Marmot and R. G. Wilkinson (eds) *Social Determinants of Health*, Oxford University Press, Oxford: 318–40.

Kelley, N. and J. Stevenson (2006) *First Do No Harm: Denying Healthcare to People Whose Asylum Claims Have Failed*, Refugee Council, London.

Kesby, M., K. Fenton, P. Boyle and R. Power (2003) 'An agenda for future research on HIV and sexual behaviour among African migrant communities in the UK', *Social Science and Medicine*, 57: 1573–92.

Kleinman, A. (1988) *The Illness Narratives: Suffering, Healing and the Human Condition*, Basic Books, New York.

Körner, H. (2007) '"If I had my residency I wouldn't worry": Negotiating migration and HIV in Sydney, Australia', *Ethnicity and Health*, 12(3): 205–25.

Mattingly, C. (1994) 'The concept of therapeutic "emplotment"', *Social Science and Medicine*, 38: 811–22.

Mills, E., V. Montori, D. Perri, E. Phillips and G. Koren (2005) 'Natural health product-HIV drug interactions: A systematic review', *International Journal of STD & AIDS*, 16: 181–6.

Mogensen, H. O. (1997) 'The narrative of AIDS amongst the Tonga of Zambia', *Social Science and Medicine*, 44(4): 431–9.

— (2005) 'Finding a path through the heath unit: Practical experience of Ugandan patients', *Medical Anthropology*, 24: 209–36.

Peltzer, K., N. Friend-du-Preez, S. Ramlagan and H. Fomundam (2008) 'Use of traditional complementary and alternative medicine for HIV patients in KwaZulu-Natal, South Africa', *BMC Public Health*, 8: 255–69.

Schumaker, L. L. and L. L. Bond (2008) 'Antiretroviral therapy in Zambia: Colours, "spoiling", "talk" and the meaning of antiretrovirals', *Social Science and Medicine*, 67: 2126–34.

Stekelenburg, J., B. E. Jager, P. R. Kolk, E. Westen, A. van der Kwaak and I. N. Wolffers (2005) 'Healthcare seeking behaviour and utilisation of traditional healers in Kalabo, Zambia', *Health Policy*, 71: 67–81.

Thomas, F. (2006) '"Our families are killing us": HIV/AIDS, witchcraft and social tensions in the Caprivi Region, Namibia', *Anthropology and Medicine*, 14(3): 279–91.

— (2008) 'Indigenous narratives of HIV/AIDS: Morality and blame in a time of change', *Medical Anthropology*, 27(3): 227–56.

— (2010) 'Transnational health and treatment networks: Meaning, value and place in health seeking amongst southern African migrants in London', Health and Place, 16(3): 606–12.

Thomas, F., P. Aggleton and J. Anderson (2010a) '"If I cannot access services then there is no need for me to test": The impacts of health service charges on HIV testing and treatment amongst migrants in England', *AIDS Care*, 22(4): 526–31.

— (2010b) '"Experts", "partners" and "fools": Exploring agency in HIV treatment seeking among African migrants in London', *Social Science and Medicine*, 70: 736–43.

Yamba, C. B. (1997) 'Cosmologies in turmoil: Witchfinding and AIDS in Chiawa, Zambia', *Africa*, 67(2): 200–23.

Yates, T., J. Crane and A. Burnett (2007) 'Rights and the reality of healthcare charging in the United Kingdom', *Medicine, Conflict and Survival*, 23(4): 297–304.

10 | Harnessing 'diasporic' medical mobilities

MEGHANN ORMOND

Mobilising 'diaspora' for development in the 'homeland'

Due to advances in transportation, communication technologies, trade liberalisation and circular migration, diasporic identity ceases to be nostalgically tied to a remote, fixed, ancestral 'homeland' and instead becomes a 'sense of being part of an on-going transnational network that includes the homeland not as something simply left behind but as a place of attachment in a contrapuntal modernity' (Clifford, 1997: 256). The potent economic and political impact of migrant diasporas on their 'homelands' – in the form of remittances, commercial investment, philanthropy and tourism – increasingly is being harnessed and mobilised by governmental and non-governmental bodies seeking to foster development. The sheer economic influence of migrant diasporas can be staggering. With 22 per cent of the Philippines' total labour force working overseas, for example, their remittances alone are responsible for generating 13 per cent of the country's GDP, such that they are relied upon as a 'foreign' source of 'aid' to the Philippines (Rafael, 1997: 268). Recognising this potential, national governments, like those of Mexico and India, began to revise their relationship to their sizeable emigrant populations starting in the 1990s, appealing to them as 'diasporas' with promises of greater political participation. This 'process of community formation' (Butler, 2001) establishes new official understandings of transnational belonging that seek to root 'de-territorialised' peoples' loyalties to a 'homeland', wherever they may be.

While transnational community bonds are forged in multiple ways between people and their places of origin, I seek here to explore how bonds can be generated through healthcare. World-class private medical care facilities are developing in many migrants' countries of origin and have their sights set on attracting middle-class patient-consumers from higher income countries and retaining their own domestic elite in the habit of turning to higher income countries for their healthcare needs. At the same time, migrant diasporas frequently have been pegged as the 'natural' markets for and 'ambassadors' to the high quality healthcare increasingly available in these places, touted as a group representing significant opportunity to burgeoning national medical tourism industries as both healthcare consumers and producers. This situation complicates the sorts of questions we have traditionally asked in studies of migration and health by drawing attention to the frequently complicated relationships between migrants and their places of origin: how different is a migrant returning 'home' for medical treatment from a 'complete foreigner' going abroad to pursue care in the same place?

The ethicist Charis Thompson has distinguished *medical tourism*, 'with its emphasis on the movement of empowered, biosocial citizens ... seeking medical care by travelling down scientific, regulatory and/or economic gradients', from *medical migrations*, those 'movements across regional and national boundaries in ways relating to health status and care and to immigration ... status and the freedom from various kinds of persecution' (Thompson, 2008: 435). Yet, the contrast she draws between tourism and migration 'superficially supposes a dichotomy separating the savvy, self-regulating patient-consumer capable of transcending and rendering irrelevant the bonds of the nation-state, on the one hand, from the dejectedly displaced for whom those bonds constitute significant obstacles, on the other' (Ormond, 2011: 148). Migrants' varied pursuits of healthcare in their places of settlement and of origin – where these elements of choice and escape are often intimately intertwined – demonstrate that the proposed distinction between 'medical tourism' and 'medical migration' is far from clear-cut.

In the pages that follow, I explore the potential of medical tourism practices and industry representations to constitute and deepen linkages between migrants and their 'homelands'. By drawing predominantly from examples in two countries promoting themselves as medical tourism destinations, India and the Philippines, I look at how migrants of Indian and Filipino origin are being strategically reimagined as belonging to national 'diasporas' and selectively enjoined to contribute to the development of their places of origin as both healthcare consumers and producers and as both citizens and noncitizens. I identify three main ways in which healthcare is being used to link these migrant diasporas with their places of origin: by capitalising on structural inequalities that constitute obstacles to care within migrants' places of settlement, by making culturally based claims to diasporas as their 'natural' markets, and by benefiting from the cultural hybridity of 'their' diasporas to connect with new markets for private healthcare in both places of settlement and of origin.

Capitalising on structural inequalities

Work on migrant health has tended to focus on structural limitations to equitable access to medical care in places of settlement. More recently, authors (e.g. Dyck and Dossa, 2007; Elliot and Gillie, 1998) have drawn attention to migrant agency in (re)fashioning healthy lifestyles and wellbeing practices for themselves and their families in ways that expand the horizons of care-pursuit by acknowledging that migrants' health practices are often transnational composites, generated through the use of health systems and practices in both places of settlement and of origin.

Though little is quantitatively known about migrants' 'return' to their 'homelands' for healthcare,[1] it is frequently assumed that motivation to seek care 'back home' is a response to the failures of health systems in places of settlement to accommodate the needs of migrants, who are either discursively framed as 'alienated' from or as failing to sufficiently 'adapt' to the dominant healthcare systems in place (Elliot and Gillie, 1998). As such, the pursuit of care in places of origin, thought to piggyback on regular return visits 'home' (Bergmark et al., 2008), is often celebrated for providing migrants the opportunity to receive greater family support, access cheaper medications and (more familiar approaches to) treatment, directly contact specialists, benefit from facilitated communication with health workers, access a broader range of traditional medicinal practices and bypass certain forms of discrimination.

Migration status and socio-economic factors are central to determining the frequency with which migrants are able to return to their countries of origin for care – if they can do so at all. Bergmark et al. (ibid.: 4) find that for Mexican migrants living far from the US/ Mexico border, returning to Mexico is 'a major decision due to the distance, time, cost, and possible legal ramifications of the trip ... The benefits of returning to Mexico tend to outweigh these challenges only in cases of severe illness or crisis.' Horton and Cole (2011), meanwhile, demonstrate that private clinics along the US/Mexican border have relatively localised catchments. They argue that this produces an out-of-pocket 'border culture of medicine' that offers a range of services and treatments specifically suited to the needs and incomes of first and second generation Latinos requiring effective and efficient treatment so that they can quickly return to their work and care responsibilities in the US. Entitlement to healthcare access in migrants' countries of settlement depends on their legal status and the varied labour protection and welfare regimes within those places. In countries where private healthcare insurance coverage is the norm, high premiums, co-payments and deductibles are prohibitive to many of those who can manage to qualify for insurance, leading some who could have coverage to remain uninsured and instead return to their countries of origin for more affordable care when necessary, leaving them susceptible in their places of settlement.

With the stated objective being 'to make healthcare affordable and accessible for all' (Diaspora.mx, 2010), the North American-based medical travel facilitator Planet Hospital has developed 'Diaspora', a 'medical tourism-based' insurance product for migrant groups in the US who encounter difficulty in qualifying or paying for private health insurance. It aims to target millions of Mexican, El Salvadoran and Filipino migrant workers by offering accident coverage within the US and, taking advantage of and fostering their temporary visits 'back home', full healthcare coverage in select medical facilities in their countries of origin for non-emergency treatment. Employing revolutionary style aesthetics, Diaspora's website reads:

> You saved me money when my healthcare options were expensive. You saved my life because you will not deny me care. You saved me from despair when I was being denied care because of pre-existing conditions. You saved me from humiliation because I can proudly say I will not be treated as an indigent at any hospital in the world in case I get sick or injured.

The provision, pursuit and receipt of healthcare in one's country of origin through Diaspora gets framed as a demonstration of identity, attachment and commitment – a 'political act of engagement' (Blunt, 2007: 690) that binds migrants to their countries of origin and to a broader sense of diasporic community derived from resistance to systems perceived to inadequately respond to them in their places of settlement.

Claiming diaspora as the 'natural' market for cultural reasons

A growing number of studies have begun to counter the common perception that cost constitutes the main factor in migrants' pursuit of healthcare in their countries of origin. Embracing the neoliberal privilege of 'shopping around' for the best quality service, Rajeev and Latif (2009) find that many non-resident Indians (NRIs) with more secure migration and employment status in the US than other migrants, for example, opt for healthcare in India as a direct result of their dissatisfaction with care in the US. Expectations of 'cultural competence' and familiarity appear to shape 'better resourced' migrants' decisions to return to their countries of origin for healthcare. Horton and Cole

(2011) suggest that migrant patient-consumers seek out particular 'cultures of medicine' that they deem more 'authentic', desiring and – in the process – reifying the competence of 'their' peoples to provide more responsive care that satisfies their diverse linguistic, religious and dietary requirements than what they have received in their places of settlement. First generation Korean migrants living in New Zealand who travel to Korea for care experience the return to Korea as 'especially therapeutic' (Lee et al., 2010: 110) and Thai migrant women married to Western men who return to Thailand for in vitro fertilisation (IVF) seek care 'at home', though the urban clinics they use are far from their families' villages (Whittaker, 2009). 'Home' comes to signify familiarity with the health systems in their 'homelands', expectations of medical authority and patient handling, proximity to family and friends and the lack of linguistic barriers that both comfort and empower.

In medical tourism destinations, entrepreneurs are slowly recognising the benefits of responding to the healthcare needs of 'their' migrant diasporas. Commonly perceived – though, as Duval (2004) suggests, not unproblematically – as being more 'at home' when visiting their places of origin, migrant diasporas are held to spend their money in ways that differ from 'completely foreign' tourists and are thought to require less 'insulating intermediation' to mitigate 'otherness' (Newland and Taylor, 2010; Scheyvens, 2007). The repeat nature of their visits generates more stable in-flows that are less affected by seasonality and less volatile at times of economic and political crisis. Furthermore, in that they often have a deeper reach into areas not visited by 'completely foreign' tourists and a greater tendency to consume local goods and services, revenue from their visits is more likely to be absorbed by local communities and less prone to economic leakages.

Health and tourism stakeholders in the Philippines currently rely predominantly on return visits by overseas Filipino workers (OFWs) to sustain their budding national medical tourism industry. A representative from the Department of Health's medical tourism programme asserts that:

Unlike other countries, the Philippines has its natural market. It is not relying on foreign patients, because the source of constant and sustainable growth for the industry is the OFWs, or the Filipinos residing and working abroad … [R]egardless if foreigners come in the Philippines or not to seek medical help, the medical tourism industry will still grow because we have growing OFWs who prefer to get medical attention in their homeland. (Calibo, in Dagooc, 12 January 2010)

Given the Philippines' substantial diaspora, Rafael (1997: 269) suggests that 'overseas Filipinos now increasingly represent novel elements in local understandings of "cultural transformations" and "national development". Their absence becomes an integral feature of vernacular narratives regarding what it means to be modern' within the Philippines itself. Because OFWs' permanent residence abroad means that their 'appearance in the Philippines is temporary and intermittent, as if one were a tourist' (ibid.: 270), the country's medical tourism strategy treats *balikbayans* (overseas Filipinos who [represent an economic] 'return to the nation') as 'medical tourists' – as 'natural' *customers* of private healthcare in the Philippines – instead of as full-fledged *citizens* with entitlements to its healthcare system (Ormond, 2011). Their return for care translates as targeted 'remittances' used to build up private healthcare to 'world-class' standards and employ Filipino medical professionals in the job scarce country. At the same time, this faith in OFWs as the core medical tourism market has been framed as a barrier to providing care to non-Filipinos (Porter et al., 2008: 15). With marketing and infrastructure narrowly focused on diasporic Filipinos who speak the national languages and are presumed to be able to turn to family members in the country for support, services for 'complete foreigners' (e.g. interpretation and personal assistants), which are common among other Southeast Asian medical tourism destinations, consequently are underdeveloped in the Philippines.

Though India attracts a larger proportion of international medical travellers beyond its diaspora than the Philippines, attempts are being made to tap the 'natural' market of NRIs (Indian passport holders who live overseas) as well as people of Indian origin (people overseas who do not hold Indian passports but are children and grandchildren of Indian citizens – PIOs). Like *balikbayans* in the Philippines, members of the Indian diaspora are considered 'medical tourists', charged the same as 'complete foreigners' and not entitled to government funded healthcare. Authors such as Pandey et al. (2004) are keen to see India cash in on the healthcare needs of its millions-strong diaspora spread around the globe. Special services are increasingly geared towards NRIs' presumed tight schedules and high expectations (Kaur et al., 2007: 418). The quickly developing Indian state of Gujarat (out of which an estimated third of the total Indian diaspora is thought to come), for example, seeks to benefit from the wealth of Gujarati NRIs by fostering transnational linkages that develop stronger diasporic identity with Gujarat specifically and encourage investment and spending in it. Among these initiatives are healthcare provider networks that link up the significant number of 'wealthy' Gujarati NRIs living in North America, the UK and East Africa with Gujarati doctors in India (Express News Service, 2007):

> [A]s cash-rich Gujarati NRIs fly home for medical treatment, doctors and hospitals are wooing them with packages, including deluxe accommodation and even English-speaking cab drivers. Doctors are organizing sight-seeing itineraries and beauty treatments for the patients, in addition to giving them attractive discounts for treatment. Along with the guarantee of excellent treatment, they also enjoy the homecoming in November, December and January — also known as the NRI season here. (Bhattacharya, 2008: 8)

This hospitality extended to Gujarat's non-Gujarati and non-Hindi speaking diaspora contrasts with assumptions in the Philippines about *balikbayans'* 'natural' cultural knowledge and affinity with their homeland. It makes apparent the work being done to not only renew but also forge diasporic relationships with politically defined, territorially based communities where they did not necessarily exist before.

Using 'their' diaspora as a bridge to access new markets around the globe

Medical tourism is increasingly used as an 'important piece of armour' for postcolonial governments to articulate 'new imaginary essences of place and a new diversity in the possibilities of collective/ national being' (Hollinshead, 2004: 33). This emancipatory enthusiasm locates agency in the recognition and mobilisation of 'their' subject's cultural hybridity, which opens up a strategic in between space of multiplicity, overlap and negotiation useful for the elaboration of 'strategies of selfhood – singular or communal – ... and innovative sites of collaboration, and contestation' within a mobile world (Bhabha, 2004: 12–13). Below I briefly explore how the hybridity of diasporic healthcare consumers and producers gets used to enter new markets and expand existing ones. I argue that migrant diasporas are increasingly enjoined to serve as – or are inadvertently co-opted into the role of – 'ambassadors' both for and within their places of origin (Edwards, 2008).

Consumption Since medical tourism largely relies on word-of-mouth, migrant diasporic patient-consumers are highly valued as 'early adopters' who serve as test subjects and pass on news of their experiences to others in their places of settlement and of origin (Bhattacharya, 2008: 7). In the case of Planet Hospital's 'Diaspora' project described earlier, for example, the structural barriers to healthcare produced by poor socioeconomic status in the US are – though undeniably exacerbated by immigration status – shared by millions of lower and middle income non-migrants living there. For this reason, and because it has so far proven difficult to convince 'complete foreigners' to pursue their healthcare needs abroad, migrant diasporas are increasingly viewed within the industry as key to helping medical tourism take root in their places of origin (Cohen, 2010). They are presumed to be familiar with healthcare services in both their places of settlement and of origin and, thus, to be able to move between these systems more easily than 'complete foreigners'. Furthermore, their comparatively higher incomes and non-resident status in their countries of origin means they can, or must, seek out private healthcare as consumers and not as citizens. Their consumption preferences get used to raise quality benchmarks 'back home' to the levels expected in their countries of settlement.

Recent studies (e.g. Adhikari et al., 2011) have explored how migration can both positively and negatively affect the health of those family members 'left behind'. While remittances enable those left behind to eat better and access previously inaccessible health services and medicines, they also risk dependency on remittances and lose out on personal support and care due to the distance that separates them. In the Philippines, where 60 per cent of families have at least one OFW parent (Santos, 2011), this is a particularly salient concern. In recognition of the continued centrality of family responsibility, special healthcare packages are now being promoted to OFWs and NRIs not for their own health but, rather, to permit them to ensure high quality care for family that has remained in the Philippines and India. The Philippines-based medical travel facilitator Contours (2011), for example, allows OFWs to 'sponsor' relatives in the Philippines, promising to 'extend the same treatment as if you were right here with them'. In India, Royal Medical Tours (Mumbai) Pvt Ltd (2011) offers a 'Parents Care Package' based on the premise that NRIs, spread throughout the world, 'are unable to attend [to] their parents' health problems to their own satisfaction'. NRIs are told that, by purchasing the package, they will be 'good children' committed to alleviating the 'burden' of care assumed by others who remain behind:

> You will make your parents feel that you really care for them. NRIs ... mostly depend on their relatives and neighbours to look after their parents. These relatives and neighbours do extend their support, but [this] has limitations because [they] too have their family problems, financial problems and many other problems beyond our imaginations. (ibid., 2011)

Tapping into the sense of guilt felt by many emigrants for leaving their families, this type of package permits OFWs and NRIs to demonstrate they are caring and competent providers to their families. It secures a way to watch over them from afar by being kept abreast of their family medical needs through routine reports from the contracted company. At the same time, it expands the market for high quality private sector healthcare domestically and further privatises care-giving.

Provision Diasporic health workers have gone from being perceived as 'a drain on national resources to a major export industry' (Harris Cheng, 2009: 111). The promotion of India and the Philippines as medical tourism destinations, for instance, hinges in no small measure on the two countries' extensive diasporas that figure prominently in medical professions throughout the world. Though constituting less than 0.6 per cent of the US population, for example, some 10 per cent of all medical students and 5 per cent of all practising doctors in the US are of Indian origin (Pandey et al., 2004). Meanwhile, more than 110,000 Filipino nurses are employed in OECD countries alone, with numbers rising in the Arab Gulf countries (OECD, 2007: 15). As a result, many Americans and Britons are used to Indian doctors, and Saudis and Emiratis are comfortable with care from Filipina nurses. The target market's familiarity at home with these countries' diasporas in healthcare delivery is frequently evoked in medical tourism promotion, drawing upon the 'brand equity' derived from them (Pandey et al., 2004: 26; Singh, 2009). While 'Filipino-ness', for example, gets mobilised 'outside the Philippines ... [by] caricatur[ing] the Filipino as caring and nurturing ... [to] facilitate access to healthcare, child-care and elder-care occupations overseas' (Kelly and Lusis, 2006: 843), medical tourism promoters also appropriate this 'mobile embodied cultural capital'. India and the Philippines are often cast as overflowing with skilled knowledge workers so expert in healthcare provision that they are 'deployed' to care for the world's most privileged populations. This promotional logic works to naturalise medical tourism destinations' claims to being able to provide the high quality service patient-consumers expect from their diasporas abroad, with the added bonus of lower medical costs in the countries of origin.

'Brain circulation' has been key for medical professionals from postcolonial countries to acquire the prestigious international experience and trans-cultural expertise that is proving essential to assuaging the concerns of international patient-consumers who seek assurance that they will receive the highest standards of care possible in a lower income country. With medical tourism increasingly recognised as a driver for economic development, some governments (e.g. India and Malaysia) are using it as justification for attracting overseas health workers back to their countries of origin (Bookman and Bookman, 2007; Mattoo and Rathindran, 2005; UNCTAD, 1997). They increasingly seek to invoke a sense of duty among returnees to contribute to the economic development of 'their homelands'. Drawing on valuable experience gained about foreign healthcare markets after years of working in Western, Arab and East Asian countries, entrepreneurial returnees can increasingly be seen setting up and revamping hospitals, clinics, eldercare facilities and medical educational institutions 'back home' (see e.g. Gamboa, 2011; Hazarika, 2010; Mullan, 2006). Their global business alliances are mobilised to thicken the transnational networks fundamental to medical tourism's success.

Conclusion

This chapter has sought to expand thinking about the ways in which 'familiarity' and 'belonging' are produced and deployed by places eager to align themselves with, and reap benefit from, the wealth, success and prestige of 'their' migrant diasporas in an ever globalising world. With their rich transnational experiences and networks, migrants are increasingly recognised as politically, economically and socially relevant to their places of origin. They are increasingly enjoined to consider themselves are part of 'diasporas' and to actively contribute to the development of their 'homelands' as both healthcare consumers and providers but not necessarily as citizens. This recognition has forged new relations of care and responsibility between these places and 'their' diasporas. The extension of healthcare to a 'nationalised trans-national' (Camroux, 2008) community seeks to ally migrant populations – particularly those living in higher income countries – with their places of origin in multiple and complex ways. Opening up to diasporic patient-consumers who cannot access or afford adequate healthcare in their places of settlement and who seek out more familiar 'cultures of medicine' may help to bolster a country of origin's moral author-ity, dispel old misconceptions, create goodwill and boost its overall reputation. Furthermore, turning to 'their' diasporas in times of global economic and political upheaval may help places of origin to sustain medical tourism flows and even increase international and domestic flows through word-of-mouth advertising. At the same time, places of origin are drawing on migrant diasporas' professional reputations and expertise, trans-cultural experience and transnational business linkages for brand recognition and improvement of service delivery and infrastructure that both suit the requirements of 'completely foreign' patient-consumers and raise the expectations of domestic ones.

Note

1 The sparse statistical information on international medical travel is marred by disagreement over how to define 'medical travellers' and quantify their consumption of medical care. Therefore, visits by migrant diasporas to their countries of origin for care frequently go largely undetected in statistics due to a persistently narrow focus on a universe of foreign passport holders that excludes non-resident nationals who still hold their countries' passports (Virola and Polistico, 2007).

References

Adhikari, R., A. Jampaklay and A. Chamratrithirong (2011) 'Impact of children's migration on health and healthcare-seeking behaviour of elderly left behind', *BMC Public Health*, 11: 143.

Bergmark, R., D. Barr and R. Garcia (2008) 'Mexican immigrants in the US living far from the border may return to Mexico for health services', *Journal of Immigrant and Minority Health*, DOI 10.1007/s10903-008-9213-8.

Bhabha, H. K. (2004) *The Location of Culture*, Routledge, London.

Bhattacharya, M. (2008) 'Advantage Gujarat in medical tourism', presented at Conference on Tourism in India – Challenges Ahead, Indian Institute of Management Kozhioke, India, 15–17 May, http://dspace.iimk.ac.in/handle/2259/581 (accessed 15 July 2011).

Blunt, A. (2007) 'Cultural geographies of migration: Mobility, transnationality and diaspora', *Progress in Human Geography*, 31(5): 684–94.

Bookman, M. Z. and K. R. Bookman (2007) *Medical Tourism in Developing Countries*, Palgrave Macmillan, New York.

Butler, K. (2001) 'Defining diaspora, refining a discourse', *Diaspora*, 10(1): 189–220.

Camroux, D. (2008) 'Nationalising transnationalism? The Philippine state and the Filipino diaspora', *Les Etudes du CERI*, 152, www.ceri-sciencespo.com/publica/etude/etude152.pdf.

Clifford, J. (1997) *Routes: Travel and Translation in the Late Twentieth Century*, Harvard University Press, Cambridge, MA.

Cohen, M. (2010) 'US reforms may boost medical tourism', *Asia Times Online*, 30 March, www.atimes.com/atimes/Southeast_Asia/LC30Ae01.html (accessed 15 July 2011).

Contours (2011) 'Who is the medical tourist?', http://contoursmedicaltourism.com/who-is-the-medical-tourist.html (accessed 15 July 2011).

Dagooc, E. M. (2010) 'Geographical concerns deter RP medical tourism growth', *The Philippine Star*, 12 January, www.philstar.com/Article.aspx?articleId=540119 (accessed 15 July 2011).

Diaspora.mx (2010) 'Diaspora you saved me', http://diaspora.mx/ (accessed 15 July 2011).

Duval, D. T. (2004) 'Conceptualizing return visits: A transnational perspective', in T. Coles and D.

Timothy (eds), *Tourism, Diasporas and Space: Travels to Promised Lands*, Routledge, London: 50–61.

Dyck, I. and P. Dossa (2007) 'Place, health and home: Gender and migration in the constitution of healthy space', *Health and Place*, 13: 691–701.

Edwards, K. (2008) 'For a geohistorical cosmopolitanism: Postcolonial state strategies, cosmopolitan communities and the production of the "British", "Overseas", "Non-Resident" and "Global" Indian', *Environment and Planning D: Society and Space*, 26: 444–63.

Elliot, S. J. and J. Gillie (1998) 'Moving experiences: A qualitative analysis of health and migration', *Health and Place*, 4(4): 327–39.

Express News Service (2007) 'Soon, docs from State to care for NRI patients', *Ahmedabad Newsline*, 25 March, http://cities. express india.com/fullstory.php? newsid= 228280 (accessed 15 July 2011).

Gamboa, R. (2011) 'Getting ready for One ASEAN', *The Philippine Star*, 30 May, www.philstar.com/ Article.aspx?articleId=691100& publicationSubCategoryId=66 (accessed 15 July 2011).

Harris Cheng, M. (2009) 'The Philippines' health worker exodus', *The Lancet*, 373(9658), 10 January: 11 –112.

Hazarika, I. (2010) 'Medical tourism: Its potential impact on the health workforce and health systems in India', *Health Policy Planning*, 25(3): 248–51.

Hollinshead, K. (2004) 'Tourism and new sense: Worldmaking and the enunciative value of tourism', in C. M. Hall and H. Tucker (eds) *Tourism and Postcolonialism: Contested Discourses, Identities and Representations*, Routledge, London: 25–42.

Horton, S. and S. Cole (2011) 'Medical returns: Seeking healthcare in Mexico', *Social Science and Medicine*, 72: 1846–52.

Kaur, J., G. Sundar, D. Vaidya and S. Bhargava (2007) 'Health tourism in India: Growth and opportunities', presented at International Conference on Marketing and Society, Indian Institute of Management, Kozhikode, India, 10 April, http://dspace.iimk.ac.in/ handle/2259/345 (accessed 15 July 2011).

Kelly, P. and T. Lusis (2006) 'Migration and the transnational habitus: Evidence from Canada and the Philippines', *Environment and Planning A*, 38: 831–47.

Lee, J. Y. N., R. Kearns and W. Friesen (2010) 'Seeking affective healthcare: Korean immigrants' use of homeland medical services', *Health and Place*, 16(1): 108–15.

Mattoo, A. and R. Rathindran (2005) 'Does health insurance impede trade in healthcare services?', *World Bank Policy Research Working Paper*, WPS 3667, World Bank, Washington DC.

Mullan, F. (2006) 'Doctors for the world: Indian physician emigration', *Health Affairs*, March/April: 380–93.

Newland, K. and C. Taylor (2010) 'Heritage tourism and nostalgia trade: A diaspora niche in the development landscape', Diasporas and Development Policy Project, USAID/Migration Policy Group, September, www.migrationpolicy. org/pubs/diasporas-tradetourism. pdf (accessed 15 July 2011).

OECD (Organisation for Economic Co-operation and Development)

(2007) 'Immigrant health workers in OECD countries in the broader context of highly skilled migration', *Sopemi International Migration Outlook*, OECD, Paris.

Ormond, M. (2011) 'Medical tourism, medical exile: Responding to the cross-border pursuit of healthcare in Malaysia', in C. Minca and T. Oakes (eds) *Real Tourism: Practice, Care and Politics in Contemporary Travel*, Routledge, London: 143–61.

Pandey, A., A. Aggarwal, R. Devane and Y. Kuznetsov (2004) 'India's transformation to knowledge-based economy – evolving role of the Indian diaspora', Evaluserve, 21 July, http://info.worldbank. org/etools/docs/library/152386/ abhishek.pdf (accessed 15 July 2011).

Porter, M. E., M. De Vera, B. Huang, O. Khan, Z. Qin and A. Tan (2008) 'Medical tourism in the Philippines: Microeconomics of competitiveness – Firms, clusters and economic development', 2 May, www.isc.hbs.edu/pdf/ Student_Projects/Philippine_ Medical_Tourism_2008.pdf (accessed 15 July 2011).

Rafael, V. L. (1997) '"Your grief is our gossip": Overseas Filipinos and other spectral presences', *Public Culture*, 9: 267–91.

Rajeev, A. and S. Latif (2009) 'Study of the knowledge, attitude and experience of medical tourism among target groups with special emphasis on South India', *Online Journal of Health and Allied Sciences*, 8(2).

Royal Medical Tours (Mumbai) Pvt Ltd (2011) 'Parents care package', www.medicaltourindia.com/ parents-health-care-package.asp (accessed 15 July 2011).

Santos, K. (2011) 'Philippines: Healing for children left behind', WFS Philippines, 4 May, http:// wfstest.weebly.com/1/post/2011/05/ philippineshealing-for-children-left-behind.html (accessed 15 July 2011).

Scheyvens, R. (2007) 'Poor cousins no more: Valuing the development potential of domestic and diaspora tourism', *Progress in Development Studies*, 7(4): 307–25.

Singh, G. (2009) 'Top Indian hospitals woo medical tourism from Canada', *Overseas Indian*, 21 November, http://overseasindian. in/2009/nov/news/20092111-103515. shtml (accessed 15 July 2011).

Thompson, C. (2008) 'Medical tourism, stem cells, genomics: EASTS, transnational STS and the contemporary life sciences', *East Asian Science, Technology and Society: An International Journal*, 2: 433–38.

UNCTAD (United Nations Conference on Trade and Development) (1997) 'International trade in health services: Difficulties and opportunities for developing countries', presented at Trade and Development Board – Commission on Trade in Goods and Services, and Commodities and Expanding Exports of Developing Countries in the Services Sector: Health Services, Geneva, 16–18 June.

Virola, R. A. and F. S. Polistico (2007) 'Measuring health and wellness tourism in the Philippines', paper presented at 56th Session of the International Statistical Institute, Lisbon, 22–29 August.

Whittaker, A. (2009) 'Global technologies and transnational reproduction in Thailand', *Asian Studies Review*, 33(3): 319–32.

11 | Access versus entitlements: health seeking for Latin American migrants in London[1]

JASMINE GIDEON

Introduction

The importance of understanding the complexities around migration and health and in particular migrants' access to healthcare has recently been reiterated in a report by WHO and the IOM (WHO/IOM, 2010). The multiple barriers that migrants can face when they seek healthcare services are well documented (Hargreaves and Friedland, this volume). At the same time one of the greatest challenges remains how far a state's human rights commitments vis-à-vis the right to health extend to migrants. It is often more vulnerable migrants who are unable to access formal healthcare services yet they are most likely to lack a voice and understand what their legal entitlements are in the host country or even during transit. While high income migrants may be able to enjoy the benefits of portability schemes that facilitate the transfer of social protection and social rights between host country and country of origin, this is not an option for the majority of migrants, particularly those who are engaged in more precarious forms of work. Indeed, at present only 23 per cent of migrants worldwide are able to enjoy access to and portability of social rights (Avato et al., 2010: 456). Yet even where migrants do have entitlements to specific social rights in the host country there may be a series of informal barriers that limit their access in other ways.

This chapter examines the case of Latin American migrants in London and focuses on their health seeking behaviour. While a significant proportion of Latin American migrants are undocumented, respondents in this study were all documented and had entitlements to use the NHS. Nevertheless, as the chapter demonstrates, many felt unable to resolve their health problems through the NHS, instead preferring to engage in a series of alternative health seeking strategies. Moreover, as the chapter argues, many of these strategies also depended on transnational networks – as a source of information, as a means of sending medication or for arranging healthcare back in Latin America. The chapter concludes that many Latin American migrants are being pushed towards more informal and precarious means of securing healthcare because of the barriers they face in securing their entitlements to health. This has important implications for long term health inequalities as well as the health and wellbeing of individuals.

Latin American migrants in the UK

Latin Americans have been identified as a 'new migrant population' in the UK and arrive through a number of channels and hold a variety of different statuses. More recently many are entering the UK via Spain and Portugal, further complicating attempts to provide realistic data on the size of the population. Reliable official statistics for the size of the Latin population in the UK do not yet exist since the 2001 census on which official monitoring forms are based did not include Latin American as an ethnic category. Current estimates range between 700,000 and 1 million (McIlwaine et al., 2011: 16). Latin American migration to the UK is mainly for economic reasons and is predominantly female. The UK Latino population is concentrated in London, largely located in four boroughs – two in the north of the city and two in the south.

As a consequence of not being officially monitored, Latinos are marginalised by UK public services and mainstream society (Carlisle, 2006: 237). Moreover they lack a voice in UK public discourse and are not able to vote in UK elections (in contrast for example to migrants from Commonwealth countries) (Peró, 2008). Their marginalisation is further exacerbated by the fact that the majority of the population group tend to be employed in low skilled and low paid jobs, regardless of their gender, educational attainments and previous experience in their country of origin (McIlwaine, 2008).

Migrants' access to NHS services in the UK

Within the UK there is considerable variation in legislation regarding health service access between England, Scotland, Wales and Northern Ireland. In England, access to free NHS care is determined both by the level of care sought (primary versus secondary) as well as the residency status of the individual seeking care. Access to primary care remains at the 'discretion of the GP' although many primary care trusts (PCTs) have issued guidance to GP surgeries advising them to not register people not deemed 'ordinarily resident' in the UK. In practice 'informal' rules are often applied by practice managers and receptionists who make decisions about who can and cannot register. At the same time, many GPs report increased pressure of work resulting from patients who cannot speak English and who may manifest multiple problems, with health only representing part of the broader social problems. GPs and other health workers are often unsure about migrants' entitlements to health (Feldman, 2006: 810).

A recent report on the wellbeing of the Latin American population in London found that out of 1,000 respondents, around 20 per cent had never been to a GP practice. Brazilians and Bolivians were predominantly those who were least likely to have used a GP and they are the population groups that are most likely to be undocumented (McIlwaine et al., 2011).

Migration, gendered vulnerability and ill-health

Migrants face a diverse range of risks, particularly to their health and wellbeing, throughout the migratory process and these may vary according to whether they are in their country of origin, in transit or once in their destination. Yet gendered norms and values can mean that female migrants may be doubly disadvantaged, both as women and as migrants. Exposure to risks can impact negatively on migrants' physical and mental health. According to Carballo and Mboup (2005: 5), 'The relationship between psychosocial wellbeing and physical health is a close one and in the context of migration is often confounded by cultural differences in the ways people think of health and health care.'

The migratory process introduces a range of threats to psychosocial health and wellbeing – including the decision to move itself and the implications of having to leave family behind. The growing tendency for partners not to be able to move together and the need to leave children behind can create high levels of stress for families. Divorce rates among migrant populations tend to be higher than in host populations and this can impact most negatively on women, particularly where their job opportunities are limited and social status may be tied to marriage and family (ibid.: 5). Where women's entry status is dependent on their husbands this can also create tensions and lead to problems that impact on women's health. Immigration status can be used a source of power and control, especially between conjugal partners with victims unable to report abuse because of fear of being deported (Carlisle, 2006). This has implications for both the physical and mental health and wellbeing of women, yet their access to support services may be limited. Anxiety and home sickness can become chronic when not treated and present serious implications for mental health and wellbeing, including depression and other stress-related disorders such as ulcers, migraines and disabling back pain (Carballo and Mboup, 2005: 5). The WHO/IOM report notes that stress-related conditions are an increasing burden on migrant populations and impose considerable demands on the health systems of destination countries (2010: 116).

Changes in roles and responsibilities can occur as a result of migration and these can pose new challenges to women and men and at times contribute to intra-household conflict and therefore impact negatively on individuals' psychosocial health. In addition, the distance between respective social positions enjoyed in the country of origin and destination can act as determinant of poor mental health (Llácer et al., 2007). It is common for economic migrants to undergo a considerable degree of deskilling, as is predominantly the case for Latin American migrants in the UK (McIlwaine, 2008). This has posed particular challenges to Latin American men who not only feel their male roles are being undermined by having to take on 'female work' but also undergo considerable deskilling to work in these jobs (ibid.: 16).

Migrants' living conditions once they reach their point of destination can also create additional stresses and pose a challenge to an individual's psychosocial health and wellbeing. In a study of Peruvian migrants in London, Wright (2011) found that the majority of respondents lived in inner city areas typified by overcrowding and high levels of crime and violence. While women and men are both vulnerable, women may be more likely to feel at risk especially when, for example, many Latin American migrants work as cleaners, often having to be at work in the early hours of the morning when public transport opportunities are limited. Moreover, Latin American migrants' housing in London tends to be dispersed rather than concentrated in one area, meaning that many feel isolated and lacking in support networks. These factors all impacted negatively on the respondents' psychosocial health and wellbeing.

Insecure working conditions among immigrant workers also pose important health challenges. A European study has shown that occupational accidents are almost twice as likely to occur among immigrant workers as in host populations (Bollini and Siem, 1995, cited in Carballo and Mboup, 2005). Yet at the same time research has shown that the health risks posed by precarious forms of employment are gendered (Menéndez et al., 2007). Women's gendered identity has been central to the international drive towards cheaper labour and higher productivity, meaning that they are more likely to be located in low status, low quality forms of work where their exposure to risk is often greater than men's working in the same industry. Other studies have pointed to the linkages between the gender division of labour, women's 'double day' and occupational health concerns. Women employed in particular types of work that may be highly monotonous can experience greater stress loads then men where they are also combining paid work with unpaid work (Artacoz et al., 2004; Borrell et al., 2004). Given the precarious lives that many migrants lead and that they are more likely to be employed in low paid, low status work than host populations, this raises particular cause for concern.

Migrants' access to healthcare services

Migrant status is critical in determining individuals' and their dependants' access to healthcare services. Yet even where migrants do have entitlements to use healthcare services, access can often depend on meeting other criteria. Using health services requires considerable work on the part of people since they have to mobilise a range of resources, including knowledge and information resources, social, language and support resources, and practical resources (Dixon-Woods et al., 2005: 7). Migrants may be particularly disadvantaged in their access to these resources and this has clear implications for addressing inequalities. In practice both formal and informal rules are in operation and access to services is highly dependent on a migrant's ability to negotiate both of these sets of rules (Sabates-Wheeler and MacAuslan, 2007). Moreover, as feminist critics have argued, such rules are often gender biased and do not accommodate the needs of 'new players' (Goetz, 1997).

Migrant groups are a diverse population with very different health needs and will experience different barriers to accessing healthcare. A common finding is that migrants may have particular cultural values and expectations associated with health systems. Several studies of Latin American migrants have noted how migrants express dissatisfaction with the type of care they receive and the inadequacy of the 'paracetamol treatment' they receive (Días et al., 2010; Hilfinger Messias, 2002; Pylpa, 2001).

The role of transnational networks and health seeking behaviour

The role of social networks in determining health outcomes has been widely discussed within the health literature (Kawachi et al., 1999). An extensive body of literature has also highlighted the importance of social capital and networks among migrant communities, both in country of origin and at destination. However, the majority of this literature has tended to focus on the economic role of networks, particularly their role in transmitting remittances back to countries of origin and their importance in helping migrants secure employment in destination countries. A small number of studies has specifically highlighted the importance of social networks among Latin American migrant groups in the US (Gurman and Becker, 2008; Menjívar, 2002) and Spain (Escandell and Tapias, 2010) for securing treatment for health problems. The studies highlight the ways in which a range of health practices, including formal and informal services, as well as biomedical and traditional practices are incorporated into transnational health treatment networks. Thomas (2010) argues that the existence of such networks serves to challenge implicit assumptions about the unidirectional flow of medical knowledge and treatments from the North to South. Moreover, networks play an essential role in supporting migrants in decision-making around health, which 'are often complex and draw upon a range of influences beyond the "biomedical"' (ibid.: 607).

Networks have been found to be essential for survival in London among Latin American migrants, yet at the same time social networks were highly fragmented (McIlwaine et al., 2011). Moreover, networks can offer both advantages and disadvantages to migrants in relation to their health and wellbeing. Escandell and Tapias (2010) have shown how Bolivian migrants in Spain rely on certain relatives to access transnational healing methods while at the same time concealing information about their health from others. In part this was out of concern for the health and wellbeing of relatives back home and the negative impact bad news about the migrant's health could have on family members, particularly if they were elderly or debilitated by illness. At the same time concealing their ill-health can exacerbate their own stress and poor health (ibid.: 7). Other studies have pointed to the central role of networks in determining individual behaviour via norms and information in terms of health service utilisation. In a study conducted among Canadian-based migrants (where universal healthcare provision means that there is no question of eligibility), Deri (2005) found that for high utilising language groups, living in areas of high concentration of the language group was found to increase access to health services, highlighting the influence of the informational channel. In contrast, for low utilising groups living in areas of high concentration of the group was found to decrease access, emphasising the influence of norms.

Transnational networks can also reproduce gendered power asymmetries and reinforce gendered roles and responsibilities, particularly around healthcare (Gurman and Becker, 2008; Menjívar, 2002). As Molyneux (2002: 181) has argued, women can therefore be doubly disadvantaged. First, women do not usually belong to the sorts of networks that bring economic advantage – valuable business or political contacts tend to operate in masculine social spaces that can exclude women – and they tend to depend on time and resources whose accessibility is gender-related. Second, female networks generally command fewer economic resources and frequently rely on more time and non-monetised labour exchanges that can be accommodated within the domestic division of labour. This is reflected in migrant health networks where women rather than men tend to be at the centre of networks to procure remedies for both unusual and serious illnesses as well as the more mundane but also more frequent ailments that affect people in their everyday lives (Menjívar, 2002: 439). The gendered segmentation of employment available to migrant labourers can also impact on networks. In a study of Guatemalan migrants in Houston, USA, Hagan (1998) found that gender differences in forms of work meant that over time women's networks become weaker and more strongly tied to those back in Guatemala since they tended to work in fairly isolated situations as live-in domestic labour; in contrast men's networks expand and strengthen as they worked in more public settings in Houston and were able to develop non-ethnic 'weak ties' with other residents in the community. It is these 'weak ties' that are often essential for facilitating better healthcare access for migrants in destination countries (ibid.: 65–6).

Migrants employ a range of transnational health seeking strategies in order to seek resolution to their healthcare problems. In particular, many continue to make use of health services in their countries of origin in a variety of ways – either directly or via friends or relatives. A number of authors have noted the ways in which migrants may seek healthcare during regular visits 'home' (Bergmark et al., 2008; Lee et al., 2010). As Ormond (this volume) notes, it is frequently assumed that this is motivated by the failure of health systems to accommodate the needs of migrants and is thus celebrated for providing migrants with an opportunity to receive greater family support, access to cheaper medication and more familiar forms of care. Lee et al. (2010) observe that returning 'home' for healthcare plays an important role in promoting feelings of wellbeing and health affirming feelings among migrants who had returned to Korea from New Zealand to seek healthcare treatment as people felt they had more 'trust' in the Korean system. Yet migrants' ability to return home is clearly affected by their migrant status and their socioeconomic position and for some migrants this may not be an option at all. For some Mexicans living in the US, the cost and possible legal ramifications of the trip back to Mexico may mean that this strategy is reserved for cases of severe illness or crisis (Bergmark et al., 2008). For other Latinos in the US, their proximity to the Mexican border allowed them to make use of private clinics established specifically to serve the Latino migrant population. Respondents reported that they preferred the more 'personal service' offered by such clinics and that services were often cheaper than paying into US insurance schemes (Horton and Cole, 2011). The prohibitive cost of healthcare in the US was also a significant factor among Brazilian migrants who reported often putting health problems 'on hold' until a return trip to Brazil (Hilfinger Messias, 2002).

Similar trends have been found among Latin American populations in Europe (Días et al., 2010). In the UK a survey of over a thousand Latin Americans in London, McIlwaine et al. (2011) found that around 30 per cent return to Latin America to seek healthcare. Peruvians are the population group most likely to do so and Bolivians, given the fact that they are most likely to be undocumented and are the newest Latin American population group in the UK, are the least likely to do so.

Horton and Cole (2011) suggest that for many their decision to return 'home' for healthcare is informed by the fact that their relatively better salaries earned as migrant workers offer them the chance to access a quality of care previously unavailable to them. The relationship between migrants' income and use of private providers is complex and requires further research. Although focusing on use of private providers in the host country, McIlwaine et al. (2011: 99) found that over 40 per cent of Latin American migrants in London had used private health services in the UK and around half had specifically consulted with a Latin American doctor in the UK. The majority of respondents cited dissatisfaction with the state-provided NHS as their reason for choosing private care and that ability to pay was not a factor in this decision. The study found that 35 percent of respondents with monthly incomes below £1,000 had used a private doctor (ibid.: 100). More work is required to determine whether migrants are able to pay for a full course of treatment that they may require if they choose to use private providers. Other studies of low income use of private healthcare in Latin America suggest that while people can afford to pay for the initial consultation they may not be able to pay for any follow up treatment or all of the necessary medication required (Gideon, 2001). Another concern is that, at least in the Latin American context, a wide variety of private providers exist and they are not always as closely regulated as public facilities, giving rise to concern about the quality of care provided. These issues raise questions about the long term viability of these 'solutions' to migrants' health problems and are particularly pertinent to lower income groups who lack the funds to pay for sustained courses of treatment.

The case study

The study draws on interviews with stakeholders working with the Latin American community, particularly around health, and with Latin American migrants living in London. Semi-structured interviews took place between May 2009 and February 2010 and were conducted in either English or Spanish, with 26 male and female respondents.[2] Respondents were predominantly from Peru, Bolivia, Ecuador and Colombia but also included one Chilean and one Argentinean and ranged in age from 22 to 58 years old. Individuals were interviewed for up to an hour and were asked about a range of health-related topics, including a number of questions about their health seeking behaviour while living in the UK. Respondents were identified through a number of avenues. The majority were users of a London-based NGO, the Latin American Women's Rights Service (LAWRS), but others were identified through 'snow balling' techniques via friends and workplace colleagues. All of the respondents claimed to be documented and had full rights and entitlements to use the NHS. A large number had Spanish passports and were therefore covered by EU legislation. The majority of respondents had sought to register with a GP and had at some point had some level of engagement with the NHS. However, as the research highlights, there are significant gaps between legal entitlements and actual access to resources. The discussion below highlights how many of the health seeking strategies employed by migrants draw on social networks in some form or other in order to secure resolution to their health problems.

In line with research findings elsewhere, lack of access to health services combined with precarious forms of employment emerged as an important issue for a number of respondents in this study. In particular there were important gender dimensions since around two-thirds of the women interviewed had children and all of them reported that they were the prime carers and had primary responsibility if a child was ill. In a number of cases the women struggled to combine paid and unpaid responsibilities when a child was ill because they were not allowed time off work and therefore had to depend on friends to provide childcare or alternatively to cover for them at work so they could stay at home. Many of the women reported that it was their responsibility to find a replacement if they took time off work and they also then had to pay them out of their own pocket, as well as having their wages docked, and spoke of the stress this involved – as well as the loss of wages. Although only a small number of men were interviewed, all had children and stated that their wives took care of them. This suggests that the gendered division of labour around household-based healthcare may remain unchanged following migration, even where other gender relations are challenged. It also points to the need for a clearer understanding of these processes since responsibility for household health and wellbeing can lead women to a position of increased socioeconomic inequality and stress, particularly if they are left to bear all the costs of care (both financial and emotional) on their own. This also reinforces the need to recognise the importance of social reproduction within the context of migration and acknowledge the shifting configuration of trade-offs and tensions between (social) reproduction and migration over the family life course (Locke et al., 2012).

The range of health seeking strategies employed by Latin Americans in the study often involved considerable resources in terms of time and money. While the majority of respondents spoke about health seeking strategies for their own health needs, further research is necessary in order to identify the strategies employed by migrants on behalf of other family members. This will reveal more clearly how far female migrants are potentially more disadvantaged than male migrants by the lack of access to services. Moreover, women often take responsibility for finding alternative means of treatment where they do not use the NHS; this can be another potential burden on their time and financial resources. Here too more work is required to understand the gendered dimensions of these practices.

Return to Latin America

Although all of the respondents in the study were entitled to use NHS services around a third had at one point or other returned to Latin America to seek healthcare treatment. In particular a large number of respondents reported using dental services in Latin America since treatment was considerably cheaper than in the UK. Others took the opportunity of being 'at home' to have a series of preventative health checks. However, in other cases some respondents had postponed surgery and other significant treatment until going back to Latin America.

In one case a university-educated Bolivian woman, who had been living in the UK for around a year, had started off with very high expectations of the NHS:

When I arrived friends told me that the NHS was awful and I should never go there but at first I didn't believe them. How could it be true? Britain is a First World country so I assumed that of course the health system would be First World and nothing like at home in Bolivia, after all we are from the Third World.

However, she later found out she was pregnant but then had an early miscarriage and then experienced some complications related to the miscarriage that meant she was hospitalised. She described her experience at the hospital as 'appalling' and this included being moved to a ward where she was left in pain for over 24 hours without any medical attention because the hospital staff had lost her notes while she was still in the hospital. The doctor who had been treating her could not locate her as she had been placed in the wrong ward. Although she spoke excellent English, her husband did not and no interpreter was found. She was in too much pain to be able to communicate effectively with hospital staff and he was unable to do so because of his lack of English. Eventually she was seen by a doctor and discharged but was supposed to return for further treatment. However, when interviewed she stated that, 'After that experience I will never go back to the NHS. I am going home in a few months and will just wait until I am there to sort things out. I know it is not the right thing to do but I can't go back ...'

A large number of respondents felt that they received 'better' treatment in Latin America and were prepared to risk future complications rather than use the NHS.[3] As argued by Lee et al. (2010) migrants often speak of their lack of trust in doctors in their chosen destinations. This was echoed in many of the interviews conducted for this study, as illustrated by the following female Colombian respondent who had lived in the UK for 12 years: 'I have a medical check-up every year in Colombia when I go home to see my family. I have tried to go to the doctor in the UK but I just don't trust the doctors here.' While she had not had any particularly negative experiences with the NHS she maintained this feeling of distrust, preferring to avoid going to the doctor except in an emergency and using the Colombian system when she could.

Similarly other respondents also noted the lack of physical contact with the GP, which they felt was a negative thing and confirmed the lack of competency on the GP's part. Another female Colombian respondent who had lived in the UK for 19 years and returned home every other year for medical check-ups explained 'doctors here [in the UK] don't look you in the eye and they don't even touch you, they just stare at their computers'. While such strategies may appear to offer a short term solution to people's healthcare problems, it also raises issues of concern regarding the longer term implications. Stakeholders working with the Latin American community warned that people are returning to the UK having consulted with health professionals at home but still requiring further treatment. Although they brought medical notes back to the UK with them they were in Spanish and GPs were often unable to understand. People then had to pay to have these translated in the UK and this could be very costly, particularly where people are employed in very low income jobs in Britain. In some instances this would delay further follow up treatment and people's health could worsen. In addition, treatment procedures for specific conditions may vary between countries and this also led to further problems where people had particular expectations about a course of treatment but then found that in the UK this was not available to them (interview with Latin American health advocates).

Use of Spanish-speaking doctors in the UK

A large proportion of respondents reported having one-off consultations with Latin American or Spanish-speaking doctors working in London. Respondents relied on both local and transnational networks to find out about London-based doctors and several referred to named Spanish-speaking GPs in different parts of London.

Interviews with stakeholders suggested that many undocumented migrants preferred to use private services because they were not asked to show any form of identification and questions about their status were rarely asked. Moreover, there is anecdotal evidence from stakeholders that these consultations are paid for through networks, particularly though Latin American churches in London, clubbing together to help people pay for treatment and then once it is paid back it is available for other migrants to use. Undocumented migrants in particular are using these mechanisms. This is an area that requires further research to build up a clearer picture of what is happening.

However, of greater concern is that some migrants are consulting unregistered, illegal doctors who have set up practices in London. Several cases were referred to during the interviews for this study but one in particular was also mentioned in the UK media. In November 2008 a high profile case was reported by the BBC of a bogus Chilean doctor who had set up a practice in South London. He was arrested at Heathrow Airport in April 2008 with large amount of prescription drugs in his suitcase. A subsequent investigation found that he had over 975 patient files, a significant number of which related to children (BBC, 2008).

One Chilean respondent reported having consulted with this particular doctor on several occasions and described the experience. A close relative was visiting her from Chile and had previously been involved in a serious car accident and as a result had some ongoing health problems. He did not speak English so she had asked Chilean friends if anyone could recommend a Spanish-speaking doctor for him to see while he was in the UK. Several friends recommended the doctor they referred to as 'El Shaman'. She described the first visit to the 'surgery':

> We were told you have to go to Elephant and Castle [an area of London with a high concentration of Latin Americans] but when we found the address it was a hairdressing salon not a doctor's surgery. We thought we must be in the wrong place but when we asked in the salon they told us we were in the right place and pointed to a small area that had been curtained off, that was the surgery.

She admitted that they realised then he was obviously not a registered GP but he told them that he was here on an internship at a London hospital and they thought he was just a young doctor moonlighting for some extra cash so they were not unduly concerned. She noted how he dispensed medication from a larger jar into smaller containers and this did arouse their suspicions:

> It was funny as I watched him in the corner, he took these pills out of a big jar and put them into a smaller pot for us, he said something about having to keep the jar which didn't really make sense.

Nevertheless, despite knowing that he was not really legitimate she also felt that he had taken her nephew's symptoms seriously and her nephew had shown significant improvement in his general wellbeing after the consultations:

> He had had all these surgical treatments in Chile and Argentina but you know, the only doctor who really listened to him was 'El Shaman' and his treatment seemed to really work. It probably was because he took the time to listen to him and that is what he needed. We saw him on a few occasions and each time he listened ...

She reflected that this was probably why he had been popular with the Latin population in London as she described him as 'a good listener'.

She had found out about the bogus status of 'El Shaman' on a return visit to Chile. She had met up with a friend whom she told about their experience. Her friend was a health professional in Chile and had seen an article in the Chilean newspaper about the arrest of the 'doctor' and had taken an interest because he came from the same town as the respondent and her friend and claimed to have studied medicine at the same university as her friend. Her friend subsequently found out that he had in fact been expelled from the university because of some form of malpractice early on in his medical studies. This too highlights the importance of transnationalism and the validity of migrants' networks (Menjívar, 2002) as well as the ways in which migrants' adaptive processes in host countries cannot be divorced from their country of origin (Hilfinger Messias, 2002: Yang, 2010).

Conclusion

This chapter has highlighted how Latin American migrants engage in a range of health seeking strategies in an attempt to resolve their health problems. Moreover, the findings reported in this chapter add to the debates around transnational health seeking behaviour of other Latin American migrant groups identified in the broader literature. For the majority of respondents in the study, who were predominantly living relatively marginalised lives in the UK, limited access to healthcare services has led them to seek alternative means to resolve their healthcare problems and has created a demand for informal care. While transnational networks play a key role in these strategies, many of these approaches are limited and do not offer long term solutions to health problems and may serve to further compound health inequalities. As the Latin American population in the UK continues to expand, more research is required to fully understand the diverse needs and cultural values of this heterogeneous community in relation to healthcare, as well as to understand more clearly the gendered dimensions of these processes.

Notes

1 This chapter draws in part on a forthcoming paper, Gideon, J. (2012) 'Exploring migrants' health seeking strategies: The case of Latin American migrants in London', *International Journal of Migration, Health and Social Care*, 7(4): 197–208, www.pierprofessional.com/ijmhscflyer/.

2 The study was intended to serve as a pilot and to highlight potential issues that require more in-depth research.

3 This echoes Horton and Cole's (2011) observation that migrants are using the private sector in Latin America rather than relying on pub-

lic services. Here too the relatively higher wages earned by migrants in the UK allows them to access private sector healthcare services in Latin America, which they may not have used prior to migration.

References

Artacoz, L., C. Borrel, J. Benach, I. Cortès and I. Rohlfs (2004) 'Women, family demands and health: The importance of employment status and socio-economic position', *Social Science and Medicine*, 59(2): 263–74.

Avato, J., J. Koettl and R. Sabates-Wheeler, R. (2010) 'Social security regimes, global estimates and good practices: The status of social protection for international migrants', *World Development*, 38(4): 455–66.

BBC (2008) 'Bogus doctor set up fake surgery', 20 November, news. bbc.co.uk/1/hi/england/london/7740329.stm (accessed 3 July 2012).

Bergmark, R., D. Barr and R. Garcia (2008) 'Mexican immigrants in the US living far from the border may return to Mexico for health services', *Journal of Immigrant and Minority Health*, doi 10.1007/s10903-008-9213-8.

Borrell, C., C. Muntaner, J. Benach and L. Artazcoz (2004) 'Social class and self-reported health status among men and women: What is the role of work organisation, household material standards and household labour?', *Social Science and Medicine*, 58(10): 1869–87.

Carballo, M. and M. Mboup (2005) 'International migration and health', paper prepared for the policy analysis and research programme of the Global Commission on International migration, www.gcim.org/attachements/TP13.pdf (accessed 24 March 2010).

Carlisle, F. (2006) 'Marginalisation and ideas of community among Latin American migrants to the UK', *Gender and Development*, 14 (2): 235–45.

Deri, C. (2005) 'Social networks and health service utilization', *Journal of Health Economics*, 24(6): 1076–107.

Días, S., A. Gama and C. Rocha (2010) 'Immigrant women's perceptions and experiences of healthcare services: Insights from a focus group study', *Journal of Public Health*, 18(5): 489–96.

Dixon-Woods, M., D. Kirk, S. Agarwal, E. Annandale, T. Arthur, J. Harvey, R. Hsu, S. Katbamna, R. Olsen, L. Smith, R. Riley and A. Sutton (2005) 'Vulnerable groups and access to healthcare: A critical interpretive review', report for the National Co-ordinating Centre for NHS Service Delivery and Organisation R&D (NCCSDO), www.sdo.nihr.ac.uk/projdetails.php?ref=08-1210-025 (accessed 1 October 2011).

Escandell, X. and M. Tapias (2010) 'Transnational lives, travelling emotions and idioms of distress among Bolivian migrants in Spain', *Journal of Ethnic and Migration Studies*, 36(3): 407–23.

Feldman, R. (2006) 'Primary health care for refugees and asylum seekers: A review of the literature and a framework for services', *Public Health*, 120: 809–16.

Gideon, J. (2001) 'The politics of health reform in Chile: Gender and participation in primary health care delivery in Chile', unpublished PhD thesis, University of Manchester, Manchester.

Goetz, A. M. (ed.) (1997) *Getting Institutions Right for Women in Development*, Zed Press, London and New York.

Gurman, T. and D. Becker (2008) 'Factors affecting Latina immigrants' perceptions of maternal healthcare: Findings from a qualitative study', *Healthcare for Women International*, 29: 507–26.

Hagan, J. M. (1998) 'Social networks, gender, and immigrant incorporation: Resources and constraints', *American Sociological Review*, 63(1): 55–67.

Hilfinger Messias, D. K. (2002) 'Transnational health resources, practices, and perspectives: Brazilian immigrant women's narratives', *Journal of Immigrant Health*, 4(4): 183–200.

Horton, S. and S. Cole (2011) 'Medical returns: Seeking healthcare in Mexico', *Social Science and Medicine*, 72: 1846–52.

Kawachi, I., B. Kennedy and R. Glass (1999) 'Social capital and self-rated health: A contextual analysis', *American Journal of Public Health*, 89(8): 1187–93.

Kofman, E. (2007) 'Gendered migrations, livelihoods and entitlements in European welfare regimes', in N. Piper (ed.) *New Perspectives on Gender and Migration: Livelihoods, Rights and Entitlements*, New York, Routledge/ UNRISD: 59–101.

Lee, J. Y. N., R. Kearns and W. Friesen (2010) 'Seeking affective health care: Korean immigrants' use of homeland medical services', *Health and Place*, 16(1): 108–15.

Llácer, A., V. Zunzunegui, J. del Amo, L. Mazarrasa and F. Bolumar (2007) 'The contribution of a gender perspective to the understanding of migrants' health', *Journal of Epidemiology and Community Health*, 61 (supplement ii): 4–10.

Locke, C., J. Seeley and N. Rao (2012) 'Neglected linkages: Migration, (social) reproduction and social protection', Draft DEV Working Paper, UEA, Norwich.

McIlwaine, C. (2008) 'Subversion or subjugation: Transforming gender ideologies among Latin American migrants in London', Working Paper, Dept Geography, Queen Mary, University of London, London.

McIlwaine, C., J. C. Cock and B. Linneker (2011) *The Latin American Community in London*, Trust for London, London.

Menéndez, M., J. Benach, C. Muntaner, M. Amable and P. O'Campo (2007) 'Is precarious employment more damaging to women's health than men's?', *Social Science and Medicine*, 64(4): 776–81.

Menjívar, C. (2002) 'The ties that heal: Guatemalan immigrant women's networks and medical treatment', *International Migration Review*, 36(2): 437–66.

Molyneux, M. (2002) 'Gender and the silences of social capital: Lessons from Latin America', *Development and Change*, 33(2): 167–88.

Peró, D. (2008) 'Political engagement of Latin Americans in the UK: Issues, strategies and the public debate', *Focaal – European Journal of Anthropology*, 51: 73–90.

Pylpa, J. (2001) 'Self medication practices in two Californian Mexican communities', *Journal of Immigrant Health*, 3(2): 59–75.

Sabates-Wheeler, R. and I. MacAuslan (2007) 'Migration and social protection: Exposing problems of access', *Development*, 50(4): 26–32.

Thomas, F. (2010) 'Transnational health and treatment networks: Meaning, value and place in health seeking amongst southern African migrants in London', *Health and Place*, 16: 606–12.

WHO/IOM (World Health Organization and International Organization for Migration) (2010) *Health of Migrants: the Way Forward. Report of a Global Consultation*, 3–5 March, Madrid, www.who.int/hac/events/consultation_report_health_migrants_colour_web.pdf (accessed 17 June 2010).

Wright, K. (2011) 'Constructing migrant wellbeing: An exploration of life satisfaction amongst Peruvian migrants in London', *Journal of Ethnic and Migration Studies*, 37(9): 1459–75.

Yang, J. (2010) 'Contextualising immigrant access to health resources', *Journal of Immigrant and Minority Health*, 12(3): 340–53.

12 | Wellbeing and community self-help: Turkish-speaking women in London

ELENI HATZIDIMITRIADOU AND
S. GÜLFEM ÇAKIR

Introduction

Migrant women, especially those arriving from developing countries, often face additional barriers to integration in the host country due to the structural constraints of immigration policies that reinforce their dependency upon male migrants. Yet worldwide, social, economic and political changes have led to increased female migration and most migratory movements from developing to developed countries are now initiated by women (Riaño, 2005). It is also widely acknowledged that migrant women often resume the role of the intermediary between their own communities and the host country as it is mostly they who will be in contact with welfare services on behalf of their families. Sales (2007: 15) comments that the mediating role they resume places additional burdens on women 'but may also provide some continuity with their previous lives, which can be particularly important where there has been a sudden rupture as in the case of refugees and allow them to make connections in the country of exile'.

This role is often materialised as voluntary work the women undertake in community organisations, providing advice and support to newer arrivals and assisting them in accessing health and social services (Tomlinson and Erel, 2005). Community self-help and mutual aid activities are considered instrumental in disadvantaged groups' claims to their right to health and welfare; such activities promote self-actualisation, social support and community empowerment.

In this chapter, we examine the role of community activism as a mechanism of empowerment for migrant women's claims to welfare and health rights. We present the case study of Turkish-speaking migrant women, a 'new' migrant community that is facing integration challenges in the British society and for whom there is little research evidence. Based on research evidence from two studies with this group, we discuss women's post-migration wellbeing status and needs for health and mental healthcare, and latent social transformations at personal and community levels. Having personal agency as our primary focus of analysis, we consider how community activism relates to the women's sense of empowerment and practices to seek help for their health and social care needs.

Post-migration wellbeing

Regardless of reasons and means of people's departure from their country of origin, living in a new environment brings about significant economical, social and health/psychological challenges to migrants. The intensity and variety of these difficulties varies according to the forms of migration (whether forced or voluntary), knowledge of language, support networks in the host country, and socio-political context of the host country (Watters, 2001). Most of these factors are linked to post-migration conditions that may increase vulnerability to physical and mental health problems. Indeed, evidence suggests that many migrants who arrive fairly healthy in the destination country may experience deterioration of health over time (Jayaweera, 2011). For example, substandard housing characterised by overcrowding and poor sanitation, and ineffective responses of care services aggravate migrants' vulnerability to serious health problems (Carballo and Mboup, 2005). Also, many newly arrived migrants experience problems in obtaining information about available health services and in expressing their care needs. Unsurprisingly, these difficulties, teamed with poverty and social exclusion, lead to poor physical and mental health for migrants (Burnett and Peel, 2001). Pre-existing risks such as country specific diseases in the regions where they come from, coupled with migratory hardship such as trafficking, material deprivation, malnutrition and mental ill-health, will inevitably raise public health concerns and increased healthcare needs among these populations (Fernandes et al., 2009). Social support from their communities helps them to recover and re-experience the feeling of belonging and independence (Coker, 2001), and thus alleviate the pitfalls of negative migratory experiences.

Migration and women

The feminisation of migration has been recognised as a major trend in international migration in recent times (Castles and Miller, 2003). In the last few decades, women have accounted for almost half of all migrants, being increasingly the principal wage earners for themselves and their families rather than dependent followers of men (Martin, 2004).

The fact that women are noted as significant actors of mobility at local and global level is not readily reflected in research and policy-making. Scholars observe that, prior to the mid-1970s, there is invisibility of women migrants in international migration studies as well as little impact of such research on policy and service development (Kofman, 2004). Focus on women and gender is mostly due to feminist and development movements of the 1970s, advancing the women's agenda in general as well as specific issues of migrant women in community development work (Engle, 2004). Women's groups have been instrumental in advancing equality and diversity policy developments since the 1960s and their political activism represents a model for community development and democratic localism (Gittell et al., 2000). This form of political agency, which takes place in the voluntary sector, is even more important for minority ethnic women, including immigrant women, who are routinely excluded from the formal political sphere (Takhar, 2011). Community organisations in the UK such as the Southall Black Sisters are at the forefront of empowering women to voice their experiences of domestic violence, forced marriage and honour killings. Personal empowerment is achieved through confidence building, economic independence and gaining educational qualifications (Takhar, 2007).

Issues for migrant women

A common depiction of migrants in Europe, and the UK in particular, is that of a 'threat' to many aspects of life, including employment, welfare and security, as well as national values and identity (Sales, 2007). The association of 'risk' and 'burden' with immigration is particularly relevant when considering migrant women as they are often perceived 'as "dangerous bodies" who pose a double risk to the nation through their fertility and their uncontrollable sexuality' (ibid.: 6). Although this view may be at the extreme end, they are indeed frequently perceived as heavy users of health and social care services, being dependent on welfare benefits and relying on social housing. This may be true for those who experience severe life changes due to migration and have to cope with trauma and psychological illness, health deterioration, lone parenthood and other post-migration hardships. However, there is a significant body of research evidence suggesting that the majority of these women do not easily access health and social care services or claim welfare entitlements they have the right to (Scheppers et al., 2006). On the contrary, it is now widely acknowledged that migrant women play a crucial role in welfare provision as informal carers and domestic workers, filling the gaps of care for the elderly and childcare for working mothers of the indigenous population (Anderson, 2001).

Notwithstanding their involvement in providing welfare, migrants' difficulty in accessing health and social care services is worsened by deterring immigration policies that aim to manage migration by restricting and stratifying migrant civil rights (Morris, 2002). Such restrictions are also highly gendered and labour market-related, potentially leaving migrant women more vulnerable to abuse, health risks and social exclusion than men.

Community self-help and user empowerment in health services

Community self-help and mutual aid are based on the concept of reciprocity that is fundamental to human development and survival (Burns et al., 2004). Closely linked to the theory of social capital, these activities are recognised as important in addressing inequalities in welfare state provision. The acceptance of organised mutual aid and the belief in personal, social and moral responsibility may also contain the inherent risk of being perceived as shifting state duties to individual citizens. Yet, writers of diverse philosophical backgrounds and beliefs such as Smiles (1886), Kropotkin (1902) and more recently Illich (1971) (all cited in Burns et al., 2004), recognise that state services are able to provide few solutions to citizens and promote a dependency culture that is corrosive of personal and community empowerment. Creative routes out of social exclusion such as community self-help and mutual aid enable disadvantaged and voiceless members of society to claim their rights and make better use of existing state provision.

Self-help and mutual aid activities can be a solution to immediate problems, a springboard into mainstream society, a resource for more formal agencies, or as an alternative to aspects of mainstream society (Burns and Taylor, 1998). The common denominator of these activities, namely empowerment, has been used with a variety of different meanings depending on the context of reference. However, in all its uses, the main elements of empowerment are the contrast to the traditional existing status quo and the emphasis on the person's control over his/her life and awareness of his/her positive influence in the community.

There are different levels of empowerment, according to the context where the term is used: the individual, the group and the community level (McLean, 1995). Individual empowerment refers to one's ability to make decisions and have control over personal life, as well as the establishment of a critical understanding of the social and political circumstances and the advancement of both individual and collective skills for social action. Empowering processes may also occur at the group level, through mutual help activities, where individuals are enabled to increase their control within the group, helping each other and legitimating their experiences. At the community level, the aim is to effect change in social policy within the community and broader society. These last two levels of empowerment refer to the 'politicisation process', according to Riessman and Carroll (1995), that occurs to individuals as they move beyond self-awareness to an awareness of larger social issues that influence their condition.

In the area of health and social care services, service user empowerment has been promoted actively and instituted in the welfare policy of the Labour government in the 1990s. The concept has been associated with the 'active citizen' model of welfare provision, whereby consumers of welfare services should be involved in their own care through choice of services, participation in designing and delivering services via consultation, and ultimately, partnership working and user controlled service provision (Thompson, 2007). In reality, it became apparent that institutionalised participation, although providing a political space for users to voice their needs, is limited due to power imbalances disadvantaging the more marginalised groups, which may be further excluded during this process (Beresford and Croft, 2008; Beresford and Holden, 2000). Indeed, 'the participation of black and minority ethnic users has often, at best, been an afterthought or marginalized and sometimes excluded altogether' (Begum, 2006: 9). The same criticism can also be made about the BME organisations that, while active in campaigning on behalf of their communities, do not always promote the involvement of their service users. This is at odds with the rich history of community activism and self-help that characterises these communities in the UK, but it is indicative of the structural barriers faced by these populations in the state welfare provision and in the national service user movement.

More recently, a move from 'users and choosers of services provided by others' to 'actors and agents in broader processes of governance' is favoured in the social policy arena and collective action is at the centre of this new approach (Cornwall and Gaventa, 2001: 4). Hence, the community activism of BME groups, including immigrant ones, is of particular importance for the understanding of their care needs, how these are met through such initiatives, and what is the role of community empowerment in promoting meaningful service user involvement among these excluded communities.

In the remainder of the chapter, we discuss findings from two related research projects that involved Turkish-speaking migrant women in London, their health and social care needs and their experiences with community activism.

Research with Turkish-speaking migrant women

The Turkish diaspora in Europe is closely linked to the guest workers' phenomenon in the 1960s when Turks were migrating to Germany and other northern European countries under bilateral labour export agreements. In the UK, the Turkish migration, although broadly economic in nature, had a different pattern and three distinct migrant groups arrived in the country due to varied historical socio-political circumstances: Turkish Cypriots, Turks and Kurds from Turkey. Turkish migration to the UK started in the 1950 and 1960s with labour migrants and was followed by asylum seekers who were mostly Kurdish in origin in the 1980s and 1990s (Yalcin, 2003). Although it is difficult to discuss a singular Turkish migrant population due to this variety in its history, character and identity, it is acknowledged that they are most likely to share the fact that they speak Turkish, hence the tendency to apply the term 'Turkish-speaking population' to characterise all these migrant groups (King et al., 2008).[1] Mainly concentrated in London, people of Turkish origin are estimated to number around 500,000, with the majority of them being Turkish Cypriots (Home Affairs Committee, 2011). In the UK immigration scene, the Turkish-speaking communities are considered fairly new and little is known about their particular experiences and needs for welfare support (Enneli et al., 2005).

Gendered empowerment experiences of Turkish-speaking women: findings from a quantitative large scale survey

A self-completed survey of the views and experiences of Turkish-speaking migrant women living in London was conducted in 2006 by the second author (Çakır) as part of her doctoral studies. It contained two parts: a set of self-reported scales examining physical and mental health status, social support, empowerment and acculturation attitudes; and a set of open-ended questions related to their views about life in London as a migrant and their experiences with health and social care services. The main purpose of the survey was to assess factors and mechanisms of resilience, acculturation and adaptation patterns of Turkish women living in London (for a detailed discussion of the study, see Çakır, 2009; Çakır and Yerin-Guneri, 2011). For the purposes of this chapter, we selectively present findings related to self-reported physical and mental health status as well as the women's views about access to services. We also comment on the women's views about life in the UK, where it relates to our discussion of their perception of themselves and their rights in the new country.

The sample (n=246) comprised different migrant groups, both economic and forced migrants, living in London boroughs where the largest Turkish-speaking community resides (Hackney, Haringey). It included women with a mean age of 34.3 years; their length of stay in the UK ranged from 6 months to 38 years, with a mean of 10 years. Most participants were married (70 per cent) and had primary or secondary education (71.6 per cent). Less than a quarter was employed (25.6 per cent), whereas the majority had either British/dual citizenship or indefinite leave to remain.

Self-reported physical and mental health status of migrant women As shown in Figure 12.1, the women who took part in the survey reported higher levels of physical and mental health problems post-migration. In particular, while 21.1 per cent (n=52) reported having health problems before their arrival to the UK, almost half (48.8 per cent, n=120) reported having health problems after arriving in the country. Similarly, while only 13.4 per cent (n=33) reported having mental health problems before migrating to the UK, 47.2 per cent (n=116) women answered that they had mental health problems after migration. In the whole sample, 32.9 per cent (n=81) of the participants had both physical and mental health problems in the UK.

Among the women who reported health problems in the UK, 108 participants provided detailed explanation regarding their problems. Based on these health problems, ten categories were developed and each problem was placed under the relevant category. As shown in Table 12.1, the most frequently reported health problems included muscle and skeletal complaints (33 per cent), followed by aches and

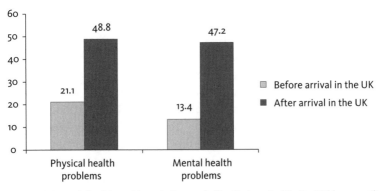

12.1 Women's health problems before and after their arrival in the UK (%, n=246)

TABLE 12.1 Health and mental health problems

Problems	Frequency	%
Health		
Muscle and skeleton complaints	45	32.8
Migraine and headache	21	15.2
Endocrine system problems	10	7.3
Hypertension	10	7.3
Asthma	9	6.6
Infections	7	5.1
Gynaecological complaints	6	4.4
Gastroenterological problems	6	4.4
Eye problems	3	2.1
Other (anaemia, dermatological problems, acute surgery etc.)	20	14.8
Mental health		
Depression	43	48.3
Nervousness	11	12.4
Loneliness	10	11.2
Bereavement	4	4.8
Panic attack	4	4.8
Anxiety	2	2.3
Post-natal depression	2	2.3
Suicide attempts	2	2.3
Sadness	2	2.3
Relationship problems	2	2.3
Other (PTSD, identity problems, family problems etc.)	5	5.9

pains (lumbago, back pain, pains in joints, legs and neck) and migraine and headache (15 per cent). Also, 32 participants reported co-morbidity of health problems.

In terms of mental health, 79 women (68.1 per cent) provided further explanation of the problems they experienced in the UK. Depression (n=43, 48.3 per cent) was reported as the most common problem among this group, and it was followed by nervousness (n=11, 15.2 per cent) and loneliness (n=10, 11.2 per cent) (see Table 12.1). Furthermore, nine participants mentioned co-occurring problems or complaints with depression in this question.

Access to health services In the UK, statutory health services, including mental health, are provided by the NHS and are free to people residing

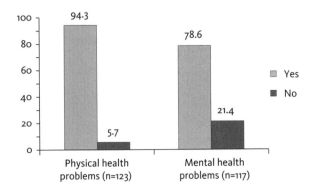

12.2 Percentage of women accessing health services for their problems

in the UK (Fernando, 2005). As shown in Figure 12.2, almost all participants had access to the NHS for their health problems. While almost all women got help for their physical health problems, only 78.6 per cent of them received help for their mental health problems.

For their physical health problems, women mainly got help from their GP and hospitals in the UK, followed by Turkish private doctors and doctors in Turkey. For their mental health problems, women were getting help from GPs and counsellors (38.4 per cent), only GPs (30.2 per cent), only counsellors or psychotherapists (17.4 per cent), hospital professionals (8.1 per cent) and others (5.8 per cent) including private counsellors/psychotherapists and doctors or psychologists in Turkey. It is worth noting that 21 per cent of the counselling and psychotherapy services were provided by community organisations for Turkish-speaking communities.

Women's perceptions and experiences related to health services Of the women, 25 elaborated on their experiences with health/mental health services. The women who answered this question perceived both health (n=11) and mental health (n=14) services as inadequate and ineffective. More particularly, they were dissatisfied with the services because they felt they were not getting sufficient care and treatment.

Among 14 participants who expressed dissatisfaction with mental health services, five participants expressed they did not get 'enough help' with no further explanation; however, all five stated that they were seen by a GP. Two other participants attributed the lack of help to language barriers: 'The general practitioner referred me to a psychologist but because of the language problem, it wasn't effective'; 'Because of the language, we can't explain ourselves.' Participants also expressed that their cultural differences prevented them from getting appropriate psychological help: 'I didn't feel being understood, I didn't find it genuine because of the cultural difference. It wasn't effective. I got more help from my friends.' Participants also mentioned their reluctance to use prescribed medication or use mental health services due to cultural differences or their distrust of them.

Life in the UK The women of the study held fairly strong positive views about life in the UK. The majority identified citizenship and gender-related issues – freedom, respect, human rights, equality – as positive elements of British life (n=125, out of 206 who answered this question). Contrary to stereotypical views of migrants as 'welfare exploiters', welfare benefits and education were mentioned to a lesser extent by the women (n=19 and n=12 respectively), as well as good economic conditions (n=19). When identified, these issues were mentioned as part of a society where the vulnerable are protected and supported and women can gain independence through education. Among the women's dislikes of life in the UK were difficulties with accessing health services (n=22) and language (n=11).

Experiences of discrimination When asked whether during their stay in the UK they experienced discrimination, almost half of the women (48.4 per cent, n=120) felt they were being discriminated against due to their culture or race. Of the women who identified some form of discrimination, 99 elaborated more on their experiences. They had experienced a general feeling of discrimination, either overt or covert, and felt they were being treated as a second class citizen and a foreigner. Experiences of discrimination were related to the workplace, how they were treated by health professionals and government institutions, experiences in education settings, and with the police.

Findings from a small scale qualitative study with Turkish-speaking women's self-help groups

Having established a range of experiences and needs linked to this population's health and social care needs during the large scale survey discussed above, in 2007 we decided to explore the role of women's community self-help in voicing their healthcare needs. To this end, we conducted a small scale qualitative study to explore experiences of community activism and empowerment of Turkish-speaking women who were taking part in self-help groups. The aim was to investigate the role of migrant women's community activism in enabling them to become more empowered and involved as users of welfare services (for a detailed discussion of the study, see Hatzidimitriadou and Çakır, 2009).

Focus group discussions were conducted with Turkish-speaking women's groups. Data from the focus groups were complemented by a brief questionnaire to collect basic demographic information about the members who participated in the discussions, as well as some information about their group membership. The criterion for identifying groups to study was the focus of change, according to Hatzidimitriadou's typology (2002), whereby self-help groups may be focused on personal change of their members or social change that deals with their shared problem/issue. Two groups were selected: one focused on personal change (Group A) and one focused on social change (Group B).

The themes of the focus group discussions were: the nature of involvement in the group, the experiences of Turkish-speaking women as members of a self-help group, group participation and coping with post-migration adversity, and mechanisms of change that the group aims to achieve. Each focus group meeting was attended by four or five group members. Participants were between 30 and 44 years old, all married and all bar one with children. They had lived in the UK for a long time – 6 to 18 years – and two of them were born in the UK. Most women were long term members – 5 to 18 years – and were regular attendees of group meetings that were held fortnightly or monthly.

Motivation to join a self-help group Group A members offered a combination of personal and social reasons for joining the group, including familiarity and friendship with other group members, before they joined or during their membership, as a strong motivator for being members. Overcoming stereotypes and prejudice about 'different communities, different groups, different backgrounds' was cited as an important reason for them.

Group B members identified social responsibility and mutuality as reasons for joining the group and as ways forward for them as women, mothers and migrants. Social action was a reason mentioned by these women and gender inequality was the prompt of such social action.

Benefits of self-help group participation Members of the two groups identified a number of different benefits from participation. Group A emphasised aspects of personal change and development, such as the value of learning new things, self-esteem, exchanging information with other group members, friendship, social support and being supported as a newly arrived immigrant. The experience of helping others was a very powerful benefit for them, as well as breaking down stereotypes about Islam and Muslim women (especially related to wearing the headscarf).

Group B acknowledged social change aspects as more beneficial. Finding voice and taking action regarding the challenges that immigrants are faced with were among the benefits identified by this group. They also recognised that being a member of the group was another form of political action they wished to take. Information and knowledge were also mentioned by the members as tools to support their children's education and to seek help such as healthcare services for their families when needed.

Views about women's community activism Both groups strongly agreed that it was very valuable to them to be a member of their group and they related this view to the gendered character of their community activism, namely that being a woman had significance in the ways they sought to effect personal or social change. In Group A, members talked about the practical approach that they take as women to undertake action, fitting it with their conventional roles as mothers and housewives. They also recognised the power of community activism as a strategy for self-development and social support.

In Group B, the empowering nature of these activities, the strong impact on their communities and the positive change in migrants' views of themselves were emphasised. The members identified that community activism is important for dealing with post-migration adversity and for promoting their rights for welfare services. According to members, the awareness-raising character of their activities had the potential to lead to more active participation in the statutory mechanisms of the host country and they pointed to the impact that these activities had on their local environments, being noticed by service providers and the wider host society. However, Group B members also noted that groups did not have the role of the 'saviour' and their expectation from other members was self-help and self-actualisation as well as mutual aid.

Discussion

Gender considerations were only recently introduced into migration studies. Yet, a gendered analysis of mobility is crucial in understanding upcoming public health needs and strategies to address them. The case of Turkish-speaking migrant women offers an intriguing opportunity to review gendered conceptualisations of wellbeing, the development of empowered identities and how these changes may influence the provision of health and social care for migrants.

The findings from our survey suggest that Turkish-speaking women experience significantly more physical and mental health problems post-migration. This echoes previous findings that migrants' health and mental health may deteriorate when they arrive in the host country (Burnett and Peel, 2001; Jayaweera, 2011). Also, consistent with previous literature, aches and pains tend to be one of the most prominent physical symptoms, which may reflect 'somatisation tendencies' among Turkish migrant women or may also be due to culturally prescribed ways of referring to stress rather than actual symptoms (Mirdal, 2006). Participants provided fewer explanations of their mental health problems than their 'somatic' health problems, indicating a tendency to look for a physical explanation of stress and anxiety (Green et al., 2006), hence to somatise psychological difficulties among migrant women from non-Western cultures.

Also, survey responses indicate that Turkish-speaking women are experiencing discrimination due to culture or race. Such experiences are known to exacerbate mental health problems and the association of migrant mental health issues with perceived discrimination has been reported in studies of Turkish migrants in other European countries (Liebkind and Jasinskaja-Lahti, 2000).

In terms of healthcare services, the higher use of GPs and primary care services reported by Turkish-speaking migrant women is consistent with that observed in other studies with migrants compared to the white population (Stronks et al., 2001). However, our findings also suggest that there is a noticeable difference in terms of getting help for physical and mental health problems that may be due to problems in the referral system for these populations (Smaje and Le Grand, 1997). The fact that fewer women were receiving help for their mental health than their physical health problems draws attention to the need for raising awareness around mental health issues among migrants and ethnic minorities through providing further education and information (Anand and Cochrane, 2005).

Finally, the results of the survey highlight the role of community organisations as providers of mental health services for migrant groups. In the UK, during the last decade, there has been a considerable shift in health and mental health policies addressing inequalities and managing diversity (Papadopoulos and Lees, 2002). Despite the positive changes that have taken place in terms of service development and provision for BME groups, health and mental healthcare services are still struggling to satisfactorily meet the needs of an increasingly diverse population and especially the needs of newly arrived migrant groups. Community organisations in the voluntary sector have the potential to act as a 'bridge' in identifying and addressing the needs of ethnic minority and migrant groups (Çakır and Hatzidimitriadou, 2006). Our findings suggest that collaboration and consultation with such organisations would assist in developing services responsive to and appropriate for a multicultural society (Bhui and Sashidharan, 2003; Fernando, 2005).

Our follow-up study on women's self-help groups revealed that community activism was affecting migrant women's lives in different ways. Depending on the groups' focus of change, members became more politically active, empowered and had a voice to communicate their needs to the host society or they improved their knowledge and skills as individuals and helped to build bridges with the host and other communities.

Female migrants may be able to use the socio-legal system of their new country to promote their health and social care rights in both the sending and receiving countries. However, Muslim women in Europe are confronted with particular tensions between their legal and cultural citizenship, namely their 'gender submission' – symbolised by the headscarf as an immediately visible sign – which is taken as one of the hallmarks of their incompatibility with 'European' values. Community activism appears to be the mechanism through which migrant women express their political agency, crucial in understanding and advocating their own and their families' healthcare needs (Takhar, 2011).

Interestingly, latent social transformations at personal and community levels were also noted in the Turkish-speaking women's post-migration views about life in the UK. For example, citizenship rights and social opportunities became important in the new country, giving the women a new sense of freedom to determine their own present and future life and to ascertain their rights as service users. The women's agency is not confined only to participation in the labour market and their resulting financial independence, hence a 'pseudo-emancipation'; instead, it refers to broader citizenship and human rights, which potentially penetrate both their private and public roles (Erel, 2009).

In conclusion, our findings suggest that Turkish-speaking women in London are faced with a range of healthcare needs that are not always met by the existing healthcare system. In addition, the women experience social transformations that impact on the way they perceive themselves as social and political actors. They may acquire formal access to citizenship, yet they are still far from substantial citizenship – being a citizen – in their new country (Castles and Davidson, 2000). Nonetheless, new opportunities are presented to them to develop agency in promoting gender equality and equality of access to healthcare services.

Self-help and mutual activities of migrant women aid their successful integration in the new country; therefore mechanisms of change should be studied more closely in these organisations/groups. More research is needed to explore in depth how migrant women's community activism is promoting personal and collective empowerment and its role in communicating and advocating the healthcare needs of immigrant communities.

Note

1 The authors acknowledge that the term has been challenged and debated as it does not attribute accurately the identities of all three groups that merit particular recognition. Both Turkish Cypriots and Kurds from Turkey are counted as 'Turks', i.e. Turkey-born populations, by the UK Census, a practice that complicates and obscures accurate demographic representations (King et al., 2008).

References

Anand, A. S. and R. Cochrane (2005) 'The mental health status of South Asian women in Britain: A review of the UK literature', *Psychology and Developing Studies*, 17(2): 195–214.

Anderson, B. (2001) 'Servants and slaves: Europe's domestic workers', *Race and Class*, 39(1): 37–49.

Begum, N. (2006) *Doing it for Themselves: Participation and Black and Minority Ethnic Service Users*, Social Care Institute for Excellence and the Race Equality Unit, Bristol.

Beresford, P. and S. Croft (2008) 'Democratising social work – a key element of innovation: From "client" as object, to service user as producer', *The Innovation Journal: The Public Sector Innovation Journal*, 13(1), Article 2, www.inovation.cc/scholarly-style/beresford_2_democrat_sw.pdf (accessed 15 June 2011).

Beresford, P. and C. Holden (2000) 'We have choices: Globalisation and welfare service user movements', *Disability & Society*, 15(7): 973–89.

Bhui, K. and S. P. Sashidharan (2003) 'Should there be separate psychiatric services for ethnic minority groups?', *British Journal of Psychiatry*, 182: 10–12.

Burnett, A. and M. Peel (2001) 'Asylum seekers and refugees in Britain: Health needs of asylum seekers and refugees', *British Medical Journal*, 322: 544–7.

Burns, D. and M. Taylor (1998) *Mutual Aid and Self-Help: Coping Strategies for Excluded Communities*, The Policy Press & Joseph Rowntree Foundation, Bristol.

Burns, D., C. Williams and J. Windebank (2004) *Community Self Help*, Palgrave Macmillan, London.

Çakır, S. G. (2009) 'Factors and

mechanisms of resilience among Turkish migrant women', unpublished PhD Thesis, Middle East Technical University, Ankara.

Çakır, S. G. and E. Hatzidimitriadou (2006) 'A bridge for migrants: The role of migrant/refugee community organisations in promoting and enhancing mental wellbeing', paper presented at the 3rd Annual Conference of International Mental Health: 'People on the Move', 30 August–1 September, King's College London, London.

Çakır, S. G. and O. Yerin-Guneri (2011) 'Exploring the factors contributing to empowerment of Turkish migrant women in the UK', *International Journal of Psychology*, 46(3): 223–33.

Carballo, M. amd M. Mboup (2005) 'International migration and health', paper prepared for the policy analysis and research programme of the Global Commission on International Migration, www.gcim.org/attachements/TP13.pdf (accessed 15 June 2011).

Castles, S. and A. Davidson (2000) *Citizenship and Migration: Globalisation and the Politics of Belonging*, Palgrave Macmillan, Basingstoke.

Castles, S. and M. J. Miller (2003) *The Age of Migration: International Population Movements in the Modern World*, 3rd edn, Palgrave Macmillan, Basingstoke.

Coker, N. (2001) 'Asylum seekers' and refugees' health experience', www.kingsfund.org.uk (accessed 15 June 2011).

Cornwall, A. and J. Gaventa (2001) 'From users and choosers to makers and shapers: Repositioning participation in social policy', *IDS Working Paper 127*, Institute of Development Studies, Brighton.

Engle, L. B. (2004) *The World in Motion: Short Essays on Migration and Gender*, International Organization for Migration, Geneva.

Enneli, P., T. Modood and H. Bradley (2005) *Young Turks and Kurds: A Set of 'Invisible' Disadvantaged Groups*, Joseph Rowntree Foundation, York.

Erel, U. (2009) *Migrant Women Transforming Citizenship: Life Stories from Britain and Germany*, Ashgate, Farnham.

Fernandes, A., B. Backstrom, B. Padilla, J. Malheiros, J. Perelman and S. Días (2009) 'Conceptual framework', in A. Fernandes and J. Pereira Miguel (eds) *Health and Migration in the European Union: Better Health for All in an Inclusive Society*, Instituto Nacional de Saude Doutor Ricardo Jorge, Lisbon: 23–32.

Fernando, S. (2005) 'Multicultural mental health services: Projects for minority ethnic communities in England', *Transcultural Psychiatry*, 42: 420–36.

Gittell, M., I. Ortega-Bustamante and T. Steffy (2000) 'Social capital and social change: women's community activism', *Urban Affairs Review*, 36(2): 123–47.

Green, G., H. Bradby, A. Chan and M. Lee (2006) '"We are not completely Westernized": Dual medical systems and pathways to health care among Chinese migrant women in England', *Social Science and Medicine*, 62: 1498–509.

Hatzidimitriadou, E. (2002) 'Political ideology, helping mechanisms and empowerment of mental health self-help/mutual aid groups', *Journal of Community and Applied Social Psychology*, 12: 271–85.

Hatzidimitriadou, E. and S. G. Çakır (2009) 'Community activism and empowerment of Turkish-speaking migrant women in London', *International Journal of Migration, Health and Social Care*, 5(1): 34–46.

Home Affairs Committee (2011) *Justice and Home Affairs area of the accession of Turkey to the European Union, Tenth Report of Session 2010–2011*, The Stationery Office, London.

Jayaweera, H. (2011) *Briefing: Health of Migrants in the UK: What Do We Know?*, The Migration Observatory, Oxford.

King, R., M. Thompson, N. Mai and Y. Keles (2008) *'Turks' in London: Shades of Invisibility and the Shifting Relevance of Policy in the Migration Process*, Working Paper No. 51, University of Sussex, Sussex Centre for Migration Research, Brighton.

Kofman, E. (2004) 'Gendered global migrations: Diversity and stratification', *International Feminist Journal of Politics*, 6(4): 643–65.

Liebkind, K. and I. Jasinskaja-Lahti (2000) 'The influence of experiences of discrimination on psychological stress: A comparison of seven immigrant groups', *Journal of Community and Applied Social Psychology*, 10: 1–26.

Martin, S. F. (2004) *Women and Migration*, United Nations, Division for the Advancement of Women (DAW), Consultative Meeting on 'Migration and mobility and how this movement affects women', Malmo, Sweden.

McLean, A. (1995) 'Empowerment and the psychiatric consumer/ex-patient movement in the United States: Contradictions, crisis and change', *Social Science and Medicine*, 40(8): 1053–71.

Mirdal, G. M. (2006) 'Stress and distress in migration: Twenty years after', *International Migration Review*, 40(2): 375–89.

Morris, L. (2002) *Managing Migration: Civic Stratification and Migrants' Rights*, Routledge, London.

Papadopoulos, I. and S. Lees (2002) 'Developing culturally competent researchers', *Journal of Advanced Nursing*, 37: 258–64.

Riaño, Y. (2005) 'Women on the move to Europe. A review of the literature on gender and migration', in M. G. da Marroni and G. Salgado (eds) *Latin American Diaspora: Migration within a Globalized World*, Autonomous University of Puebla and Institute of Developing Economies, Japan External Trade Organization, Mexico and Japan: 207–39.

Riessman F. and D. Carroll (1995) *Redefining Self-Help: Policy and Practice*, Jossey-Bass Publishers, San Francisco.

Sales, R. (2007) 'Giving more than they receive? Migrant women and welfare in Britain', *International Journal of Migration, Health and Social Care*, 3(3): 6–19.

Scheppers, E., E. van Dongen, J. Dekker, J. Geertzen and J. Dekker (2006) 'Potential barriers to the use of health services among ethnic minorities: A review', *Family Practice*, 23: 325–48.

Smaje, C. and J. Le Grand (1997) 'Ethnicity, equity and the use of health services in the British NHS', *Social Science and Medicine*, 45(3): 485–96.

Stronks, K., A. C. J. Ravelli and S. A. Reijneveld (2001) 'Immigrants in the Netherlands: Equal access for equal needs?', *Journal of Epidemiology & Community Health*, 55: 701–7.

Takhar, S. (2007) 'Expanding the boundaries of political activism', *Contemporary Politics*, 13(2): 123–37.

— (2011) 'The construction of political agency: South Asian women and political activism', *Community Development Journal*, 46(3): 341–50.

Thompson, A. (2007) 'The meaning of patient involvement and participation in health care consultations: A taxonomy', *Social Science & Medicine*, 64: 1297–310.

Tomlinson, F. and U. Erel (2005) *Refugee Women: From Volunteers to Employees*, London Metropolitan University, Working Lives Research Institute, London.

Watters, C. (2001) 'Emerging paradigms in the mental health care of refugees', *Social Science and Medicine*, 52: 1709–18.

Williams, F. (2002) 'The presence of feminism in the future of welfare', *Economy and Society*, 31(4): 502–19.

Yalcin, C. (2003) 'The Turkish existence in the United Kingdom', *C.Ü. Sosyoloji Tartismalari Dergisi*, 1: 11–27.

Contributors

Rosalind Bragg is the director of Maternity Action, which is a UK charity working on maternity and equalities. Rosalind has worked in the voluntary sector and civil service in the UK and Australia on issues of social exclusion and health access. Rosalind has qualifications in law, economics and public policy.

Dr Báltica Cabieses is a Chilean nurse-midwife, and holds a certificate in health education and a master's degree in epidemiology. She has a PhD in health sciences (health inequalities) from the University of York. She currently works as a faculty member at the Universidad del Desarrollo in Chile and her current areas of interest are health inequalities, migration and global public health.

Dr Gülfem Çakır is an assistant professor in the Faculty of Education, Guidance and Psychological Counselling Program at Akdeniz University, Antalya and teaches courses at undergraduate and postgraduate levels. She received her BSc (Hons), MSc and PhD in psychological counselling and guidance from the Middle East Technical University (METU), Ankara, Turkey. Her research interests include the psychological consequences of migration, empowerment identity development in adolescence, and burnout and self-care among service providers.

Dr Elaine Chase is based at the University of Oxford's Institute of Social Policy. Since 1990 she has conducted policy-focused research in relation to the health, wellbeing and the rights of children, young people and families, particularly those most likely to experience disadvantage and marginalisation. She has a particular interest in youth migration and, more specifically, the wellbeing of unaccompanied children and young people seeking asylum as they make the transition to adulthood in the UK and across Europe.

Professor Jon Friedland is Hammersmith campus dean and Head of Infectious Diseases and Immunity at Imperial College London as well as lead clinician for infection at Imperial College Healthcare NHS Trust. He is also co-director of the International Health Unit at Imperial investigating health issues associated with international migrants. His major research interest is in tuberculosis, for which he was awarded the Royal College of Physicians Weber-Parkes Medal. He is a fellow of the Academy of Medical Sciences.

Mary Haour-Knipe currently works as an independent adviser on migration, health and HIV/AIDS. From 1999 to 2007 she served as senior adviser on migration and HIV/AIDS, then on migration and health, at the International Organization for Migration. She has carried out several evaluation studies, and extensively advised on policy concerning HIV issues among migrant communities. She is the author of *Moving Families: Expatriation, Stress and Coping* (Routledge, 2001), editor of *Crossing Borders: Migration, Ethnicity and AIDS* (Taylor and Francis, 1996), *Health, Medicine and Society: Contributions to the Sociology of Health* (Seismo, 1999), and *Mobility, Sexuality and AIDS* (Routledge, 2010), and has published numerous articles and chapters in the fields of HIV and migration, social equity and health.

Dr Sally Hargreaves holds a PhD from Imperial College London. Her research has explored healthcare provision for migrants arriving in the UK and Europe, in particular assessing the impact of policies to restrict access to services for new migrants. She was made an honorary research fellow of Imperial College London in 2007. Prior to that she worked as a freelance journalist and senior editor for the *British Medical Journal* and *The Lancet*, and overseas with the international aid organisation Médecins Sans Frontières.

Dr Eleni Hatzidimitriadou is a reader at the Faculty of Health and Social Care Sciences, Kingston University and St George's University of London. She is a clinical and community psychologist and holds a BSc (Hons) in psychology, an MSc in clinical psychology (Aristotle University of Thessaloniki) and a PhD in psychology (University of Kent). She has conducted national and international research and published on self-help and mutual aid for socially excluded populations, welfare and social care in old age, and health and social care of migrants and ethnic minorities.

Dr Siân Oram is a post-doctoral research fellow in the Section for Women's Mental Health at the Institute of Psychiatry, King's College London. Her doctoral research, completed at the London School of Hygiene and Tropical Medicine in 2011, examined the UK public policy response to the health needs of trafficked people between 2000 and 2010. She was a member of the Human Trafficking and Harmful Traditional Practices subgroup of the NHS taskforce on the health aspects of violence against women and girls (2009–10) and the joint ministerial NGO stakeholder group on human trafficking (2007–10).

Meghann Ormond is assistant professor in cultural geography at Wageningen University. Her research uses the lens of healthcare to examine the politics of hospitality, care and mobility. Her forthcoming book is entitled *Neoliberal Governance and International Medical Travel in Malaysia* (Routledge).

Rebecca S. Shah has a PhD in global public health ethics and currently works for the UK's Foreign and Commonwealth Office. She has worked and published on social justice, public health ethics, human rights and international development and lectured in professional ethics. Recent publications include 'Global social justice and public health' (in Widdows and Smith (eds), *Global Social Justice*, Routledge, 2011) and *The International Migration of Health Workers: Ethics, Rights and Justice* (Palgrave MacMillan, 2010).

Dr Helena Tunstall is a health geographer with a PhD in health geography from the University of Bristol. She has significant research experience in health inequalities and health and place, especially migration and health in the UK. She is a research fellow at the Department of Health Sciences at the University of York and her areas of interest are related to the effects of place and geographical movement on health and inequalities in health.

Sue Willman is lead solicitor in the International and Human Rights Law team at Deighton Pierce Glynn solicitors; the firm represented a Palestinian migrant in the main test case on access to healthcare for migrants in the UK, *R(YA) v Secretary of State for Health*. Since 1996 she has taken a leading role in litigation, teaching, writing and campaigning for improved socioeconomic rights for migrants. She continues to collaborate with organisations such as Detainee Action, Doctors of the World, Medical Justice and the Refugee Council to ensure access to healthcare for individual migrants, especially detainees, and to challenge government policy. She is author of the handbook *Support for Asylum Seekers and Other Migrants* (Legal Action Group, 2009) and was specialist adviser to the UK Parliamentary Joint Committee on Human Rights during their inquiry into the treatment of asylum-seekers (2006). She has a law degree from Oxford University and a masters in international law from Georgetown University in Washington DC.

Index

Mental Health Act (1983) (UK), 101

Mexicans, in USA, health behaviours of, 169–70

Mexico: borderland clinics, 170; returning to, for healthcare, 152

midwives, 127, 134; survey of, 130

migrant-friendly hospitals, 35

migrant health, rights-based perspective *see* human rights approach

migrant workers: exploitation of, 16; returning home ill, 19, 21

migrants: awareness of health rights among, 87; deterioration of health post-migration, 181; discrimination against, by healthcare staff, 32; gendered health vulnerability of, 165–7; health-seeking strategies of, 171; heterogenity of composition of, 89; multi-nationality of, 11; new (health status of, 29–30; impact on European health services, 30–1); official labour recruitment of, 12; right to equality of healthcare, 46–8; seen as health threat, 1

migration: as a family affair, 12; barriers to, 19; benefits of, 11; clandestine, 14; complexity of, 1; composition of migrants, 10–26; data regarding, 5; feminisation of, 84, 181; health effects of, 14; heterogeneity of experience of, 6; major issue in Europe, 10; of health workers, 6, 62–78; patterns of, 4, 5, 11 (circular, 13); phases of process, 13; push and pull factors, 11; research into, 4; rights of, 44–61

migration-development-social policy nexus, 1

mobile telephones, use of, 11

mobility, gendered analysis of, 191

Moldova, 113

multiple medicaments, 137–49

murder of women, 132

Muslim women, and wearing of headscarf, 191, 193

mutual aid activities, 180

National Health Service (NHS), 4, 163, 187; charging regulations for migrants, 117–20; dissatisfaction with, 170; expectations of, 172–3; migrants' access to, 164–5; trafficked migrants' access to, 114–16

NHS National Research Ethics Service, 114

National Referral Mechanism (NRM) (UK), 7, 115–16, 120–1

Nepal, 18

nervousness among migrants, 187

Netherlands, 33, 34

networks: of migrants, essential for survival, 168; women at centre of, 169

New Zealand, 169

non-resident Indians (NRIs), 153, 155

Norway, 30, 56

nursing, work done by migrants, 12

obesity, 15

occupational accidents among migrants, 166

occupational illnesses of migrants, 19

ontological security, 7, 94–5, 96, 97, 104, 105, 107; threats to, 98–102

overseas Filipino workers (OFWs), 154–5, 157

Palestine, 56

Papua New Guinea, 16

passports, confiscation or withholding of, 117

paying for healthcare, 15, 33, 54, 56, 86, 88; debt arising from, 122; impact on vulnerable women, 130; pursuit by payment officers, 119

persecution, criteria of, 96

Peruvian migrants in Chile, 83–4, 88, 90

Philippines: as healthcare destination, 151–62; remittances of migrants, 150

About Zed Books

Zed Books is a critical and dynamic publisher, committed to increasing awareness of important international issues and to promoting diversity, alternative voices and progressive social change. We publish on politics, development, gender, the environment and economics for a global audience of students, academics, activists and general readers. Run as a co-operative, Zed Books aims to operate in an ethical and environmentally sustainable way.

Find out more at:

www.zedbooks.co.uk

For up-to-date news, articles, reviews and events information visit:

http://zed-books.blogspot.com

To subscribe to the monthly Zed Books e-newsletter, send an email headed 'subscribe' to:

marketing@zedbooks.net

We can also be found on **Facebook**, **ZNet**, **Twitter** and **Library Thing**.